Find it on the Intern

Your complete guide to search engines, databases, directories,
libraries, people finders, yellow pages, portals, gateways
& thousands more amazing internet research tools

Internet Handbooks

Books & Publishing on the Internet
Careers Guidance on the Internet
Chat on the Internet
Creating an Effective Web Site
Creating Your First Home Page
Education and Training on the Internet
Email for Everyone
Find It on the Internet
Finding a Job on the Internet
Gardens & Gardening on the Internet
Graduate Jobsearch on the Internet
Homes & Property on the Internet
Internet for Business
Internet for Schools
Internet for Students
Internet for Writers
Linking Your Web Site to the Internet
Managing Staff Using the Internet
Marketing Your Business on the Internet
Maths on the Internet
Music on the Internet
News and Magazines on the Internet
Newsgroups for Everyone
Overseas Jobs on the Internet
Personal Finance on the Internet
Shops & Shopping on the Internet
Travel & Holidays on the Internet
Using Internet Explorer
Using Netscape Communicator
Wildlife & Conservation on the Internet
Working from Home Using the Internet

Other titles in preparation

Find it on the Internet

Computers

Your complete guide to search engines, databases, directories, libraries, people finders, yellow pages, portals, gateways & thousands more amazing internet research tools

Kye Valongo

www.internet-handbooks.co.uk

Copyright © 1999 by Kye Valongo

First published in 1999 by Internet Handbooks, a Division of International Briefings Ltd, Plymbridge House, Estover Road, Plymouth PL6 7PY, United Kingdom.

Customer services tel: (01752) 202301
Orders fax: (01752) 202333
Customer services email: cservs@plymbridge.com
Distributors web site: http://www.plymbridge.com
Series web site: http://www.internet-handbooks.co.uk

All rights reserved. No part of this work may be reproduced or stored in an information retrieval system without the express permission of the Publishers given in writing.

Note: The contents of this book are offered for the purposes of general guidance only and no liability can be accepted for any loss or expense incurred as a result of relying in particular circumstances on statements made in this book. Readers are advised to check the current position with the appropriate authorities before entering into personal arrangements.

Printed and bound by The Cromwell Press Ltd, Trowbridge, Wiltshire.

Contents

List of illustrations		7
Preface		10
1	**Getting started – a little essential know-how**	**15**
	Web sites and browers	15
	What are web sites and browsers?	15
	Viewing a web site	16
	Offline viewing	17
	Searching the internet	19
	Is the internet full of rubbish?	19
	Search strategies	20
	Directories	20
	Search engines	21
	Using keyword searches	21
	Metasearch tools	24
	Some good search sites	25
	Metasearch sites	26
	Asking people	27
	For children	29
	Some specialised sources	29
	Forums, mailing lists and newsgroups	30
	Forums	30
	Mailing lists	31
	Usenet	31
	What is a newsgroup?	32
	How to find a newsgroup	32
2	**Work – business and education**	**34**
	The arts	34
	Books and literature	34
	Performing arts	37
	Visual arts	39
	Museums and galleries	41
	Geography and history	43
	Science and technology	45
	General science	45
	Computers and the internet	47
	Your security on the internet	49
	Physical and chemical sciences	51
	Biological sciences	55
	Military technology	56
	Business and finance	58
	Online banks and building societies	58
	Finance and investment	60
	Law	63
	Finding businesses	63
	Miscellaneous	64
	Couriers	64
	Careers, jobs and education	66
	Finding jobs	66
	Schools	70

Contents

	Government and politics	71
	Human rights and ecology	73
3	**Rest – private life**	76
	Family and health	76
	General health and fitness	76
	Hospitals and medical organisations	78
	Addictions	80
	Disability and chronic illness	80
	Children and young people	81
	Relationships, sex and health	82
	Alternative health and medicine	84
	Hobbies and interests	85
	Quizzes and games	85
	Sites for children	87
	Younger children	89
	Home and garden DIY	90
	Cinema and theatre	91
	Food and drink	91
	Music	94
	MP3	95
	Music publications and news sites	97
	Religion and spirituality	97
	Western religions	97
	Eastern religions	98
	Others	99
	Buying products and services	101
	How to avoid being conned	101
	Shopping directories and malls	102
	Auctions	104
	Books and magazines	104
	Cars and bikes	105
	Used cars	106
	New cars	106
	Classic and special cars	107
	Homes and property	108
	Small goods	110
	Tickets	111
	Electrical goods	112
	Fashion	113
	Food and drink	113
	Food	113
	Beers and wines	115
	Spirits	116
	Travel and holidays	116
	General travel information	116
	Health and safety abroad	119
	Transport	119
	Motoring	120
	Driving	121
	Classic cars	122
	Travel agencies and airlines	122
	Hotels and other accommodation	126
	Maps and guides	126
	Britain	126
	Other countries	128

Contents

Currency and other necessities	130
National and international information	130
Towns and cities	130
Government and national organisations	130
Royalty	131
World information	132
Humour and general knowledge	134

4 Play – social life 136

Sport and recreation	136
Soccer	136
Cricket	138
Rugby	138
Golf	139
Outdoor sports	139
Motor sports	142
Others	142
People	144
Friendship and romance	144
Finding someone's email address	145
Some other sites	146
Animals	147
News and entertainment	149
Television	149
Films	149
Radio	151
Newspapers online	151
Other news sources	155
Weather	156
Cartoons	157
Computer games and software	158

Appendix: your safe use of the internet 159

Viruses and the web	159
The reliability of information on the web	159
Electronic copyright	160
Privacy on the internet	161
The invisible eavesdroppers	161
What can we do?	163
Children and the web	163
Blocking software	164
Ratings	165
Parental control	167
FAQ – frequently asked questions	167

Further reading	169
Glossary of terms	173
Index of web sites	183
General Index	189

List of illustrations

Figure		Page
1.	Pure Fiction	18
2.	AltaVista search engine	22
3.	The Google search engine	25
4.	The British Library	35
5.	The Shakespeare Birthplace Trust	36
6.	The Ballet.co	37
7.	The History Channel	44
8.	Nature Magazine	46
9.	Cnet	48
10.	Epic	50
11.	Applied Space Resources	52
12.	National Geographic	54
13.	Janes Defence	57
14.	Internet Banking	60
15.	Motley Fool	62
16.	Company Sleuth	64
17.	Royal Mail	65
18.	Golden Square	67
19.	London Student	69
20.	Department for Education and Employment	70
21.	Number Ten	72
22.	FreeSpeech	74
23.	Samaritans	78
24.	The Virtual Medical Centre	79
25.	Hitched	84
26.	Colouring	89
27.	Garden Web	90
28.	Dotmusic	94
29.	MP3.com	96
30.	Salem Tarot	100
31.	Advertising Standards Agency	102
32.	Lastminute	103
33.	New Car Net	107
34.	UpMyStreet	109
35.	Ticket Links	111
36.	FinestWine	115
37.	Worldwide Tourism Directory	118
38.	Virtual London	118
39.	The Trainline	120
40.	The Royal Society for the Prevention of Accidents	121
41.	Deckchair	123
42.	Epicurious Travel	124
43.	National Trust	127

Illustrations

Figure	*Page*
44. National Map Centre	129
45. Time Out	131
46. The British Monarchy	132
47. Hitch Hiker's Guide to the Internet	134
48. The Fantasy League	137
49. Scrum.com	138
50. International Amateur Athletic Federation	141
51. Racenews	141
52. Boxing Monthly	143
53. Introduction	145
54. Telephone Directories on the Web	146
55. RSPCA	149
56. Channel 4	150
57. BBC Radio	152
58. The Star	154
59. The Drudge Report	155
60. The Met Office	157
61. The Copyright Website	161
62. Anonymiser	162
63. SurfMonkey	164
64. Internet Freedom	166

Preface

Do you want to find something on the internet? If you know where to look, it's easy. If you don't, it's a nightmare. The internet is a vast ocean of useful information and a fabulous resource once mastered but it is also a soggy marsh full of an unbelievable amount of rubbish. Without solid ground, the beginner is likely to become overwhelmed and frustrated very quickly.

Most subjects of everyday interest and relevance are covered here, but if what you want is not here, the section on search tools and tips will give you a flying start to enable you to find it quickly. It would be impossible to include everything in one book, but *Find it on the Internet* contains a listing of some of the highest quality sites on the internet – and many of them are relevant to the UK. This book breaks new ground because most other books written about the internet are by American authors who, naturally, favour sources in the US. In the UK, we have many wonderful web sites that are more relevant to people in the UK and better quality than similar sites in other countries.

The tips offered in this book are easy to understand and are included on a 'need to know' basis. Too many authors make the mistake of trying to explain the internet in too much detail assuming this will help a new user to understand. The opposite is often true: too much information can be very confusing! Anyone interested in finding out more is invited to refer to the Further Reading section on page 169. For the simple tips, read on.

The people I would like to thank in producing this Internet Handbook are too numerous to mention but special thanks go to the people that made me 'walk the plank': to Roger, who provided the plank, and Anette, who pushed me.

Kye Valongo

Email: kyevalongo@internet-handbooks.co.uk

Introduction: what is the internet?

In this introduction we will explore the basics of the internet:

- ▶ *the world wide web – web pages and web sites*
- ▶ *email – electronic mail*
- ▶ *usenet – newsgroups*

The world wide web

▶ *World wide web* – a part of the internet that basically consists of a series of interconnected documents called web pages. It is perhaps better thought of as a way to bring products, services, and information into your home via your computer.

The most useful part of the internet for finding something is the world wide web. The world wide web is the part of the internet that allows you to view information composed mainly of text and graphics, in the form of 'web pages'.

Individuals, organisations and companies put the information on the web for others to see. This information can range from a simple family holiday diary with photos up to the largest of corporation and government information services. In this way it is similar to a notice board, a shop front, or a tourist information centre, but it is also much more.

The internet used to be purely the territory of universities and governments, but now it is being used for much wider practical purposes – useful to the average person in almost every country of the world. In fact you can find sites that will help you in every conceivable aspect of your 'work, rest and play'. For example:

1. If you don't work, you can find a job using an online agency or by browsing through a company's own online job adverts.
2. The self-employed can complete a self-assessment online, and financial prospectors can check the state of world stock markets online.
3. If you fancy a rest, you can book a hotel room anywhere in the world, plan a holiday, take a course in creative writing, or learn how to meditate.
4. When you feel like playing, you can check where the weather is best for skiing, or how your favourite team is going on, or go to the many online gaming sites.

Introduction: what is the internet?

The list goes on and on, almost endlessly. There are many advantages to using a service on the internet: many of the products and services are cheaper, the news is often more up-to-date, and people are often more helpful. For example, suppose you want to plan a holiday. Traditionally, you may have had to get hold of guide books to find an idea, calculate timings of transport, find a cheap flight or train ticket, book a hotel and check the weather and local tourist information. Imagine how much time and work this would take if you were to go into town – taking the bus, driving and walking, and walking. Chasing up the best prices can take days and lots of wasted telephone conversations and shoe leather. 'Where did you say I could find a map of the French metro or a list of hotels in Cyprus?'

The same task can be completed on the internet in minutes, even if you are not yet sure what type of holiday to plan for. For example:

(a) Find an idea for a trip at Epicurious Travel – http://www.epicurious.com.

(b) Check with the Foreign Office to make sure there is no trouble in the country you choose – http://www.fco.gov.uk/travel

(c) Get health information at Travel Health Online – http://www.tripprep.com

(d) Book the cheapest flight at Travelocity – http://www.travelocity.co.uk

(e) Reserve a hotel room from Hotels and Travel on the Net – http://www.hotelstravel.com

(f) Check out the restaurants and local attractions at The Sidewalk – http://www.sidewalk.com

Even if the whole process took an hour, at weekend telephone rates this would cost you less than a pound – and you don't even have to put your socks on!

The same kind of systematic search can be useful for almost any situation: finding lost relatives, contacting people that share your interests, doing research for homework or some other project, in fact you name it and there will be something on the internet. Finding it may not always be easy but with the help of the key sites and tips in this book, you will save hours of frustration. You will be able to find sites of such quality that you may wonder why people still waste time going to the library or shopping in the High Street. Search methods are dealt with on page 19. The internet is set to change our ways of life for ever.

Email

▶ *Email* – short for electronic mail, a computer to computer version of the post-office mail. Email uses electronic documents instead of envelopes and letters, and telephone lines instead of postmen.

Sometimes, the web itself is not enough – we need to ask someone a

---

Hotels/Travel Information
Links to more than 100,000 Hotels and lodgings worldwide in over 120 countries. Links to local guides, maps, transportation, cultural facilities and more.

Hotel Chains
Large and small hotel chains and affinity groups.

TravelChat!
An informal forum to let others know about your travel

.... **Introduction**

question. Email is the way we send a message to someone else on the internet. Email is cheaper, faster and easier to send than normal mail – no matter which country you send email to. There are no stamps to buy and no forms to fill in; all you need to do is write your message, address it, connect to the internet then send it. Your connection is usually done using a local or national phone number and the time taken to send a message is only seconds.

The only disadvantage is that you must learn some new concepts and techniques before you can use email. These techniques will be detailed in the help file of your email software to some extent. If you are interested in more information, see the other books in the **Internet Handbook Series** on the back cover of this book, or visit the web site:

       http://www.internet-handbooks.co.uk

Usenet

▶ *Usenet* – a collection of special interest discussion groups

Usenet is rather like a vast collection of public notice boards. You can read messages from people all over the world, on almost every topic under the sun, and in almost every language. You can also place messages for others to read or reply to the messages that others have 'posted'. There are many of these notice boards, called newsgroups, each with a defined area of interest. A single post, especially if its subject is emotive, can start off a chain reaction of comments developing into many separate but simultaneous discussions called threads. Newsgroups are great places to learn about things because they are often frequented by experts in the specific area of knowledge covered by the group. The subject of forums is covered in more detail on page 30.

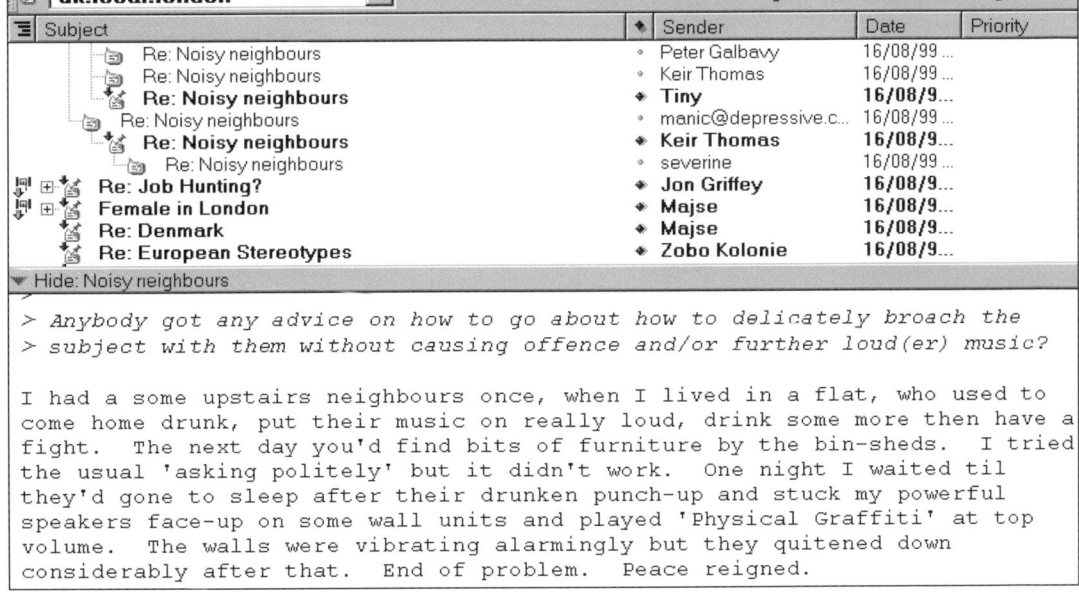

Welcome to aol.co.uk - Microsoft Internet Explorer
File Edit View Go Favorites Help
Back Forward Stop Refresh Home Search Favorit... Print Font Mail Edit
Address http://www.aol.co.uk/
Links
aol.co.uk
AOL Services
NetFind
AIM
NetMail
Channels
My News
Webcards
Try AOL For Free!
AOL Information
Press
Jobs
aol.co.uk Today
Einstein, Darwin and Nobel provide our online introduction to science at aol.co.uk Learning.
aol.co.uk Entertainment gets fashionable
Download AIM 2.0 for chats galore!
Daily Essentials
• Horoscopes
• Fact of the Day
• NetMail
• Join a Chat
aolnetfind
Search
AOL NetFind UKPlus
Business Finder • Advanced Search • Kids' AOL NetFind
News Headlines
NEWS: THREE DIE AS AIRCRAFT HITS CARGO
Read Your Mail
The new British bookshop on the Internet
click here
bol.com
Click Here
www.ebay.co.uk
bid
£1 £5 £10
Additional

ihome - Netscape
File Edit View Go Communicator Help
Back Forward Reload Home Search Guide Print Security Stop
Bookmarks Location: http://www.internet-handbooks.co.uk/
This site contains over 100 pages. Please remember to press your VIEW/REFRESH or RELOAD button to view current pages. Updated: 12 September 1999
internet handbooks
Check out the new series of Site Finder titles - hundreds of web sites reviewed on key educational, business, consumer and other topics.
Internet Handbooks - Helping you get the most out of the internet
New titles for 1999 New!
Internet Handbooks Sitefinders...
Secure online ordering
Plymbridge Distributors...
Your internet kit New!
Email Search Newsgroups Chat ...
Email services
Bigfoot Hotmail Yahoo ...
Authorship New!
Proposal material Author form
Internet privacy issues
Big Brother Surveillance Encryption
Search engines
Altavista Dejanews Lycos Yahoo
Access providers
AOL BT Demon FreeServe Virgin
Review web sites for cash
Guidance Samples Terms ...
Glossary of internet terms
E-commerce New!
Site index A to Z New!
The Internet is coming. Millions more people around the world are now scrambling to get connected. Internet Handbooks meet the pressing need for information to help ordinary people start discovering and enjoying all these new possibilities. The books are aimed at private individuals, students, job hunters, people at work, business managers and professional people through the private and public sectors. Internet Handbooks show how to acquire the necessary skills, and start enjoying all this
Document: Done

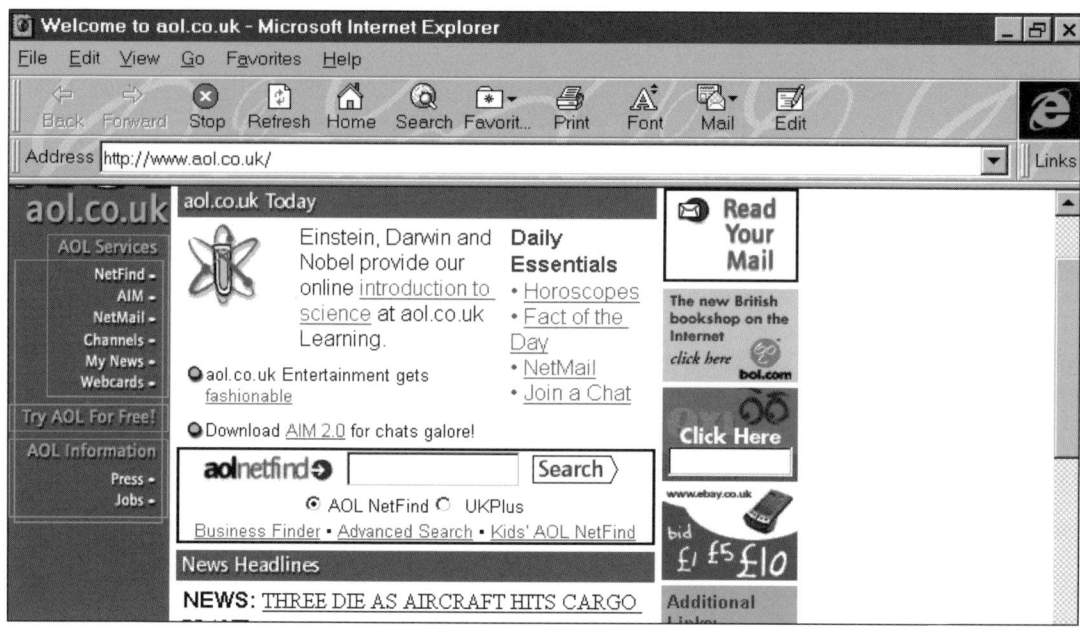

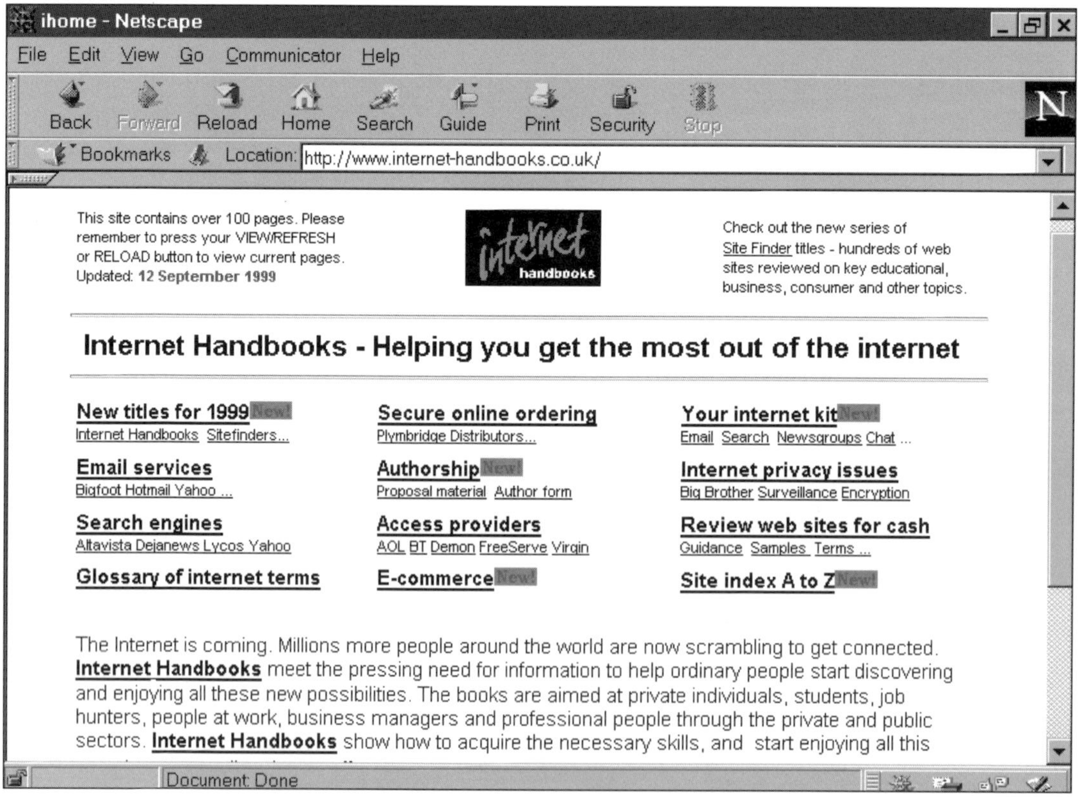

1 Getting started: a little essential know-how

In this chapter we will explore:

▶ *Web sites and browsers*
▶ *Searching the internet*
▶ *Forums, mailing lists and newsgroups*

WEB SITES AND BROWSERS

What are web sites and browsers?

The documents that make up the world wide web are called web pages. They are little more than text and pictures, somewhat like the pages of a magazine. Occasionally, you will come across web pages that have more advanced content such as animated images, sound clips or even short video clips. Usually, web pages are grouped together into web sites. A web site is a collection of web pages with a similar theme, again similar to a magazine. The BBC web site, for example, follows the theme of television and radio, and includes aspects such as news, entertainment, films and others that you would associate with the BBC. There are probably thousands of pages that constitute the BBC web site.

▶ *Browser* – a computer program that allows you to retrieve and view web sites. The two most common browsers are Internet Explorer and Netscape Navigator. One of them should already be installed on your computer – otherwise you can get them free from the CDs that come with the monthly internet magazines. Don't worry too much about which one you have. They both have broadly the same features. Try and make sure you have at least version 4 of either one.

When you view web pages, you are said to be browsing, or surfing, the web. Words such as browsing and surfing imply that you are physically moving around the web, but this is misleading and makes it hard to appreciate what is really happening. You may fidget or stand up and stretch occasionally, but that is usually as far as you can move physically without losing sight of your monitor.

When you view a web page, it is fetched ('downloaded') from wherever it is stored and saved onto your computer. Perhaps a better name for the 'browser' software would be 'internet downloader'. This downloading is almost invisible to you; all you see is a momentary message or two at the bottom of the browser and then, after a short while, the web page itself will appear. Whenever you view a web page, you are really viewing a document that is saved on your computer.

Getting started

Viewing a web site

Viewing a web page is simplicity in itself. Try this: connect to the internet according to the instructions of your internet service provider[1] then start your browser program. You should now be watching a web page appear as it is retrieved in stages. The text will become visible first followed, one by one, by the images. You are now browsing the web. By default, every time a browser starts, it tries to find a page called the 'home page'. Initially, the location of the home page is set by the browser manufacturer or your ISP and is usually one of the main pages of that company – Netscape, Microsoft, BTinternet or AOL for example.

▶ *Internet service provider (ISP)* – the company that provides you with the ability to access the internet. They usually also provide you with internet software and other online services.

Finding a different site after the home page has loaded is a simple step. All but the most basic web pages contain references or links to pages on the same and on other sites. These links – also called hyperlinks – contain information that tells your browser where the page is located. You just click on a link using your mouse cursor, and the page at that location is retrieved for you. Links are easy to spot – you can recognise them in a number of ways:

1. Underlined text usually indicates that it is a link. Often these links are arranged in a menu system at one edge of a web page. A text link might look like this:

   Click here for more info

2. Images that look like buttons are usually links.

3. Wherever your mouse cursor changes into a pointing hand.

When you click on a link, you are telling the browser to find and retrieve the document at the location the link refers to.

Finding a web page is similar to finding someone's house; you first need to know the address. The address of a web page is called the URL, or uniform resource locator. This is a unique piece of information, just like a house address. You use the URL of a page to 'point' your browser at that page.

▶ *Uniform resource locator (URL)* – the unique web address of a web page, image or other document on the internet.

This is an example of a URL:

http://www.ukwriters.com

---

1 Most ISPs configure your computer to connect when you start the web browser.

Offline viewing

It looks complicated and makes little sense to the eye. But if you study it, you will be able to make out the words 'writers' and 'UK' so you might guess that it is the URL of a site for writers in the UK. You would be right, and it is called UKwriters. There is a meaning to every part of the URL but all you need to know is that your browser will take you to the UKwriters web site if you give it that address. In that respect, your browser is just like a taxi – you don't need to know where the address is or even which language it is in as long as your taxi driver (browser) does. Most URLs will begin with

> http://

followed by the rest of the address, but modern browsers let you miss out the http:// to save typing. For example with the UKwriters site, if you just type

> www.ukwriters.com

the browser would fill in the rest. Try it out by typing the shortened version into your browser's 'address' or 'location' box.

Offline viewing

Because these pages are retrieved and stored on your computer, it should follow that you will still be able to view them after you disconnect. You can to an extent – the browser keeps the pages on your computer's hard disk on a part of the hard disk called the **cache**. The pages are kept until the cache becomes full then the older pages are automatically deleted to make room for the new ones.

Initially, the cache is limited to a few megabytes but you can change its size according to your needs. You can make the cache smaller to save disk space or, if you have plenty of disk space, set it higher. Mine is set to a huge 500 megabytes and acts almost like a library of information. A large cache means that you have many sites stored on your computer and you will not need to connect to the internet if you have visited a site before. When the cache becomes full, the URLs are not deleted, only the saved pages. The URLs will remain in your 'favourites' menu so you can revisit the site by connecting to the internet again.

To view the sites offline just type the URL into your browser or open your 'Favourites' menu ('Bookmarks' in Netscape Navigator) and select the site you want to view. Of course, many sites such as news sources change daily or more often and to retrieve the latest news you must connect.

Try it yourself with a site called Pure Fiction ('for anybody who loves to read – or aspires to write – bestselling fiction'). Go online and type into your browser this URL:

> http://www.purefiction.com

Getting started

then press 'enter'. Wait until the page (Figure 1) finishes loading, then press the key shortcut 'Control-D' to add the page to your favourites menu in Internet Explorer. Netscape Navigator uses the same key shortcut but calls the stored URLs 'bookmarks'. Now disconnect (to save telephone charges).

▶ *Key shortcut* – two keys pressed at the same time. Usually the 'control' key (Ctrl), 'Alt' key, or 'Shift' key combined with a letter or number. For example to use 'Control-D', press 'Control', then tap the 'D' key once firmly, then take your finger off the 'Control' key.

To prove offline viewing works, make sure you are offline, then start your browser program. Now perform the following steps:

1. Select the 'File' menu then 'Work Offline' (Navigator: 'Go Offline').
2. Open the 'Favourites' Menu ('Bookmarks').
3. Select the Pure Fiction entry.
4. Watch the site load. Simple!

Fig. 1. Pure fiction is a pure delight with stories to whet the appetite of the short-story connoisseur. In fact, if you have ever thought of writing yourself, take a look.

You do not have to disconnect each time you add a page to your favourites, just press Control-D and move on. Offline viewing is especially useful if you want to read a page with lots of text such as an in-depth news report or a short story.

.... **Search engines**

SEARCHING THE INTERNET

Isn't the internet full of rubbish?

Some people think that the internet is full of pornography and terrorism. You could say just the same of 'the printed word'. It may be true that there is a lot of rubbish out there but, with a few good starting points, you will find a vast number of valuable sites, and make the web an enjoyable and very useful experience. In fact, it can save you lots of time and money. For example:

▶ Buying books is cheaper online.

▶ Booking air flights is more efficient.

▶ Doing all kinds of research is easier.

▶ You can meet like-minded people without having to travel miles.

▶ You can keep your children safely and quietly entertained while you do other things.

If you start with a number of high quality sites, your browsing experience will be cleaner and more enjoyable than you ever imagined. Some sites help you in this by providing high quality links in a categorised menu system so you can explore the internet and find most of the subjects that you may be interested in by clicking a link or two. UK Directory, which is designed to be such a site, is at:

http://ukdirectory.com/

It has links to shopping, travel, sport, education, government and much more. By customising your browser, you could even make a site like this your home page and have it come up each time you connect – instantly having useful links available. 'My Yahoo' at

http://uk.my.yahoo.com

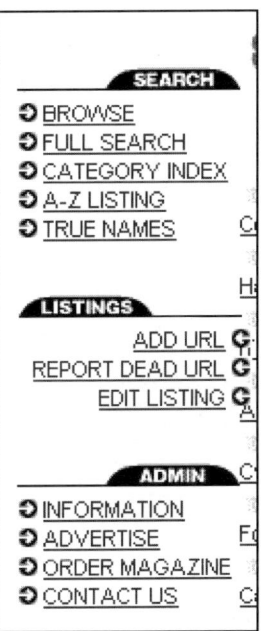

goes a step further by letting you personalise the page so that you see the items you want to see when you visit the site. You can select what kind of news headlines, weather, stock quotes, sports information and more. Once you have selected the content, My Yahoo will remember your settings for next time you visit.

The web is becoming more and more like the high street every day. Almost every kind of shop, club and organisation is racing to build a presence online. An article in April 1999 issue of *The Scotsman* predicted that the value of online business will grow from £230 million in 1998 to a massive £3.9 billion in 2003. At present, the number of internet users in Britain is growing by 10,000 a day. There is a gold rush on and everybody is getting in on the act. During the writing of this book, Barclays Bank, Waterstones and WH Smith – to take just three examples – have started to offer free internet access. Competition is building, and prices are falling. Already, many products and services are

Getting started

cheaper bought over the internet than they would be in the high street. Technology may never replace real shops and real organisations, but the internet is offering a totally new experience.

There is a lot of useful stuff out there and it is becoming easier to find. The sites selected later in this book should give you some excellent starting points but at some stage you will want to find something that is not covered in these pages.

Search strategies

Trying to find anything on the internet without help can be like trying to find a needle in a haystack. You will be glad to hear that help is abundant on the web, with special sites like directories and search engines. These powerful sites are designed and maintained to help you to find information. Using these tools efficiently is one of the keys to finding and keeping up to date with good sites.

▶ *Directory* – a special web site with information about other sites classified by subject area and further subdivided into smaller categories.

▶ *Search engine* – a directory compiled with the help of a computer program that automatically scans the world wide web storing and categorising information about other sites as it goes. As it stops at each site, it finds keywords to add to the directory entry.

Directories

Online directories are very similar to the good old BT Yellow Pages – sites are classified by subject area and further subdivided into smaller categories. However, unlike the traditional Yellow Pages you can enter a keyword and let the site do the searching for you. One of the best known directories is Yahoo! from California. You can find at:

http://www.yahoo.co.uk

Yahoo! contains information on hundreds of thousands of sites – from the personal 'this is me' site to the largest global corporations. Yahoo! organises everything by categories similar to the way a library organises its books, with sections for entertainment, arts and humanity, business and economy, computer and internet, and masses more. The classifications start as general and become more specific as you make more specific choices. For instance, if you choose 'Entertainment', you are shown a page where the selections are broken down further into 'Food and drink', 'Games', 'Music', and so on. By following the links, you will eventually find the topic area you are interested in and you receive a list of relevant web URLs and a short description for each site; for example a list of vegetarian restaurants in London.

Using a directory like Yahoo! is very much like climbing a tree: first you clamber up the main trunk then out onto one of the main branches,

---

Inside Yahoo!

- Yahoo! Address Book: Keep your contacts safe
- Web Access For Free! With Yahoo! Online
- New to Yahoo!? - For help click here

[more features...]

Search engines

then to a smaller branch, and so on until you find the information you want – the fruit. The sites listed in a directory are placed there by humans. If nobody 'registers' the URL and description of a site with a directory, you will not find it. In that case you would probably do better with a search engine.

Search engines

Search engines collect and contain information about many more sites. A search engine automatically scans the web following links from site to site, storing and categorising information as it goes. As it stops at each site, it finds keywords to add to its index. Search engines also keep their information current by constantly searching for new sites and updating the ones already in their lists. Some search engines collect specific information limited to a subject area (such as education) or a particular country (such as Brazil or the UK).

Imagine a little robot wandering around the web from site to site, busily collecting information like a bee collecting pollen, and you may get an idea of what is happening. Actually, these automatic systems have been termed robots, spiders and web crawlers – cute if you are not afraid of creepy-crawlies.

The large number of sites listed on search engines makes them more difficult to use but once mastered they can be much more effective than directories. The information you find is only as good as the search you perform: ask a general question and you get a vague answer, ask a question that is too specific and you will get no answer. To carry out a meaningful search, you need to know how to use keywords.

Using keyword searches

With search engines and directories, you can search for sites matching keywords that you type into a form on the search site. Keywords help you to:

▶ Find sites on a specific subject.

▶ Filter out the unwanted information.

Using the wrong combination of keywords can bring you hundreds of thousands of matches or none at all. It is like opening a child's toy-cupboard – you never know what is going to fall out until you open it. Using keywords effectively may seem complicated at first but using the right syntax and combination of keywords will give you a manageable and useful list. One that is relevant to your area of interest but not too short a list that there is little to choose from.

Let's take an example. Suppose you want to find some sites that deal with house auctions. Let's first go to a popular search engine called 'Alta Vista' at:

http://www.altavista.com

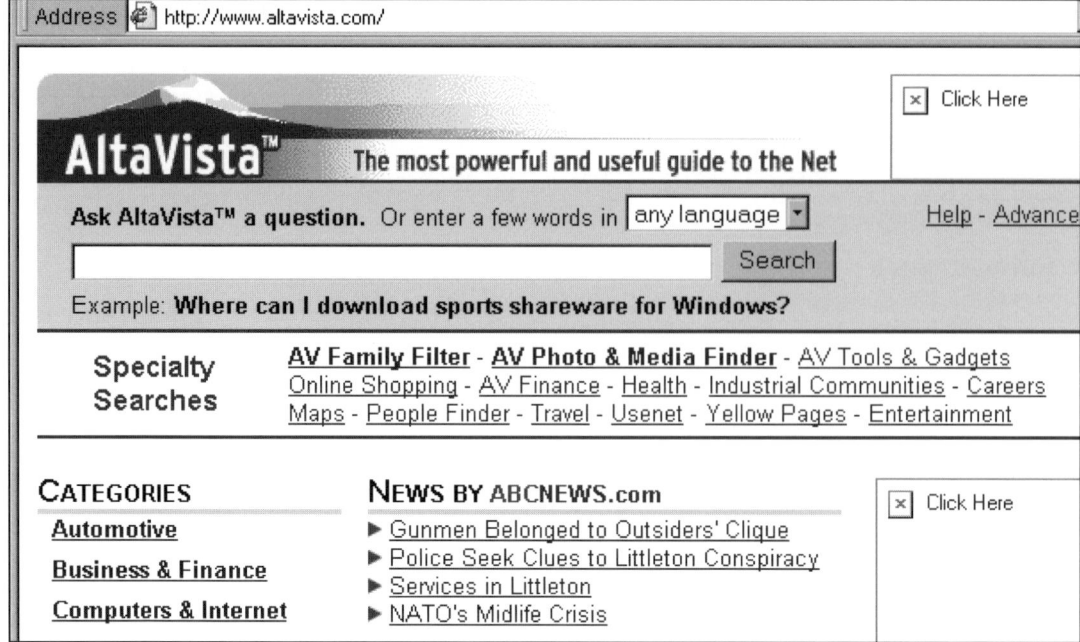

Fig. 2. AltaVista is a great search engine – probably the best on the internet for a good all-round search. Once you have mastered the use of keywords, AltaVista is a joy to use.

1. Type **buying a house** in the search box.
2. Click the 'Search' button.

My attempt came back with thousands of matches – not many of them were relevant to auctions and some of them were about buying something else. The search engines were looking separately for the words 'buying' or 'house' so there were topics such as 'buying a new car' and 'decorating your house', and many others weird and wonderful sites. Adding more keywords made it even worse. For example, entering **buying a house in an auction** returned over 20,000 matches – it would take weeks to check them all.

Enclosing a phrase in quotes usually narrows down a search. The quotes ensure that only references using the whole phrase will be listed, excluding all those ufologists and masseurs. Using

"house auctions"

returned 5,000 matches, better, but it would still be a lot of work to find the best sites. The next step is to exclude the US sites part – we are only interested in buying a house in the UK.

"house auctions NOT USA"

came up with no matches because the phrase inside the quotes is meaningless – remember the search engine looks for the exact phrase if it is enclosed in quotes. However, we can split it into two phrases, and then the special word 'NOT' will act as a command telling the search engine to ignore sources containing 'USA' anywhere in the text.

Search engines

"house auctions" NOT USA

brought up about a thousand matches. Not too bad but the list contained lots of entries for one particular company that dealt only with commercial property – Wright and Sons. To get rid of those entries the keyword phrase was changed to

"house auctions" NOT USA NOT commercial

Now there was a list of about thirty five – ideal.

Another special keyword is OR. This word is useful if two or more different names or terms refer to the subject you want. It is also useful if you are interested in either of two or more options. Your child wants to find sites about either dragons or witches: you could enter

dragons OR witches

as a keyword search. A third useful word is AND. This forces the search site to look for both words in the search. Say your child is interested in knights slaying dragons but is scared of trolls:

knights AND dragons NOT trolls

would ensure that the sites with trolls would be excluded. These features can be combined to give you very precise control over a search as in

"short stories" AND witches NOT trolls

which picks out short stories about witches but not if they contain trolls.

Some search engines treat capitalised words as different from those in just lower case letters. If you don't capitalise a word, the engine will search for both capitals and lower case. If you add a single capital letter in the word, the engine will search for that exact capitalisation and no other. Searching is often a matter of juggling with keywords until you have found a number of matches you feel able to handle. Too many and you should try to make the search more specific. Too few and you should either use more general terms or find an alternative keyword. For example, instead of house try property. These techniques should be sufficient for most searches but for more information about keywords, go to:

The Spider's Apprentice
http://www.monash.com/spidap.html - or -
http://daphne.palomar.edu/TGSEARCH/

Search engines differ in the syntax of search phrases. Some may use single quotes but others only double. Some may not recognise the

---

MP3 Search

FAQ
Search Strategy
How Search Engines Work
Search Wizard
Rankings
Top Page

Find books, articles on search engines, web site promotion

Search All Your Favorites Engines

Getting started

special words such as AND, OR, NOT etc. To get the most out of a search engine, it is helpful to know the syntax it uses. Aim to stick to a few favourite search sites and, once you become familiar with their quirks, you will be able to find anything you want.

Advantages of directories	*Disadvantages of directories*
Directories are easier to browse at leisure, something you can't do very well with a keyword search engine. Reports from a search engine are not evaluated, but in a directory, human beings have evaluated each page listed.	You may have to branch through the categories repeatedly before arriving at the right page. If you're looking for some obscure topic, the people that maintain the directory may have excluded those pages. Search engines would be a better strategy. Directories are often several months behind the times because of the need for human organisation.
Advantages of search engines	*Disadvantages of Search Engines*
If you've used the right keyword strategy, you can quickly find the relevant web pages. You can find pages that human experts (of the directories) would exclude from their lists. New web sites are accessible within days or even hours after publication.	Keyword searching can be difficult to get right. It may be difficult or impossible to use a keyword search if the vocabulary of the subject is unfamiliar. You must have a clearer idea of what you're looking for. Search engines don't evaluate the pages they find and a certain amount of poor quality pages will be displayed. No single engine searches the entire internet, so it's often necessary to use several search engines.

Metasearch tools

There are thousands of different search engines available covering both general areas and specific subjects. Some of them are particularly effective and sophisticated, but none of them is comprehensive. Most of them only have a small database of sites, or they may not be up to date (some sites take weeks to update their database). Consequently, you may need to use several search engines before you are satisfied

Good search sites

that you have found everything you require. A metasearch engine may save you the trouble of using many different sites to run your search, or it may point you to a search engine that you didn't know about.

A metasearch tool is simply a site that sends a keyword search to many different search engines and directories so you can use many search engines from one place. This kind of site is especially useful if you have found no information using search engines. Sometimes, if you are trying to find out about an obscure topic or one that is very new, many search engines may not have found a site, or the site designer may not have publicised it effectively.

Some good search sites

AltaVista
http://www.altavista.com
AltaVista (Figure 2) is a popular site and has one of the largest databases on the internet. The use of keywords is a must to get the most out of a search. Often, if you get the keywords right, you can get better results from AltaVista than you can from a dedicated UK search engine.

Google
http://www.google.com
A new and innovative site is Google. Google matches the text in its index with your query to find pages that are both important and relevant. For instance, when analysing a page for indexing, it looks at what the pages linking to that page have to say about it. So the rating does not depend on what a site says about itself but what others say about it.

Fig. 3. Google sounds like a happy newborn baby and it certainly has the freshness of one. Google is also intelligent in that it tries to figure out what is important and relevant to your search.

Getting started

Another nice feature of Google is that instead of static summaries of the web pages, it gives you excerpts of the text that matches your query – with your search terms in bold. This means you don't have to load a web page that has nothing to do with your query.

Yahoo! UK
http://www.yahoo.co.uk
Yahoo! was the first search site and is still one of the best for general searching. Yahoo! contains over a half a million links categorised by subjects. You can browse the categories or search through them using keywords. The site also contains links to specific information such as world news, sport and weather. Yahoo! is probably one of the sites you will visit time after time.

Excite
http://www.excite.com
Excite has a Search Wizard that can be a useful tool to help you weed out unwanted entries from your search results. The Wizard presents a list of terms that may be related to your search. For example, searching the word 'oesophagus' brings up a list that includes words such as 'reflux,' 'swallowing,' and 'heartburn.' To refine your search, simply click the check boxes next to the words you want to add and then click the Search Again button.

The Ultimates
http://www.theultimates.com
This is a new type of index with twenty-five net services at your fingertips. There are resources from all over the net like phone books, email directories, and trip planners. As they say on the site, 'This isn't just another list of links. The form for each resource is integrated into the site, and the information is copied from one blank to another so you can use everything out there with a minimum of time and effort'.

FilePile.Com
http://img.filepile.com
FilePile is the world's largest indexed collection of shareware files with over a million free software programs you can download free for all platforms of computer operating systems including applications, games and pictures.

> ▶ *Shareware* – software that you can try before you buy. Usually there is some kind of limitation to the game such as a time limit or limited features. To get the registered (uncrippled) version, you must pay for the software.

Metasearch sites

Metasearch tools do not take advantage of the strengths of individual search engines, so it is useful to learn those strengths should you need that extra advantage.

Asking people

The Internet Sleuth
http://www.isleuth.com
A metasearch tool with over 3,000 databases to choose from. If you want to find something that may be rare or unusual, this is a great place to start. It is an easy site to use and provides an excellent base-camp from which you can explore the web and find information. This kind of site can easily bury you under a mountain of information so you have to be very specific in your search keywords and phrases. The site is not just a search site, though – there are many sections devoted to business users and a new market place with 300 merchants and over one million products.

Country Specific Search Sites
http://www.twics.com/~takakuwa/search/search.html
This site is a link to search engines by country. It appears to be a way of narrowing a search to a specific country. It is an interesting site – especially for travel and current events info. The site has links to hundreds of search engines, from Afghanistan to Yugoslavia.

WebFerret
http://www.ferretsoft.com
This is not really a search engine, but an offline search utility. You formulate your query offline and then, when you connect, it searches the web until it has collected the number of references you have specified. WebFerret queries large web search engines to find sites matching the keywords you specify. It queries all configured search engines simultaneously and discards duplicate results. URLs that are found can be visited immediately even as WebFerret continues to run. New or updated search engines are added automatically to WebFerret as they become available. The program is free but you can purchase a more advanced commercial version that lets you turn off the adverts that otherwise nag you as the program is running.

Asking people

The web is a great place to find information, but sometimes we do need to talk to real people. Emailing the owner of the web-site is one way but a better one is to find a place that they gather.

Sites full of experts
It is not easy to find someone willing to give free help; one only has to think about the high cost of legal or technical advice to realise how difficult it is. However, there is a growing number of people who are willing to literally give away information and answer questions on the internet. Before contacting an expert, make sure you have explored other sources first. Although the experts have volunteered to share their knowledge, they are likely to redirect you to your local library if the question shows that you expect the expert to do all the work.

Some of the sites below are a part of a large company or government site and therefore may have a hidden agenda, but they may none-

Getting started

theless be useful. The best sites are those that classify the experts by their specialist field.

Pickable Brains List
http://www.scalar.com/mw/pages/pickable.shtml
Many writers are experts in some field and many offer their knowledge on this site. The page is called the Pickable Brains list and is categorised under many general headings and some more specialised headings such as musical theatre, old Icelandic literature, confectionery manufacturing, newspaper publishing, history of Christianity, computational finance, and pizza delivery.

AskA Locator
http://www.vrd.org/locator/subject.html
This is the mother of all 'ask someone' sites! Organised in a wide variety of categories by their subject matter AskA lists those Ask an Expert sites in alphabetical order by subject, and then title name. You can find an expert for just about any topic.

Electronic Emissary
http://www.tapr.org/emissary
Holds a database of volunteer experts. You can search the Emissary's database of experts by keyword. The search should come back with a list of experts and description of the specialist field for each. You then choose an expert from the list and record an application number (which appears in the description). Finally you complete a form to request a match with the expert whom you have selected. This site is aimed at teachers but is open and very useful to others.

NJ NIE Project
http://njnie.dl.stevens-tech.edu/curriculum/aska.html
This site, hosted in New Jersey, USA, is called the New Jersey Networking Infrastructure in Education project (NJ NIE). Although having an unwieldy title, this site should probably be the first place (after the Pickable Brains list) to look for an expert. The site is classified into major subject areas and is simple to navigate. It is aimed at educators but is accessible and useful to anyone. The site is easy to navigate and the vast majority of the links are useful and up to date. Finding the relevant expert is easy. Perhaps the only limitation is that the content is mainly American biased.

The Internet Public Library
http://www.ipl.org/ref/
The *Ask-A-Question* service at the Internet Public Library is experimental. They say 'We're doing the best we can with what we've got. Right now, our biggest problem is volume: each day, we receive more questions than we can answer with our current staff resources.' The librarians who work at the IPL Reference Centre are mostly volunteers with other full-time librarian jobs. Your question is received at the IPL Reference Centre and the mail is reviewed once a day and questions are forwarded to a place where all the librarians can see them and

answer them. Replies will be sent as soon as possible, advising whether your question has been accepted or rejected. If it has been accepted, you should receive an answer in a day or two – a week or so if it is a harder question.

For children

Although aimed at children, these sites can be useful to adults, as long as you have a child to supervise you.

KidsConnect
http://www.ala.org/ICONN/kidsconn.html
If you have children or if you are around twelve years old yourself, contact this site. KidsConnect is a question-answering, help and referral service for children around the world. The goal of the service is to help students access and use the information available on the internet effectively and efficiently. The site is an experimental project run by the American Library Association. School library media specialists from throughout the world are collaborating on KidsConnect to provide direct assistance to any child who is looking for resources for school or personal interests. Children can contact the main KidsConnect address by email and will receive assistance within two school days from a library specialist. Are there any librarians reading this book? Isn't it time the UK had a service like this?

Homework help
http://www.nypl.org/branch/teen/homework.html
The site is divided into sections covering different subject areas. Questions and answers are treated as a discussion – questions are displayed on the relevant page of the web-site and answers from volunteer teachers are displayed within 24 hours. If you cannot find a discussion on the subject you are interested in, you should start a new discussion. For example, you might start a discussion to ask a new question on a new subject. The title for a discussion can be anything like 'Mummies' or 'Spaceflight' or you can elaborate and say exactly what it is you need to know about 'Mummies' or 'Spaceflight'.

Some specialised sources

Ask Grammar Queen
http://www.grammarqueen.com
The Grammar Queen, Wendy Weiner, is a business and academic writing consultant. She teaches English composition and conducts business-writing seminars. Besides answering grammar questions, she provides editing and proof-reading to businesses and individuals. Wendy says 'Although I DO answer each question personally, your question may be selected for display on the site.' For more information or to ask a question, email Wendy at: thequeen@grammarqueen.com.

Ask an Astronaut
http://www.nss.org/askastro/
One for lovers of science fiction – Ask an Astronaut receives on average

Getting started

7,000 to 10,000 questions per astronaut each session. The National Space Society selects 25-30 questions that the astronaut will answer. The questions selected include the more popular and well-thought-out submissions. To better your chances to have your question selected, try to make your questions specific. Unfortunately, questions take at least one month to be answered due to the astronauts' schedules so this option is only realistic for long-term projects. There should be only one question per person, no multi-part questions, and the subject matter should be related to the astronauts' professional lives. In January 1999, Alan Bean answered various questions about his life and thoughts including 'What it is like to be in space?' – 'What were his feelings while standing on the moon?' – 'Why he retired from NASA'. If you are interested in space exploration in any way, take a look.

Drug InfoNet: Ask the Doctor
http://www.druginfonet.com/askprof.htm
If you have ever wanted to know more information about the drugs you are taking or if you have any health related questions, you should bookmark this site. Not only do you have personal access to skilled physicians, but you can also use a number of large databases categorised under: drugs, manufacturers, medical reference, hospitals online, and more. The site is well laid out and easy to navigate, and is probably a good first point of call for medical questions although the site is not as comprehensive as you would expect a medical site to be. Another drawback is that experts may take weeks to reply to your questions.

Go Ask Alice
http://www.alice.columbia.edu/
Alice is the Health Education Program of the Columbia University Health Service. They say, 'We are committed to helping you make choices that will contribute to personal health and happiness, the well-being of others, and to the planet we share.' Unfortunately, at the time of writing there seemed to be no easy way to send a question. There are, however, plenty of questions and answers on the site, one of which will probably answer your question.

FORUMS, MAILING LISTS AND NEWSGROUPS

Forums

If you have been unable to find an expert on the web, check a special interest group. There are tens of thousands of special interest groups on the internet covering almost every subject you can imagine. There are two major kinds: mailing lists, and usenet.

▶ *Usenet* – a network of special interest forums (tens of thousands) which are accessible by anyone. You can post a message to the public forum, a newsgroup, where other newsgroup users can read and reply to it.

▶ *Mailing list* – a forum where messages are distributed by email to

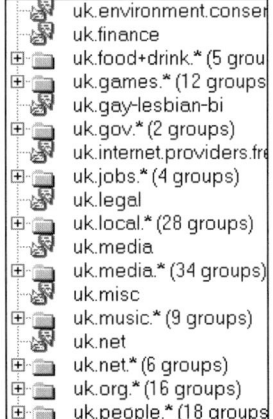

Mailing lists

the members of the forum. The two types of lists are discussion and announcement. Discussion lists allow exchange between list members. Announcement lists are one-way only and used to distribute information such as news or humour.

Lists and usenet work in slightly different ways. A mailing list is a community that discusses a certain subject by e-mail. Messages in a list are emailed directly to its members whereas those in a newsgroup are collected by their ISPs. Usenet discussion groups are publicly available to anyone who chooses to fetch the messages; a mailing list, on the other hand, can be private and exclude people.

Mailing lists

To join (subscribe to) a list, all you usually need to do is to send an email message to the list subscription address. The site owner or an automatic program will then acknowledge your request and send you further information and instructions on sending messages to the list. Try this: to get a daily fix of interesting web destinations emailed to you just send email to:

majordomo@web-today.net

with no subject and

subscribe webtoday-l

(that's a small L) in the body of the message. You will receive one email each day with reviews of four or five sites of general interest. Once you have tried it out, you can unsubscribe by sending mail to the same address with no subject and

unsubscribe webtoday-l

in the body of the message. There are thousands of mailing lists covering many subjects. To find a list with your interest, go to

Liszt
http://www.liszt.com/about.html.
Liszt is a directory of more than 90,000 different internet discussion groups, including mailing lists and newsgroups. On Liszt, you will be able to find almost any subject, from banjos to stamp collecting, or travel. Liszt says, 'There's other stuff, too, like humour lists and business and technology newsletters and alternate role-playing universes – basically, anything two or more people can do together via email.'

Usenet

My mother used to say 'he who asks never gets' in my early years. However, it became apparent that the opposite is actually true. Internet forums are great ways to ask for help and information. For example, a

Getting started

newsgroup called

misc.writing

is a great example of a helpful community – ask any question related to writing and you are likely to get a large number of responses. But even in such a good-natured group, questions that are unrelated to writing are likely to draw some sarcastic responses. The details of newsgroups are complex and will be covered by other books in the Internet Handbook series, detailed at:

http://www.internet-handbooks.co.uk

A brief introduction here, however, will enable you to quickly find people who are knowledgeable, or share an interest, in your topic of interest.

What is a newsgroup?

A newsgroup is a discussion forum dealing with a specific and defined area of interest. You can join in a discussion simply by sending or posting a message according to the instructions of your particular newsreader software (e.g. Outlook Express). To find out which usenet software you have, open your browser program and type into the address box:

news:

Your browser will then automatically start your news software (usually Outlook Express or Netscape Message Center) if you have one installed.

When you send a message to the group, you can reply to someone else's message or start a new discussion. There are often many different discussions taking place in a newsgroup at the same time. For instance in a music newsgroup, among the many discussions, you may see one on the latest concert at Wembley, and another one debating the merits and disadvantages of acoustic and electric guitars. Newsgroups are a great place to meet people with similar interests as well as a good place to find experts, but remember – they are not there to serve you personally. Be polite when asking your questions and don't assume that you will automatically receive the answer you want.

How to find a newsgroup

The solution is to go to Liszt (see mailing lists above) or to

Deja.com
http://www.deja.com/home_if.shtml.
There you can find forums that talk about the keyword or phrase you specify. In its own help page, Dejanews uses the example of 'Captain Kirk' (of the *Star Trek* television programme). The search results included alt.startrek.creative and alt.startrek.

Newsgroups

Reference.com
http://www.reference.com
Reference.com is another well known site dedicated to searching newsgroups and mailing lists. Aside from searching in the normal way, like Dejanews and Liszt, you can also submit an Active Query that will keep working even when you are not online. Reference.com will remember your query and run it periodically and as soon as something appears that matches your query, you will be sent an email message. For example, if the tickets are sold out for your favourite football team, you might want to receive the first ten messages every day about ticket sales from now until the day before the match.

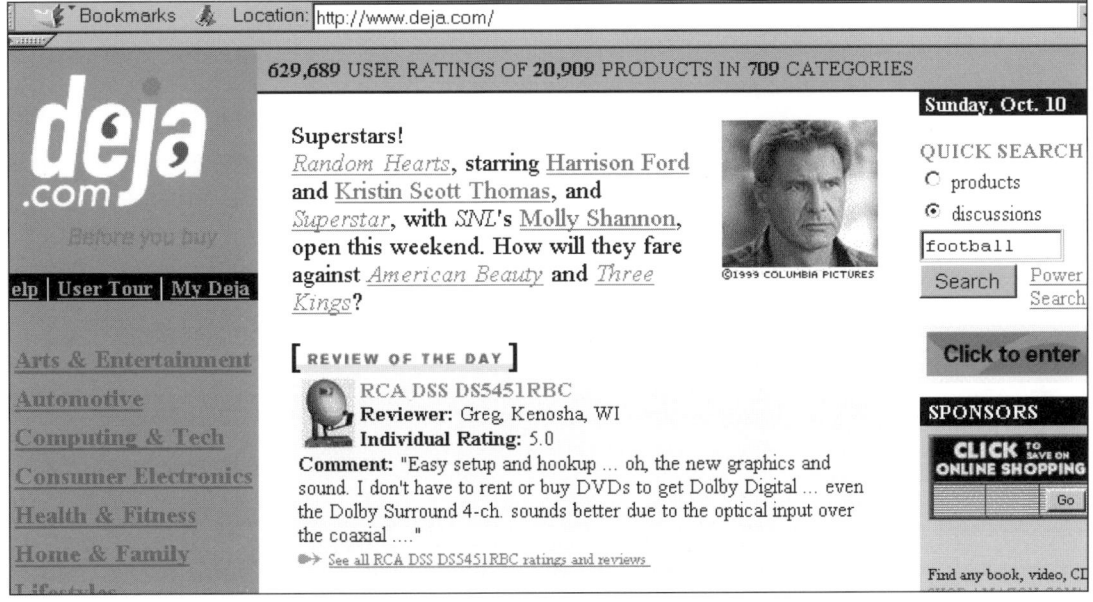

2 Work: business and education

In this chapter we will explore:

▶ *The arts*
▶ *Science and technology*
▶ *Business and finance*
▶ *Miscellaneous*
▶ *Careers, jobs and education*
▶ *Government and politics*

THE ARTS

Books and literature

Assorted Encyclopaedias
http://edis.win.tue.nl/encyclop.html
Assorted Encyclopaedias on the Web is just that – a collection of links to various encyclopaedias including biology, environment, medicine, crafts, hobbies, sports, cultures, geography, history, economics, finance, general knowledge, internet, mathematics, computing, mysticism, mythology, philosophy, physics, cosmology, religion and social sciences.

Bookwire
http://www.bookwire.com
This is an essential site for anyone interested in books – whether it is reading, writing, selling, publishing or editing. This site is the book industry's most authoritative source of information with book news, lists of best-selling titles, and touring authors. There is a best-sellers list for the current week, a job section contributed by *Publisher's Weekly* magazine, and a book review section called the Hungry Mind Review.

BookBrowse.com
http://www.bookbrowse.com
One of the disadvantages of buying something via the web is that you can't pick it up and feel it. With books, for example, you usually flick through the pages and read a little to see if you like the feel of the writing. A web site that comes close to this ideal is BookBrowse.com. They publish chapter long excerpts from most of the current best sellers, and shorter excerpts from hundreds of other recent fiction and non-fiction titles. Many excerpts are unique to BookBrowse; others are often available on the site before anywhere else on the web.

British Library
http://www.bl.uk
The vast resources of the British Library are not so easy to get at on the

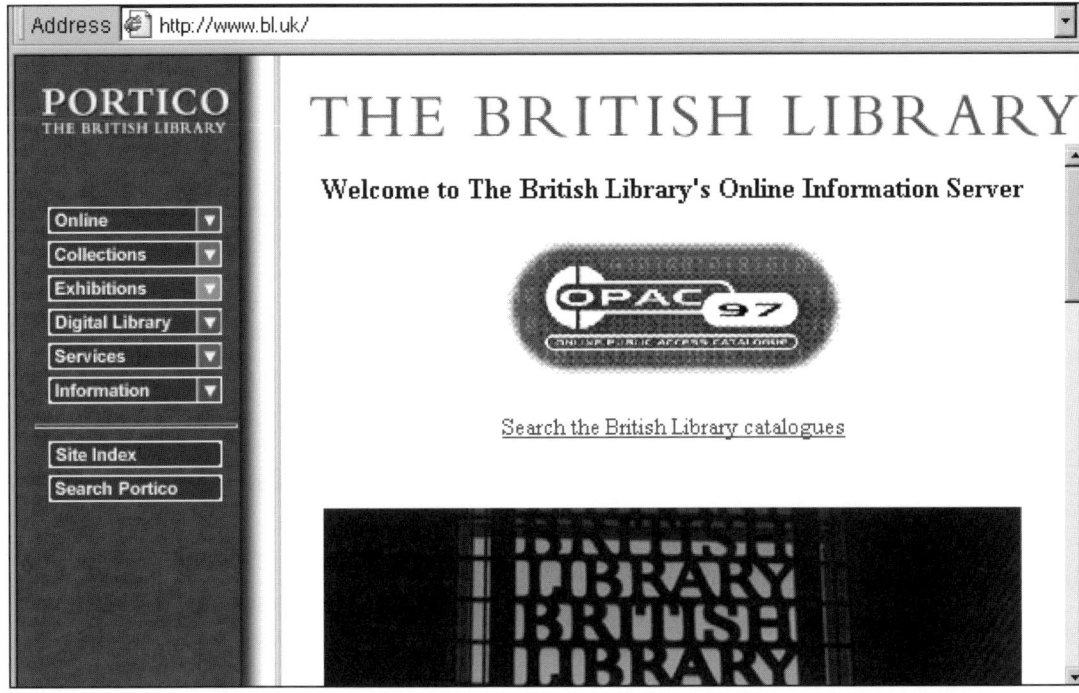

Fig. 4. The web site of the British Library. Imagine having the British Library in your front room! Well, you might not fit all of those books in there but at least you can look through the indexes at this enormous site.

site. It may look good but finding your way around is not as simple as it could be. You can do a free search of the main catalogue during opening hours but you must pay to look at some of the other more specialised book catalogues.

The Internet Classics Archive
http://classics.mit.edu
'Classics' are defined as ancient Greek and Roman texts and anyone with a liberal arts background will have had some experience with them. The Internet Classics Archive is extensive and covers hundreds of works. The main section is an author directory that leads to electronic texts, commentary and interactive discussions of each title. You can also test your knowledge in the trivia section. The content doesn't stop there – there's also a virtual bookstore where you can buy print versions, an exhaustive link section with pointers to other classics sites and a help page to ensure that you get the most out of the site.

National Library for the Blind UK
http://www.nlbuk.org
Take advantage of this free library service for visually impaired that provides monthly and yearly updates, a quarterly bulletin, and some electronic texts. The site uses high contrast colours and a large text size. The National Library for the Blind is the free library service for visually impaired readers who want books in accessible formats. Topics on the site range from astrophysics to Wilbur Smith including music scores and more. You can request a braille book from the site and it will be delivered the next day or you can download an electronic version from the site. Joining is easy, there are no formalities and you don't need to be registered.

Work: business and education

OneLook
http://www.onelook.com
OneLook allows you to search over four hundred online dictionaries to find the definition or spelling of a particular word. More than two million words are accessible through its site. You enter a word and OneLook provides a listing of dictionaries containing that word. You have the option to limit your search to standard sources, such as various versions of Webster's dictionaries, or to include specialist dictionaries such as the phrase and fable dictionary, a Shakespearean dictionary, an acronym finder, and Jane's defence Index.

The Online Books Page
http://www.cs.cmu.edu/books.html
There are thousands of books that you can read for free on the internet and many of them are classics. This site will help you to find them by performing a search. Just enter the title, author, or subject and the site will give you a list of matches and links to where you can read or download them. More titles become available constantly and are described in the new listing section. There is also a list of banned books with histories and links.

Project Gutenberg
http://www.aether.com/Aether/gutenberg.html
You are free to copy and download books and other texts that are out of copyright or in the public domain. Project Gutenberg is collecting such texts at its site. Their goal is to have ten thousand books by 2001.

Shakespeare Birthplace Trust
http://www.shakespeare.org.uk
'Let Shakespeare do it his way, I'll do it mine. We'll see who comes out

Fig. 5. The web site of the Shakespeare Birthplace Trust. The Russian writer Leo Tolstoy expressed his admiration of Shakespeare by describing his writing as, 'Crude, immoral, vulgar and senseless.' Could this be why Shakespeare's work has remained so popular down the centuries?

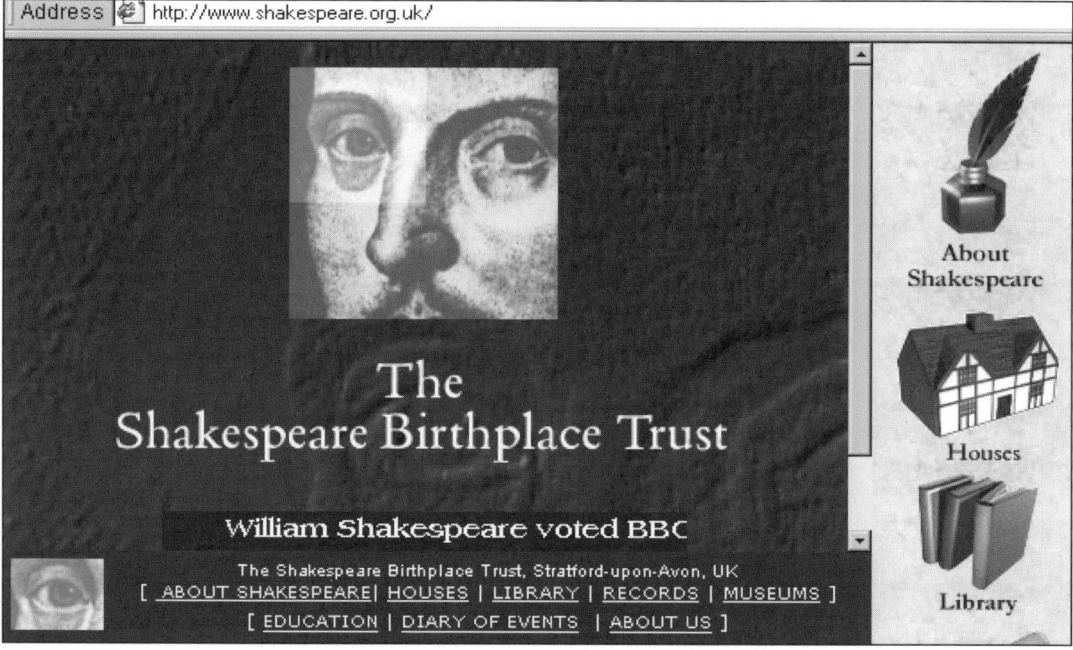

Performing arts

better' (Mae West). The trust came into existence after the purchase of Shakespeare's Birthplace in 1847 in order to preserve it as a national monument. The Trust is a registered charity incorporated by Act of Parliament. The main objects of The Shakespeare Birthplace Trust are: to promote understanding and enjoyment of Shakespeare's works, to maintain the five houses connected with Shakespeare and his family, and to provide a museum and library with particular reference to Shakespeare, and the history of the Stratford-upon-Avon area.

Shakespeare Online
http://www-tech.mit.edu/Shakespeare/works.html
All of Shakespeare's plays are available for download at this simple but functional site. The plays are arranged in four categories: tragedy, comedy, history and poetry. The site also has a discussion area, a 'What's New' section and a chronological and alphabetical listing of plays, and Bartlett's familiar Shakespearean quotations. Not a commercial quality site but at least there are no ads pushing themselves in your face. The site may be simple but it is a very useful resource.

Virtual Library
http://www.mth.uea.ac.uk/VL
You can use the virtual library to find resources on a large range of topics. Tim Berners-Lee, the creator of the world wide web itself, also created this library. It is the oldest catalogue of the web. It is non-commercial and run by volunteers, who compile pages of key links for their particular areas of expertise. It may not be the biggest index on the web but it is probably one of the highest quality.

Performing arts

Ballet.co
http://www.ballet.co.uk
The site 'about all things ballet and dance in the UK.' The site is divided

Fig. 6. The professional looking Ballet.co site is full of useful information and is easy to use. The subtlety and grace of the site matches that of the dancers it serves.

37

Work: business and education

into sections: magazine, listings, and update. The magazine section contains a mix of the latest reviews, interviews, views, articles on ballet history and a regular column by dancer Josephine Jewkes. The magazine is updated monthly and the listings section lets you know what's happening where and how you can get tickets. The update section keeps you informed about what is happening during the current week. There is also a postings page for exchanging ideas, views and questions with others, and a weekly newsletter that sums up the events and happenings.

English National Ballet
http://www.ballet.org.uk
Read all about the English National Ballet on this site. Plans for the season including highlights of past tours and details of future tours and the latest press releases with current news. You can start a chat about ballet, dance and the arts or join in one of the ongoing conversations in the discussion forum. The forum is organised into topics and articles, so you can reply to previous postings and develop conversations. The site is a good source of information and reference material about the history of English National Ballet and includes a list of links to other related sites.

OperaData
http://www.operadata.co.uk
OperaData was constructed for opera professionals and is the most comprehensive source of inside information on opera. The site is open to everyone 'from the casual enquirer to the dedicated operaphile.' The information is supplied by the team that contribute to *Opera Now*, the printed opera magazine. Material is checked daily and updated when needed. Regular users of the site must register but you can sample the information first.

Royal Opera
http://www.royalopera.org
Where are the buskers? Although the attractions of Covent Garden are lacking from the online Opera House, the site is still stylish and, well, operatic. The site is elegant, easy to navigate and authoritative with content that is educational and informative. Learn about the history of the ROH or simply book a seat to your favourite ballet or opera using a sophisticated interactive seat plan.

The Stage
http://www.thestage.co.uk
The Stage provides news and information on the business of entertainment including auditions, features and reviews. The main purpose of the site is to draw people to the paper version although the site in itself is useful. There is an auditions and recruitment section for thespians wanting to find some work and plenty of links to other sites of theatrical interest.

Visual arts

Royal Shakespeare Company
http://www.rsc.org.uk
Formerly the Shakespeare Memorial Company, the Royal Shakespeare Company is an English theatrical company based in Stratford-upon-Avon and in London. Their performances consist mainly of the plays of Shakespeare but include some other Elizabethan and Jacobean plays. The London-based Company performs modern plays and non-Shakespearean classics. The site offers free membership of a web club, which will send you up-to-date information on the company's activities.

To find all the information for dates and venues for this seasons productions CLICK HERE.

UK Theatre Web
http://www.uktw.co.uk
The UKTW started life on 14th February 1995 and claims to be the 'definitive WWW guide to professional and amateur performing arts in the UK.' It certainly displays lots of awards on the home page. The site mainly deals with theatre but also has sections for dance and opera. There are also sections dealing with jobs and training for those in the theatre business.

Visual arts

World Wide Arts Resources
http://www.wwar.com
This site should be the first stop in your exploration of the online world of art. The service is free once you have registered and there are links to most of the web pages with online art. The directory is organised into over 3,000 categories and has a mailing list and several chat rooms. This is a functional and reliable site.

Architectural Association
http://www.arch-assoc.org.uk
'The Architectural Association was founded in 1847 by a group of students and teachers who were unhappy with the education being provided by the articled system and wanted to develop an education that was self directed and independent of the profession and the state establishment. At that time no formal architectural education was available outside of the offices of practitioners.' The site contains details of events, lectures, exhibitions and publications open to anyone with an interest in architecture.

Architectural Web Sites
http://www.fbe.unsw.edu.au/misc/ArchSite
This site is a collection of links collected by Stephen Peter, of the University of New South Wales, to architecture and related web sites. The current shortage of architectural sites on the internet means that this site is worth bookmarking if you have an interest in architecture.

Art-Connection
http://www.art-connection.com
So, you want a Picasso hanging on your wall, do you? It is easy, all you need to do is to log onto this site, choose a suitable work of art from one

Please select gallery...
20th Century British Art Fair
A Art99
Affordable Art Fair
Agnews
Alberti Gallery
Andrew Mummery Gallery
Anna Hunter Fine Art
Anne Faggionato
Art Attack
Art First
Art on Paper
Atlantic Bay Gallery
Begbie
Bernard Jacobson Gallery
Blains Fine Art
Bowie Art
Brandler Galleries
Bruton Street Gallery (The)
Burlington Paintings

Work: business and education

of over thirty London commercial art galleries, order it, and then sell your house and your car to pay the deposit. The paintings are searchable by artist, gallery and subject. You can't buy online but that painting is only a phone call away.

ArtRes
http://www.artres.com
This is the world's largest and most comprehensive archive singularly devoted to images of painting, sculpture, architecture, and the minor arts, ranging in time periods from the prehistoric to modern art. There is access to over three million images on the site.

Art Review Magazine
http://www.art-review.co.uk
'Art Review is the UK's leading independent visual arts magazine designed to serve the art buyer and gallery visitor. In particular, we aim to cater for those who have an interest in art and wish to buy, but may need help and encouragement in developing their interest and knowledge.' The magazine serves as a taster for the paper magazine to which you can subscribe for £12. Sections on the site include: art under £1,000, editor's letter, bookshelf, exhibitions, features, focus, art on the net, news update, and shop window.

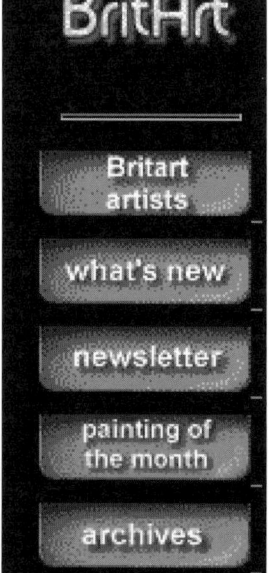

BritArt
http://www.britart.com
Anyone who has a few thousand pounds to spare can buy work by contemporary British artists, such as Chris Gollon, Maggi Hambling and Peter Howson. To purchase a work simply email the sales department and arrange packing, shipping and insurance. BritArt.com is updated every month with reviews, general information and details of forthcoming shows for each artist. They feature a 'painting of the month' at a 10 per cent discount, and display an archive of works sold. The site makes art buying simple and accessible, and the works are exclusive. Admit it, a wall looks bare without a painting or two.

British Journal of Photography
http://www.bjphoto.co.uk
The *British Journal of Photography* is the world's oldest photography magazine, first published in 1854. The magazine is aimed at professional photographers, and is published weekly. The site says, 'This is the online companion to our weekly printed edition of the *British Journal of Photography*. We don't attempt to duplicate the contents of our magazine; instead we use the Web to bring additional benefits that would otherwise be impossible in printed form each week.'
You will find a gallery of images from top photographers, a listing of exhibitions, a discussion area, and many other features useful to professional photographers.

The Electric Gallery
http://www.egallery.com/
The Electric Gallery has collected a unique collection of artwork from

Museums and galleries

renowned artists such as Picasso and Renoir. The Electric Gallery also showcases new artists whose work is not widely known. There is a section on Abstract realism, and another on the Amazon Project dedicated to preserving the traditions of the Peruvian Amazon, there is even a section containing images of, among others, Bob Marley and Jimi Hendrix.

ICA
http://www.newmediacentre.com
The Institute of Contemporary Arts (ICA) is 'a public playground for developing and presenting new and challenging work across the arts; for forging innovative ways of thinking about the wider culture; and for experimenting with the presentation of the arts. From exhibitions to performance, music to bands, independent films to video technology, literary events to conferences on digital culture and scientific issues, the ICA brings together the most exciting new ideas from around the world.' The ICA is always on the frontline of the art world, and the internet is a part of the battlefront. You specify your interests and the site tailors the information to your requirements and suggests other areas that might interest you. By the time this book is published, the site should also have a live camera for you to preview the events in the ICA.

The Louvre (Paris)
http://mistral.culture.fr/louvre/louvre
Is that a smile or a smirk? The Mona Lisa has fascinated people for years and it's still probably the most famous work of art in the world, and its home, the Louvre, is the most famous art gallery in the world. It is the French national museum and art gallery of France, housed in part of a large palace in Paris that was built on the right-bank site of the twelfth-century fortress of Philip Augustus. Take a virtual tour around the gallery at this site and look at the other resources, although many of them are in French, the artwork speaks for itself in any language.

New British Artists
http://www.newbritishartists.co.uk
Traditional dealers are being left behind as new British artists take their work to internet galleries. The traditional dealers have always been unwilling to take a chance on new artists but the internet now seems the obvious solution. This site asks 35 percent commission for each painting sold.

Museums and galleries

Cornucopia
http://www.cornucopia.org.uk.
By 2001 Cornucopia is intended to provide a complete picture of the museum collections in the UK.

MuseumNet
http://www.museums.co.uk
This is not just a site for the public, but also for museum professionals,

Introduction
Teacher's Guide
Museums
Museum Maps
Objects & Collections
People
Places
Picture Gallery
Search

Work: business and education

academics, and families. There is an A to Z listing of exhibits, and email addresses and links to many museums. For professionals, there is a chat area and an industry section.

Museums and Galleries Commission
http://www.museums.gov.uk
The MGC provides a gateway to UK museum information. At present, the site has an extensive range of facts and figures about museums, as well as the latest museum-related news and full details of all MGC publications and links to other museum related sites. Full details of museum collections are available via the new MGC database at Cornucopia (see page 41).

Museum of London
http://www.museum-london.org.uk
What was London like in the Victorian era? What was the fire of London like? What was entertainment like in London in the past? All these and many more questions are answered on this easy to use site. Many aspects of London's history, including the darker side, are explored in depth. The museum claims to be the most comprehensive city museum in the world. Indeed, the site covers London's history in great depth and breadth.

Museum of Science and Industry
http://www.msim.org.uk
Do you have intelligent children who continually become bored? Get them to play some of the games on the MISM site such as a co-ordination game or the Towers of Hanoi. These high-tech Shockwave games are really quite entertaining. Or encourage them to watch a streaming video and explore virtual landscapes. Try it yourself.

▶ *Shockwave* – a browser plug-in that gives you powerful multi-media playback. It lets you view interactive web content like games and presentations from your web browser. If you have not already got Shockwave, you can download it for free from Macromedia at: http://www.macromedia.com

National Gallery
http://www.nationalgallery.org.uk
This is the art museum in London, on the north side of Trafalgar Square, that houses Great Britain's national collection of European paintings. Most of the works of the National Gallery are paintings from the year 1240 onwards. You can view these online on more than 500 pages of art. Most of the paintings have excellent in-depth descriptions to accompany the image. Downloading the image may take a few minutes, though.

Natural History Museum
http://www.nhm.ac.uk
The Natural History Museum has been open to the public since 1881 and is much more than just a collection of stuffed animals. The

History and geography

museum's collection includes almost 70 million specimens from all over the world including historical collections such as those of Captain James Cook from his expeditions to the Pacific, and of Charles Darwin on the *HMS Beagle*. The collections are organised under the headings of botany, entomology, mineralogy, palaeontology and zoology. That's plants, insects, stones, fossils and animals to us common folk. There are also popular displays in the museum on such subjects as the Earth, ecology, *The Origin of Species*, dinosaurs, mammals, and human biology. The site is very comprehensive with something for everyone – from the casual tourist to the dedicated researcher. Take a virtual tour of the museum or visit the interactive exhibition, Quest.

National Portrait Gallery
http://www.npg.org.uk
The National Portrait Gallery houses the national collection of portraits of British men and women. If, like me, you are not very good at drawing faces, you might like to go to the Gallery to see the efforts of some other people – people a little better at drawing faces. The site is a simple and elegant introduction to the gallery and gives you an idea of what is available and the interactive site plan will help you to plan your visit. And, if you are a young artist, you can enter the NPG annual portrait competition for young artists.

Victoria and Albert Museum
http://vam.ac.uk
If you want to see what is probably the world's greatest collection of the decorative arts, visit the Victoria and Albert Museum in South Kensington, London. The home page welcomes you to the museum with a good-looking brightly coloured page. The site itself introduces you to the current exhibitions and gives you information about the museum. You can read about art news, educational events, research programmes, current listings and membership.

Geography and history

Ancient Sites
http://www.ancientsites.com/index.rage
Archaeology is the theme on this site, from Rome to Machu Picchu. You will find digs, site reconstructions, pictures and much more. Take virtual tours of places such as Ancient Rome, Greece, Egypt, Babylon, Nieuw Amsterdam, and Machu Picchu. The site is mainly for history buffs to discuss related topics but it also has wider appeal with some good graphics and some historical games. Ancient Sites has instant messaging, free homepages, group forming, editor elections, and bulletin boards.

Eurodocs
http://library.byu.edu/~rdh/eurodocs
Many interesting and important documents can be found on this site including political, economic, social and cultural history. The site contains documents on most of the European countries. The collection deals mainly with modern history but some earlier periods are included.

Fig. 7. The History Channel prepares you for the future by telling you what happened in the past. Here, you can find out what anniversaries are likely to be celebrated and who died or was born on a certain date.

The History Channel
http://www.historychannel.com
How much do you really know about history? Well, find out by visiting this site. Unlike many history classes at school, history is a fascinating subject, especially when presented as this site does. The History Channel is likely to make the most entrenched history-haters sit forward in their chairs. The home page pulls you into the main features with headings like 'Hear the words that changed the world' or 'story of the gun'. There is also a compelling 'this day in history' section where you can, for instance, enter the date of your birth and see what was happening of significance at the time.

Hyperhistory
http://www.hyperhistory.com
Hyperhistory.com is devoted to the idea that history is best learned by understanding synchronistic concepts. In other words, the site lets you access historical information through a timeline. You can see what else was happening in the world around 1812, for example, when the US was in a war over Canada, Napoleon was in Moscow, and the Maratha wars were being fought in India. Clicking the history button takes you to a master timeline, which is colour-coded to help you keep track of the region you're viewing. You can also view timelines that show only the life spans of famous figures or ones that show events in more detail but over smaller periods. In any timeline, you can read more about a topic. The number of options can be overwhelming at first, but you just may become hooked on viewing history in this fascinating manner.

Is Today Monday?
http://www.calendarzone.com
With the year ending, why not explore some different ways to look at 1999? The Calendar Zone helps you get more out of a calendar than just the day of the week. You can find calendars of historical and celestial

General science

events, interactive calendars, thought-of-the-day calendars, calendar software, and much more.

On This Day in History
http://dmarie.com
Click on 'Inspirations' then 'dMarie Time Capsule'. Almost everybody is curious about what was happening at the time of their birth – this site will give you a brief list of events for a specific date and an idea of what was happening around the time. When you select a date and activate the form, you are shown the top news and sports headlines, a list of the most popular songs of the day, the best film, actors, and some average income details.

Renaissance
http://renaissance.dm.net/
Renaissance, literally meaning rebirth, is the period in European civilisation immediately following the Middle Ages and characterised by an increase in popular classical learning such as the new Copernican system of astronomy where it was acknowledged that the planets revolved around the Sun instead of the Earth. Inventions of the time included paper and gunpowder. Despite these practical advances, the period was well known for its pomp. The Renaissance site has plenty of information on the Elizabethan period as well as a lot of quality links to other sites. Register for email notification when the site changes.

Tudor England
http://tudor.simplenet.com
The Tudor period saw the breaking of relations with the Catholic Church in 1534 and the beginning of the Reformation. The site includes resources and links to all the Tudor monarchs as well as sections on life in Tudor England. Other sections include architecture, who's who, maps, Tudors in the news, dates in Tudor history, Tudors in the movies, electronic texts and documents, a student's guide to Tudor England, and a pen pals section.

SCIENCE AND TECHNOLOGY

General Science

CNN: Sci-Tech
http://cnn.com/TECH
A news service concentrating specifically on the sciences. It is updated daily and is comprehensive, with excellent pictures and video clips. At time of writing, the main news item featured the discovery of a Taiwanese hacker who admitted creating the Chernobyl virus that ravaged computers world wide. There are sections dealing specifically with computers, personal technology and space news.

The Exploratorium
http://www.exploratorium.edu
The Exploratorium is a hands-on museum of science, art, and human perception that provides interactive online exhibits and exhibitions,

Work: business and education

activities, science news, and publications. The Exploratorium has many interactive 'hands-on' exhibits. 'Each year more than 600,000 visitors go to the Exploratorium, over 100,000 students and teachers go on field trips, and more than 10,000 teachers attend professional development programs, which focus on inquiry-based teaching and learning for the primary school.'

The London Science Museum
http://www.nmsi.ac.uk
The National Museum of Science & Industry comprises the Science Museum, London, the National Museum of Photography, Film & Television, Bradford, and the National Railway Museum, York. It holds 'the world's largest and most significant collection illustrating the history and contemporary practice of science, technology, medicine and industry.' The site lets you take tours of the museum and has details of the exhibitions and collections, the picture libraries, visitor information and a diary of events.

Nature
http://www.nature.com
Nature is perhaps the most authoritative publication for the frontiers of science. The site features a number of articles and offers you a single free sample full-text magazine. The publication and the site deal mainly with biological science but both have the occasional general feature. At time of writing there was a piece on scientific fraud. There is also a job section and a new product section. Beware, though, the site can be very technical and academic, but fabulous if that is what you need.

Fig. 8. The authoritative journal *Nature* takes you to the frontiers of science. Of benefit mainly to the scientific community, especially biology, but a fascinating read for anyone interested in the details of how and why the world works.

.... **Computers and the internet**

New Scientist
http://www.newscientist.com
The paper version of New Scientist is 'a science magazine for everyone, both young & old, amateur & professional.' It puts about a third of its paper content online and makes no charge for accessing the site. There is a selection of articles from the current week's issue of the magazine and searchable archive of back issues. The site has two sections besides New Scientist, Sciencejobs and NSPlus. Sciencejobs is a searchable database of jobs in the science sector and NSPlus is a little like a supplement and includes an archive of everyday science questions & answers and sections on topics like cloning and global warming. NSPlus also contains Hotspots – a guide to science sites on the web.

Science Frontiers
http://www.knowledge.co.uk/frontiers
The site is a supplement to the printed version of Science Frontiers and has plenty of information on weird discoveries and phenomena. General science subjects covered include archaeology, astronomy, biology, geology, maths, and physics. It is an interesting view into the possible future.

Computers and the internet

A List Apart
http://www.alistapart.com
There are dozens of sites out there intended to help web page authors create great sites. Many of them are excellent. Most of the pages focus on the practical aspects of HTML tags, programming and multimedia. 'What we found ourselves wanting was a resource that delved into the conceptual side of electronic publishing and that's just what A List Apart is.' This monthly newsletter features articles by some of the internet's best respected personalities on topics including writing for the web, the pitfalls of banner adds and the stultifying effects of trying to maintain browser compatibility. This is an outstanding site that every page designer should bookmark and visit often.

Ask Dr Internet
http://www.promo.net/drnet
Understanding a single computer is difficult enough but understanding a global network of millions of computers can be totally overwhelming. Ask Dr Internet explains email, FTP, the web, gopher and more. In each issue of Ask Dr Internet the editors take a selection of questions and answer them with information and advice.

CNET
http://home.cnet.com
The Computer NETwork claims to be 'The centre of the digital universe'. It is really a computer-related search site and quite a good one too. You will find information on games, hardware and software as well as news and articles on the issues of the moment at the sister site at News.com.

Fig. 9. Computer buffs, Cnet's site is unmissable. Whether it is games or technical details that attract you, this is a great site to start your quest. Once hooked, you'll be hanging around for quite a while.

Computerworld
http://www.computerworld.com
Computerworld serves as a channel of information for the IT marketplace – a weekly venue to find news and analysis of information technology events with sections on online communication, annual events, access to market research, and connection to global resources. News is updated three times a day and there's an audio version of the news and audio profiles of people in the IT news.

eFUSE.com
http://www.efuse.com
eFUSE.com is intended to make web publishing for small businesses understandable and easy. The site includes a step by step tutorial which guides you from basic web page design through to dynamic content and registering properly with search engines. The articles are very clear and helpful. Even seasoned online publishers will find something of use.

News.com
http://www.news.com
News.com is faster than Silicon News (see below) but not as comprehensive or customisable.

NoWonder!
http://www.nowonder.com
Amazingly, NoWonder! is a free technical support centre for almost any kind of computer user. The site offers to answer emailed technical support questions within 24 to 48 hours. Just choose your operating system (Windows, Mac, etc.) and fill out a form describing your problem. The more information you provide the more accurate and

Security on the internet

useful the answer. You are even asked your level of experience with computers: answers are then put into terms that you can understand. If you have a fairly good idea what might be wrong, look at the FAQs. NoWonder! uses volunteers. If you are a computer expert, share in the prestige and volunteer yourself – it would be a great way to expand your knowledge. From their site: 'For over two years, NoWonder! has been online providing *The Answer to Technical Support*. With over 450 volunteers world wide, answering nearly 50,000 questions in 1998 alone at no cost to our users, it's easy to see why we continue to be rated as one of the Top 10 net essential sites.'

OnNow
http://www.onnow.com/
OnNow lets you know what's on now on the internet – of course! The key word is 'now'. Most other Internet guides simply have a calendar of events, OnNow informs you about what's going on *now*. The minute the page appears in your browser, you can browse for events happening at that moment. You can also search the categories that interest you and, once you've found something of interest, you can get there quickly and easily.

Silicon News
http://www.siliconnews.com
Technology news is offered at hundreds of sites on the net, most of them come with layers and layers of adverts too. Silicon does have the odd advert or two but the news service is fabulous. You can customise the site so you get information relevant to your particular interests but beware the junk mail option in the details form, though.

Tasty Bits
http://www.tbtf.com
Can't get enough technology news? Here's another site offering lots of internet news: Keith Dawson's Tasty Bits from the Technology Front. The bias is towards internet commerce, but you will find news about computers and communications technology. The site is updated daily and you can sign up for a weekly email newsletter.

Your security on the internet

You would think only large corporations and international criminals (the terms are not always synonymous) need to be careful about sending information over the internet. You would be wrong – you may be giving away much more information about yourself than you think. Almost every time you visit a web site, some details about you or your computer are being recorded. Someone somewhere will be able to tell what kind of computer, operating system and browser you are using. Other sites compile information on your browsing and shopping habits. Most sites only use this information so you can personalise your browsing but an increasing number track your every step on their site to build a profile of your habits – for marketing purposes. Many sites even store information on your hard disk to 'make life easier for you'. This kind of invasion may be acceptable for most people but if you are for

Work: business and education

example a Chinese national wanting to look at the Free Tibet site, be careful. If you want to understand more about the privacy issue, which is complex, visit the following sites. Some of them are heavy going but the knowledge contained there is invaluable.

Anonymizer
http://www.anonymizer.com
Anonymizer provides a free anonymous surfing service. To quote their site, 'a web site can track your movements through their pages and monitor your reading interests. For example it is widely agreed that governments and organisations publish dummy web sites on controversial topics for the purpose of monitoring interested parties. In addition, this information – in combination with your email address – can be used to increase the number of targeted advertisements fired at you by the marketers. Anonymizer Surfing hides your address – the web site only sees that Anonymizer fetched the page. A web site can automatically exploit security holes in your system using ready-made, free hacking programs.' Anonymizer helps to prevent this.

EPIC
http://www.epic.org
EPIC stands for Electronic Privacy Information Centre. It was established in 1994, and one of its aims was to focus public attention on civil liberties issues and to protect privacy. EPIC works in association with Privacy International, an international human rights group based in London, UK.

Fig. 10. Epic is probably a site you have never heard of; nonetheless, it is one of the most important players in the future of the internet. The internet is a battleground – the disputed territory is your personal online privacy, and Epic is one of the strongest defenders you have.

Physical and chemical sciences

PGP home page
http://www.pgpi.com
The PGPi project is a non-profit organisation, whose purpose is to make PGP encryption software freely and legally available world wide. They write, 'Because of the strict US export regulations, strong encryption programs such as PGP cannot be exported electronically without a special license. In order to get around this problem, every time a new PGP version is released in the USA, we purchase the PGP source code books from a US book store, ship them to Europe, and scan and proof-read the entire books (currently over 12,000 pages) to recreate the original program.'

▶ *PGP (Pretty Good Privacy)* – a method of encoding a message before transmitting it over the internet. With PGP, a message is first compressed then encoded with the help of keys. Just like the valuables in a locked safe, your message is safe unless a person has access to the right keys.

The Privacy Site
http://www.privacy.org
Did you know the new Intel Pentium III chips each have a unique serial number that can be used to trace you all over the internet? The privacy site has information and news concerning privacy and security on the internet. If you value your privacy, check this out before you agree an upgrade to Pentium III.

Zero Knowledge Systems
http://www.zks.net
This company produces a product called Freedom that 'provides a simple method for any internet user to obtain cryptographically assured anonymity.' The system is similar to the Anonymizer in that it prevents a user's personal information being used without consent.

Physical and chemical sciences

Applied Space Resources
http://www.appliedspace.com
Some of the aims of the ASR are: to identify, develop and commercialise interplanetary resources, lead the opening of near-Earth space to private, commercial ventures, deliver a spacecraft to any destination with precision, and return resources and information to Earth with equal precision. ASR is planning the first commercial lunar mission for launch in 2001 to Mare Nectaris and collect new lunar samples. ASR will make part of the sample available to consumers. The Lunar Retriever spacecraft will carry several scientific experiments.

The Arthur C Clarke foundation
http://www.acclarke.co.uk
Anybody who enjoys science fiction novels will know who Arthur C Clarke is. The site is almost as memorable – it is an educational resource, which documents the history of technological progress

Fig. 11. Space is the greatest source of untapped wealth that you can imagine. ASR aims to be the first extra-terrestrial plumber and fit the first tap.

including the oceans, communications and space. This is a cleverly designed site that is both entertaining and educational.

Chemistry
http://www.dayah.com/periodic
Are there any people who need to know the Periodic Table out there? Even if you don't, this site has a great example of the table of elements. Use of complex tables and JavaScript allows for a remarkable presentation. Click on an element and you get a description of it as well as where it comes from. An outstanding resource!

▶ *JavaScript* – A simple programming language that can be put on a web page to create interactive effects such as buttons that change appearance when you position the mouse over them.

Edinburgh Engineering Virtual Library (EEVL)
http://eevl.icbl.hw.ac.uk
This is a vast resource for sorting through all the engineering information available on the web. The EEVL catalogue boasts reviews of more than 3,800 engineering-related sites. Fortunately, you can search the catalogue by subject or resource type, and you can further limit searches by selecting a filter from a drop-down list and/or by specifying sites inside or outside of the United Kingdom. Another great feature allows you to search more than 100 engineering journals, which are available in PDF format. In addition, you can search an archive of newsgroup messages posted over the last forty days.

European Space Agency
http://www.esrin.esa.it
An independent European space power was talked about in the early

Physical and chemical sciences

1960s and was formed on 30 October 1980. ESA comprises of Belgium, France, Germany, Italy, the Netherlands, United Kingdom, Australia, Denmark, Spain, Sweden, Switzerland, Ireland, Austria, Norway and Finland. Canada takes part in some projects. The organisation has been involved with the Hubble Space Telescope, Spacelab, and the SOHO and Cassin-Huygens project.

Hubble Space Telescope Public Pictures
http://oposite.stsci.edu/pubinfo/pictures.html
There is always something fascinating about high-resolution pictures taken from space. This is NASA's official archive of publicly released Hubble images with hundreds of pictures organised into categories that cover everything from neighbouring planets to distant galaxies. Each can be downloaded in several formats including high and low resolutions and each is accompanied by scientific data and detailed explanations.

NASA Spacelink
http://spacelink.nasa.gov
Spacelink is an educational resource aimed at teachers and students. It is a comprehensive electronic library with current information related to research at NASA. You will also be able to find teacher guides and pictures that may be useful for the classroom.

NASA Spaceflight
http://spaceflight.nasa.gov
Probably all you need to know about space exploration and development can be found at NASA spaceflight. You can now access information previously located on other sites such as NASA's Shuttle Web, NASA's Shuttle-Mir Web and NASA's Station Web. Further improvements are planned which include access to information from other sources such as international partners and academic institutions and the inclusion of an intelligent search engine, an animated real-time telemetry display, Audio/Video streaming, and a library search tool.

NASA's Quest Projects
http://quest.arc.nasa.gov
These projects, which are also called Sharing NASA, allow students to share in the excitement of NASA's authentic scientific and engineering pursuits like flying the shuttle and the International Space Station, exploring distant planets with amazing spacecraft, and aeronautics/ aeroplane research. In these project students 'engage in scientific content and processes with NASA scientists and discourse is facilitated with online chats, email Q&A and live audio/video programs.'

National Geographic
http://www.nationalgeographic.com
The National Geographic Society, one of the world's largest non-profit organisations, was founded in 1888 with the purpose of increasing geographic knowledge, it represents the world through magazines, books, maps, films, television and other media. *National Geographic*

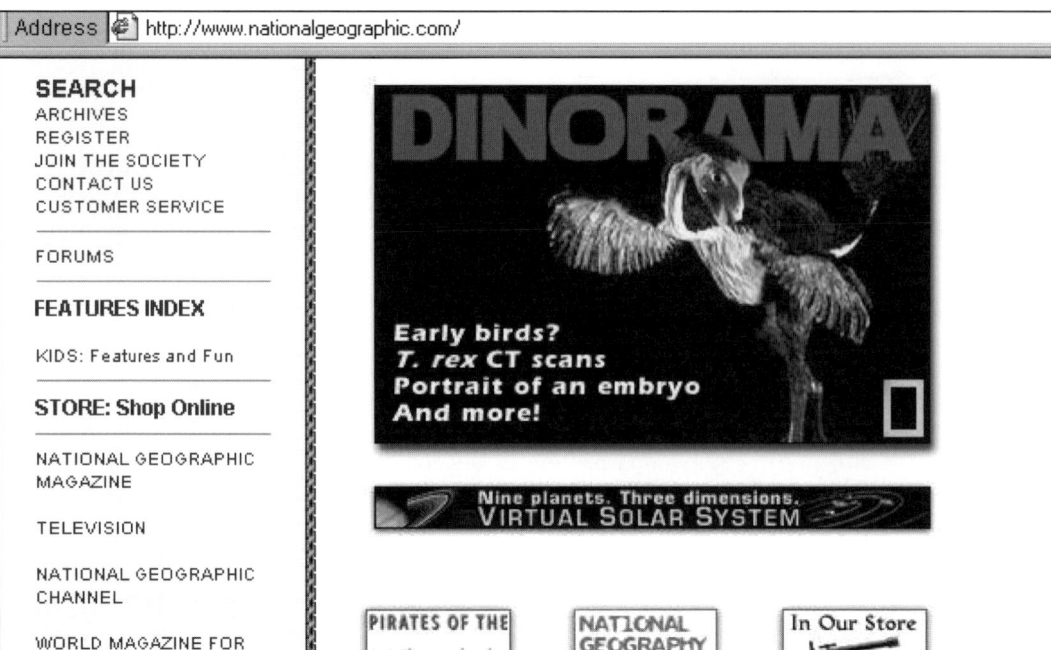

Fig. 12. National Geographic is the source for stunning information and images from every corner of the world. National Geographic will convince you that there are no corners in fact, and that we are but a small part of an incredible world.

magazine, the official journal of the Society, is read in every country in the world. The Society has supported thousands of explorations and projects and also funds an education program to encourage geographic literacy.

Physics Time-Line
http://www.weburbia.com/pg/historia.htm
What have string theories and Greek philosophers in common? They are both part of the story of physics. This site records the time-line of discoveries in physics and cosmology. It is a collection of the 'Eureka moments' of the greatest physicists. These pages contain a list of most of those moments, which have helped to form the science of physics – a chronology of discoveries in physics and cosmology.

PhysicsWeb
http://physicsweb.org
PhysicsWeb offers ten online services including three news services: weekly news, in depth news, patent news, book reviews, web watch, online letters, PhysicsWorld, events calendar, web resources, physics jobs, and physics net. Web Watch consists of reviews of other sites by the editor of PhysicsWeb. PhysicsWorld includes enhanced versions of articles from *Physics World* magazine; and Physics Net provides information on online equipment available online. Certain services will be restricted to *Physics World* subscribers, PhysicsWeb subscribers and members of the Institute of Physics. At time of writing the subscription charge was £25.

Spacestation.Com
http://www.spacestation.com
The Space Station is where the real action is. And whether you're curious about the USA/Russian hook-up or a die-hard enthusiast for all

things interstellar, you'll find something of interest on this site. It is presented by Encyberpedia and NASA and offers the opportunity to view real-time space station data and gives a chance to meet the crew, discover the history of space travel, and view various launchings.

Biological sciences

Botany.com
http://www.botany.com
Botany employs many terms. This site may not give you all of them, but you do get databases of common plant names, botanical plant names, a dictionary of botanical terms and a listing of botanical organisations. The site is designed to be an encyclopaedia of plants, 'your complete resource for all of your gardening needs.' It provides general descriptions of the plants, the methods of cultivation such as indoor or outdoor planting, soil and temperature requirements, pruning, the means of propagation and the different varieties and hybrids. The directory of plants is easy to use and includes, annuals, bulbs, fruit, grass, cacti, herbs, succulents, water plants, spices, houseplants, perennials, shrubs, bushes, trees, vegetables, vines, crawlers and wild flowers.

Dinosaur Interplanetary Gazette
http://www.dinosaur.org/frontpage.html
'All the dinosaur news that is fit to print.' If you are interested in dinosaurs, this is the place to go, but watch out – the site itself is a bit of a dinosaur. The individual pages are chaotic to view – unbearably long and composed of almost every imaginable combination of colour, font, image, animation and special effect. This is probably one of the few sites on the internet where you can get lost without even leaving the home page.

Human Anatomy Online
http://www.innerbody.com
Human Anatomy Online offers fun with interactive and educational displays of the human body. The site contains over one hundred illustrations of the human body with animations and thousands of descriptive links. To use the site, you need to have Java enabled in your browser. Java applets are used to show the images and to allow you to select anatomy parts. One of the best ways to find your way round a complex land is by taking a tour, and this site will give you the equivalent for the human body. The content of the site is aimed at older children. Students can click on Interactive Anatomy, choose one of several different anatomy systems, and then select and learn the names and functions of various organs. They can choose the Anatomy Lessons, which will teach the student about the human body organ-by-organ. The whole of the site features colourful and well-labelled diagrams.

The Human Body: An Online Tour
http://www.education-world.com/a_lesson/lesson065.shtml
The human body is the most fascinating and fantastic machine in existence. Did you know that:

Work: business and education

- More than half the bones in the human body are in the hands and feet?
- A new-born baby has 350 bones, but a fully-grown adult has only 206?
- Everyone is colour-blind at birth?
- The average adult is made up of 100 trillion cells?

This site is meant for teachers but the lessons will be interesting, entertaining and very readable for anyone.

Online Surgery
http://www.onlinesurgery.com
This gruesome site broadcasts live surgery over the internet, using the latest techniques and technology. Past surgical procedures are also available in the surgical archives. Online surgery was at time of writing covering cosmetic surgery, but plans are afoot to expand to cover subjects such as child birth, brain surgery, and orthopaedics.

Psychology
http://www.unipissing.ca/psyc/psycsite.htm
Have you ever considered that you might be interesting or weird enough to be the subject of a psychological experiment or are you in two minds about it? Now is your chance to find out for sure. This site, besides acting as a jump-off point for many excellent psychology sites, provides links to institutions, which are looking for volunteers. The experiments may not sort out your head, but they will be a talking point the next time you are in a bar. The site would be useful for anyone interested in the science of psychology but sites dealing with self-help or parapsychology are not listed.

Military technology

Imperial War Museum
http://www.iwm.org.uk
The Imperial War Museum, consists of four sites in one:
1. Imperial war Museum itself showing off the museum's outstanding collections of film, photographs, diaries, letters, art, firearms, medals, printed material and sound recordings, and includes a comprehensive guide to exhibition programmes.
2. Duxford Station in Cambridgeshire, which is a former Battle of Britain fighter station that now houses most of the Museum's aircraft exhibits.
3. Cabinet war rooms in London which were the nerve-centre of the war cabinet and the chiefs of staff during the second world war.
4. HMS Belfast, a cruiser moored on the Thames near Tower Bridge.

Janes Defence
http://defence.janes.com
Janes is perhaps the most authoritative source of information on military technology in the world. And the site does not stop at

Fig. 13. To understand the technology behind the wars, Janes' publications are essential reference all over the world. Often the technology is the deciding factor in a war; at other times, it is the cause of the war.

technology; there is regular news on the conflicts in the various parts of the world. The war in Yugoslavia has been covered in fine detail with profiles of the equipment of all of the armies involved and in-depth analysis of the capabilities of the forces and their equipment.

Operation Desert Storm Debriefing Book
http://www.nd.edu/~aleyden/contents.html
What is the difference between a map of Saudi Arabia and a piece of sandpaper? The sandpaper is more useful if you are lost in the desert. This site is the online version of the book by Andrew Leyden. It contains a comprehensive analysis of the Gulf War – Operation Granby/Desert Storm. Colour illustrations are plentiful and there is even a section offering people who were involved the chance to tell their own story.

Secret Kingdom
http://www.cc.umist.ac.uk/sk
Sssh! The secret services are listening. Secret Kingdom describes the various British secret military organisations such as MI5, MI6, GCHQ, SBS, SAS, and others. The site attempts to keep up to date with the latest changes in the intelligence community but the site appears to have been unchanged since 1996. Even so, it makes interesting reading. The site reports that the SBS has now been combined with other sections of the Royal Navy to form the MCT unit – (Marine Counter Terrorism) and the SAS Headquarters are moving to Credenhill, a disused RAF base a few miles north of Hereford. 'Who Dares Wins' is the motto of the Special Air Service based in Hereford. The details of the methods and operations by the SAS and other Special Forces and intelligence organisations remain mostly hidden from public view. The Secret Kingdom site, however, has lots of scary inside information and news updates. Dare you visit?

Work: business and education

Business and finance

TheBiz
http://www.thebiz.co.uk/finstk.htm
The Business Information Zone gives UK-relevant business information, products and services including an index of stock and commodity markets. However, The Biz doesn't just limit you to information on the internet. It also gives you information about organisations not on the internet from extensive database listings.

UK Directory
http://ukdirectory.com
UK Directory is business oriented and has a very comprehensive database of business related and general sites. 'Our aim is to provide the most comprehensive guide to everything in the United Kingdom on the world wide web.'

WebData
http://ns4.webdata.com/
WebData is an internet database portal, specialising in finding, categorising and organising online databases. WebData provides business and researchers a centralised location for searching and accessing web databases with targeted access to information that text-based search engine sites do not. The databases are specially chosen – professionally reviewed, and are categorised using strict standards for evaluating their nature, quality and content. WebData features even allow a user to interact with many different databases simultaneously.

▶ *Portal* – web site that is designed to be used as a 'home base' from which you can start your web experience. Portals often serve as general information points and offer news, weather and other information that you can customise to your own needs. Yahoo! is a good example of a portal: http://www.yahoo.com.

Online banks and building societies

According to a survey by accounting company Deloitte Consulting, one in three banks will disappear before 2005. Banks, in their race to provide better services to customers, are taking the banking war onto the internet. Services offered range from simple balance enquiries to the full services offered by the walk-in branches: bill payment, cash transfers, standing orders, chequebook ordering and the rest.

There are two main kinds of banking that you can do using your home computer: PC banking and internet banking.

▶ *PC banking* – uses the software supplied by the bank and bypasses the internet and connects you directly with the bank's computer system.

Online banks and building societies

▶ *Internet banking* – works over the internet and can use third-party software such as Microsoft Money.

In 1999, about half a million people in Britain were already using internet banking. And it is predicted that most banks will allow some kind of access to personal accounts over the telephone by the year 2000. PC banking is thought to be more secure but more expensive and not as flexible as internet banking. However, internet banking carries all of the risks associated with the internet such as hackers and other internet problems.

Banks and building societies are constantly competing and competing hard. Whenever one of them comes up with a new idea, the others follow fairly quickly. By the time this book is published, there will undoubtedly be different features on probably every site listed. As an example, Barclays started free internet access in April 1999 to go with their free link to its stockbroking facility. Here are some of the main banks:

Abbey National	http://www.abbeynational.co.uk
Barclays	http://www.barclays.co.uk
Bank of Scotland	http://www.bankofscotland.co.uk
Co-operative Bank	http://www.co-operativebank.co.uk
First Direct	http://www.firstdirect.co.uk
Lloyds	http://www.lloydsbank.co.uk
HSBC	http://www.banking.hsbc.co.uk
National Westminster	http://www.natwest.co.uk
Nationwide	http://www.nationwide.co.uk
Royal Bank of Scotland	http://www.rbs.co.uk
TSB	http://www.tsb.co.uk

Bank of England
http://www.bankofengland.co.uk
The Bank of England, 'The Old Lady of Threadneedle Street', is the central bank of the UK. The Bank has many roles such as setting interest rates to meet the Government's inflation target, managing the Government's stock register and printing bank notes. It also collects and publishes money and banking data in order to monitor financial developments in the country.

Internet Banking
http://www.internet-banking.com
To avoid the confusion, why not start your look at banks at the Internet Banking Barometer, which has articles on online banking and links to the most of the major banking sites in Europe. To quote their site, 'The Unisys banking site is designed to give a measure of the current status of Internet Banking in Europe. As well as providing information describing how banks are using this new medium, the site rates the Banking industry's use of the internet in the form of the Unisys Barometer Index.'

Fig. 14. If there is such a thing as an independent evaluation of the banking system, Internet Banking will be it. Don't commit yourself until you take in the information on this site.

Finance and investment

It has been estimated that the number of people using online broking services will increase fivefold from around 150,000 to over 700,000 by 2003. The volumes of shares traded will probably add up to hundreds of millions of pounds. Here are some sites to help you out.

Better Business
http://www.better-business.co.uk/home.htm
Self-employment can be a lonely and overwhelming experience and finding information can be painful. Better Business is a wonderfully clear site that offers practical, money saving, time saving and profit boosting information for small businesses. You will find down-to-earth advice, news, contact points and technology updates. It helps people at all stages from start up to established and growing businesses. It also offers motivation, inspiration and support.

Charles Schwab Europe
http://www.schwab-worldwide.com/Worldwide/Europe
One of the more enterprising share dealing companies to take advantage of the trend towards internet dealing is Charles Schwab who signed up over ten thousand customers and traded over £200 million worth of shares in its first year of business. They say they have about 500 new customers joining every week. Some of the services on offer are: web access, deal equities, monitor accounts, real-time prices, in-depth news, research and analysis, savings for web and electronic dealing, and personal assistance seven days a week.

The Euro
http://europa.eu.int/euro
The Euro site provides general and technical information on the

Finance and investment

changeover to the new European currency. 'Whether you are a citizen interested in your future currency, a specialist working on technical preparations for the changeover, or a surfer passing by, this site has useful and interesting information in all eleven official languages of the European Union.' The site is regularly updated with applicable documents when they become available and also provides access to an electronic version of *Infeuro*, the Commission's own newsletter on the euro, plus links to other sites with useful information on the single currency.

FIND
http://www.find.co.uk
FIND stands for the Financial Information Net Directory. It was launched in 1996 and is owned and operated by Omnium Communications. The site is directed by people with considerable experience in the financial services industry. Although directed at the finance industry, there is a good deal of useful information for everybody. The greatest strength of the site is the collection of quantity links categorised under the headings: insurance, investments, information, advice, banking and savings, and mortgages and loans.

FT.com
http://www.FT.com
The *Financial Times* web site delivers business news, comment and analysis in a variety of formats combining articles from the printed newspaper with material specially prepared for the web. The site is updated throughout the day. The FT also aims to provide the best source of world wide business information, authoritative analysis and comment.

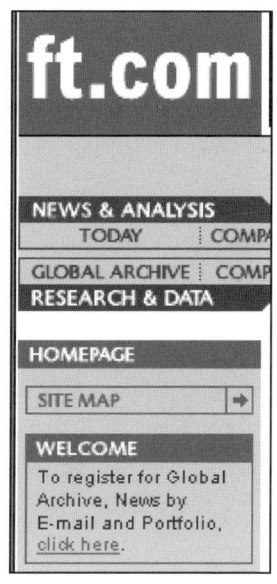

Inland Revenue
http://www.inlandrevenue.gov.uk
Microsoft has teamed up with the Inland Revenue to create this site. One of the results is that PC users can now fill in their tax returns online. Small businesses will be specially interested in the self assessment system which gives information about completing your tax returns, the effect of self assessment, record keeping and the taxpayer's charter. Plans are underway to enable taxpayers to send tax information over the internet. The site also has information on income tax, National Insurance contributions, corporation tax, capital gains tax, petroleum revenue tax, inheritance tax and stamp duties. The site is easy to use and comprehensive – some possible comfort to the small business owner.

Interactive Investor
http://www.iii.co.uk
Whatever you want to know about your investments, you are likely to find on this site. The 3i's offer free portfolio monitoring where you can inspect a valuation and a profit-and-loss statement. A clickable graph allows you to check on the performance of your individual investments over time compared to reference indexes. The news section updates

Work: business and education

you on recent stories relevant to your investments. The 3i's is a major institutional investor, backed by leading financial institutions.

The London Stock Exchange
http://www.londonstockex.co.uk
The site offers a very interesting introduction to the London Stock Exchange and the listing rules for the official List and AIM, the Alternative Investment Market. This web site tells you how the Exchange and its markets work and includes a glossary and how-to guide. There is also a news and information section, which you can search by keyword.

MoneyXtra
http://www.moneyeXtra.co.uk
This site is a partnership of the Microsoft Money software and The Exchange, who provide online financial information. There are financial features, price comparisons, personal loan information, credit card tips, mortgage information, insurance and more. MoneyXtra is an independent personal finance site. The site outlines the various investment rules. ISAs, for example, are explained in fair detail and the site will help you to decide which is the best for you.

Moneyworld
http://www.moneyworld.co.uk
A good site covering personal finance in general. There is a news service, guides and tips on many subjects like arranging a pension and finding the right mortgage. You can plan your mortgage payments to get the best tax deal with the handy calculator on the site. It lets you juggle with mortgage payments, pension contributions, PAYE income and gifts.

Fig. 15. Don't be a fool, be a Motley Fool. The Motley Fool gives an objective if humorous view of the money world. Whether you are a new or a seasoned fool, take a look.

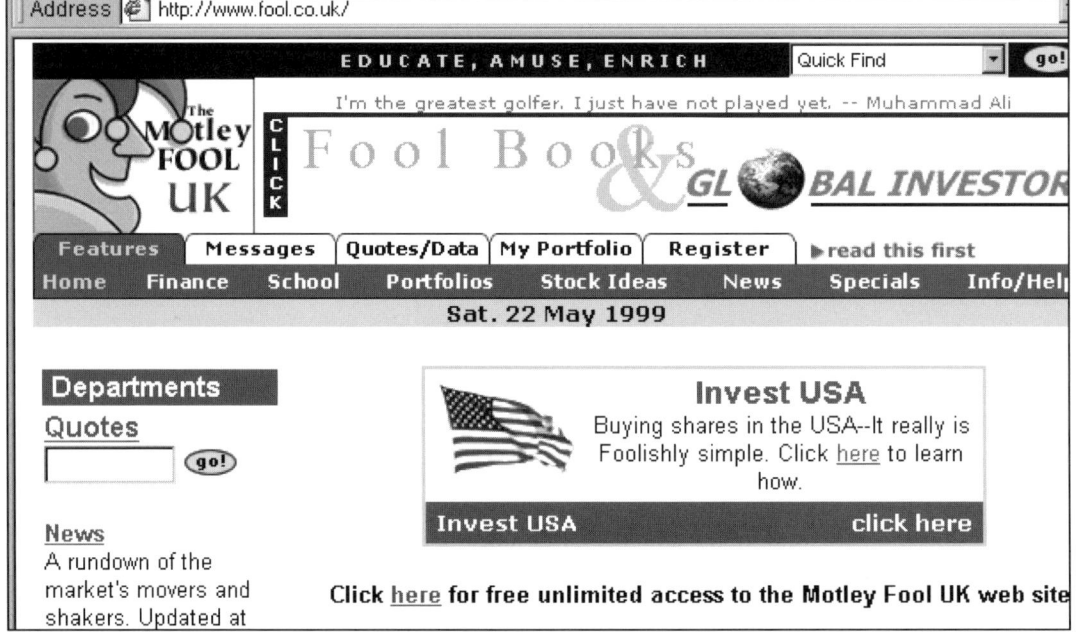

.... Finding businesses

The Motley Fool
http://www.fool.co.uk
The Motley Fool aims to give the reader an unbiased view of the money world. Many of the articles are humorous but the site has a serious base beneath the jokes. There is a Fool's School where you can 'Learn to invest the Foolish way,' a glossary of financial terms, educational articles on investment, and a message board where you can be a fool with other fools.

Self Assess
http://www.selfassess.com
Here is another useful site for small businesses. It specialises in untangling the confusion of self-assessment under the British Inland Revenue. Self Assess offer 'a wide choice of tax information and a professional, cost-effective service for dealing with your self assessment tax return forms and subsequent revenue correspondence.'

Law

Law Talk
http://www.lawtalk.co.uk
There is a weekly news page, a bulletin board and a wide range of links to other legal sites. The bulletin board is for the exchange of ideas, discussion of work related problems and general brainstorming. There is a magazine section, which is regularly updated with a selection of articles on the legal issues of the day. Topics include access to justice and reform of the criminal justice system.

Finding businesses

Britnet
http://www.britnet.co.uk
Britnet provides a range of services for British companies wishing to exploit the internet. These services include: a trading directory for British commercial internet sites, registration of the company's web URL and email addresses, site design, marketing, technical management, advertising and sponsorship opportunities, development and management of online revenue generation opportunities, email database management, online publishing, and training.

Communications Business
http://www.icbinc.com
A portal to annual reports from more than 3,500 publicly traded corporations. The site links to six annual report ordering services offered by the financial press, including the *Wall Street Journal*, *Barron's*, the *Financial Times*, and the *Globe and Mail* (Canada).

Company Sleuth
http://www.companysleuth.com
This is a great new free resource for finding information about companies and staying ahead in the stock game. 'Company Sleuth scours the internet for free, legal, inside information on the companies

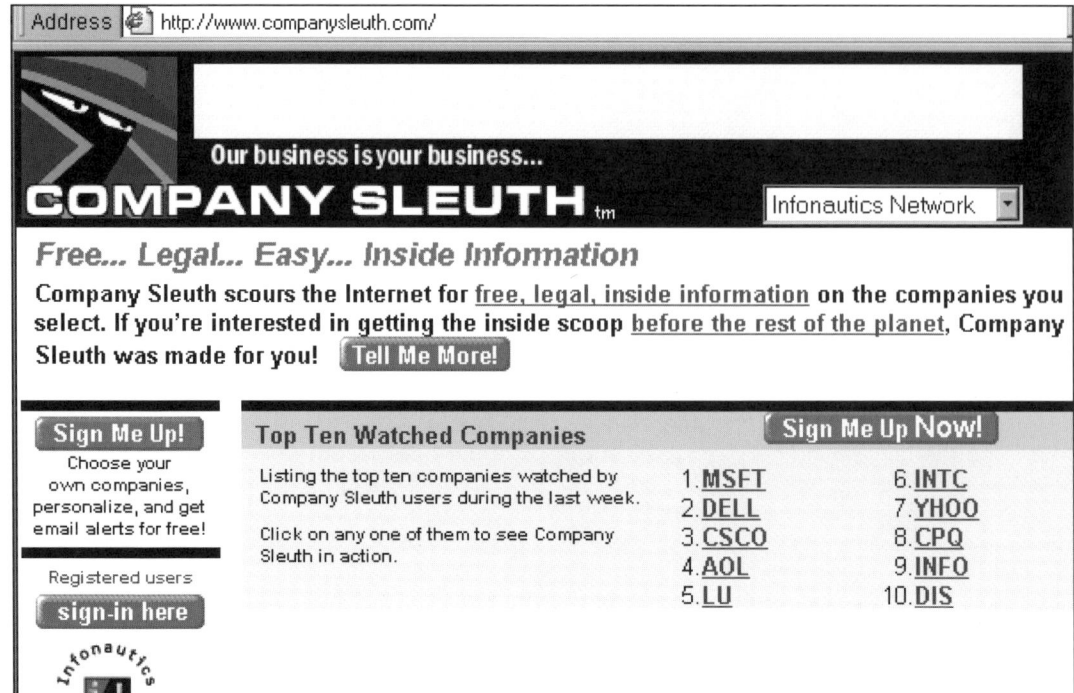

Fig. 16. It's not quite industrial espionage but nonetheless, the information could be vital if you are thinking of investing in a particular company. Be forewarned and forearmed with the Company Sleuth.

you select. If you're interested in getting the inside scoop before the rest of the planet, Company Sleuth was made for you!' The Company Sleuth often publishes news about a company before the company publishes a press release. It takes advantage of the information that is made available on the internet. Company Sleuth claims to be the only place that brings it all together.

Electronic Yellow Pages
http://www.eyp.co.uk
More than 1.6 million UK businesses are listed in this database, which is similar to the printed yellow pages. There are around 2,500 different business types on the yellow pages database. Some companies have a map and a web URL in their entry. A search returns a list of businesses with the ones that advertise in the Electronic Yellow Pages appearing at the top of the list – one of the advantages of paying.

MISCELLANEOUS

Couriers

Email is perfect for most communications but some things just can't be squeezed down a telephone line. Couriers such as TNT and Federal Express provide the fastest non-email delivery services and most companies offer a tracking service via the web so you can keep an eye on where your parcel is up to. You can find out what route it is taking or has taken, when it arrived, who signed for it and news of delays.

Federal Express
http://www.fedex.com
A US-biased site but still with the ability to serve UK customers

Couriers

effectively. The site is better organised than TNT's and information is clearly presented and accessible. FedEx supplies free packaging, advice on filling in paperwork, online preparation of waybills and commercial invoices, and information about transit times and coverage. From this site you can download free tracking and shipping software (FedEx World). The tracking package includes 'a world map so you can see the routing of your packages and has an automatic online booking option for pick-up of your shipment – without the need to call FedEx customer services.' The shipping software is multi-lingual windows-based software that 'enables you to automate the entire shipping process.'

Royal Mail
http://www.royalmail.co.uk
The Royal Mail has a site with broader interest than the other couriers do. It will also appeal to the home user or home worker – in fact anyone who would use a post office in the high street. The Postal Rates Calculator on the site helps with planning parcels and letters, and there is a post-code search section which will tell you the postcode of addresses in the UK or will find the addresses covered by a particular post code. Businesses can use the many post office services online such as the direct-mail facility and the parcel-tracking service.

Fig. 17. Don't worry if you haven't a post office in your high street or even if you haven't a high street, Royal Mail is on the web. Perhaps it's the one place where they are safe from dogs.

TNT
http://www.tntew.com
A bright, simple site that is easy to use and free of jargon but it can be a little difficult to find the information you need. Their area of operations is 'focused on the key areas of world trade in Europe, Asia, North and South America.' They also have 'strong domestic networks in Australia and Europe.' TNT provides real-time tracking information to put the nervous at ease and give the besieged manager someone else to blame when a delivery is delayed.

Work: business and education

CAREERS, JOBS AND EDUCATION

Finding jobs

Fed up of queuing up for information about a job that attracts thousands of applicants and pays peanuts? Look at sites such as Lycos, The Monster Board and JobServe – all will distribute your CV, send you job announcements by email, and give you information about companies looking for staff – in fact, all the things the local Jobcentre ought to do. What's more, a web site does not close – it is open all day and all night. Jobs can usually be searched by salary, category, company name, whether they are contract or permanent, and how recently the ad was placed on the site. In fact, many companies now prefer applications via email. The internet is particularly popular with secretaries and PAs because they are among the most computer literate people in a company.

British Army
http://www.army.mod.uk
Visit strange and exotic places, learn to ask for a beer in twenty different languages and get the chance to catch lots of different exotic diseases. The army is not all fun, though. You have to prove yourself in tests of fitness and skill, and there is a tendency for people to shoot at you occasionally. Are you up to the challenge? To get an inside view, look at the section called the Sandhurst Diary, which follows the progress of a group of officer recruits as they progress through their training.

Certes
http://www.certes.co.uk
Certes is a contract and permanent recruitment provider specialising in the IT market. They 'provide many of the UK's largest IT sites with contractors and permanent candidates nationwide, across all skills sets and at all levels.' The site's theme is that of a space journey where the sections are denoted by orbiting planets and space ships. Select a ship to guide you through your job search and, when you get bored with the job hunt, play the Java arcade games.

Golden Square
http://www.Goldensquare.com
There are a few ways of making yourself available for a job through Golden Square – fill in a 'lightning registration', 'quick registration card' and a 'full online CV'. Employers can access your information on the database and if they like what they see they will respond with an interview offer. The site also offers regular articles, and industry news. A database of company information is being compiled, and a new hot product is planned for late 1999 – 'HR Manager Online', a guide on how to quickly find a new employee. At time of writing, the agencies with Golden Square dealt with jobs in the following areas: secretarial, media and technology, secretarial, college leavers, pathfinders, recent graduates, media-based secretarial, and general.

Job Title
Packaging Artworkers
Evening Legal Secretary in Solicitors
Cold Fusion Developer
Opportunity in Banking
Administrator
Imaging Centre Managers - London/Reading
Luxury Hotel Empire
Project Manager
Graduate Researcher
Marketing Assistant/Reception

JobServe
http://www.jobserve.com
JobServe is based in the UK but about ten percent of the vacancies are drawn from other countries in Europe and the rest of the world such as: Australia, Hong Kong, Indonesia, New Zealand, Russia, Saudi Arabia, Singapore, South Africa and the USA.

Lycos Jobs
http://www.lycos.co.uk/webguides/career
Lycos says that the service contains hundreds of thousands of jobs with thousands of fresh vacancies added daily. You will also find advice on employment, education and training. For even more help, there are a number of mini-guides with titles such as employment, improve your skills, and employment sites. You can even use the CV builder to help you to compose an artful CV of yourself.

Michael Page
http://www.michaelpage.com
Specialising in the middle to senior management sector, Michael Page offers a little more than just a search site. They follow through to the next stage, which is to assess the jobseeker's needs and give advice and guidance. There are around 50,000 vacancies to search through on the site as well as information about visa and other requirements when looking for work outside the country.

Monster Board
http://www.monster.co.uk
Search over 3,000 job vacancies in the UK, and thousands more in the rest of the world. Once you get an interview, be prepared by getting an inside view of the products, services and cultures of top employers. And, to help your quest, there is the 'job search agent'

Fig. 18. Searching for a job is never easy and often wears down the shoe leather at an alarming rate. The search has become much easier with sites such as Golden Square where you can move around all day without leaving your seat.

Work: business and education

The Response Centre
http://www.responsecentre.co.uk
The Response Centre gives you a categorised list of most recruitment sites in the UK including many of the big companies' job sections. The site is easy to use if not especially attractive and there is also a 'WOTSON' section where job seekers can get a quick view of what's on a web site. They say, 'Begun in March 1998 as a simple directory of employment related sites, we now include a free A to Z listing of all employers carrying recruitment pages, agencies with vacancies, job sites and media pages.'

Royal Air Force
http://www.raf.mod.uk
Supporting each pilot, there are hundreds of men on the ground. To become a pilot needs dedication, intelligence, co-ordination, correct attitude, and many other special qualities. The other trades and specialisations need their own sets of skills and abilities. If you are not sure whether you have the right qualifications, it would be worth checking out this site.

Royal Navy
http://www.royal-navy.mod.uk
There is variety, companionship and lots of water waiting for you in a career in the Royal Navy. If you can't swim, the Navy will probably teach you. If fighting the enemy from a distance greater than a few hundred metres whilst protected in a big floating box appeals to you, then join the Navy. If you think the Navy is a little too sissy for you, try telling that to a Royal Marine Commando – then duck.

For students

Gradfinder
http://www.gradfinder.com
Gradfinder is 'made to help people stay in touch'. It allows you to contact graduates from over 70,000 schools all over the world. If you want to be found, you can add your own contact information, including a photograph and short bio, to the database. You can also plan reunions from the site. This site plans to contain every school in the world. You can search for your school in the UK or browse by country such as Australia, Canada, England, Hong Kong, India, Pakistan, Philippines, United States, and elsewhere.

London Student
http://www.londonstudent.org.uk
The London Student site covers news of interest mainly to students already at university in London but some of the features, in what is basically a student magazine, will interest prospective students. The site will give them an idea of the daily life of a London student such as sports, union activities, marches and rag week.

```
Address  http://www.londonstudent.org.uk/
```

Volume 18      1997/1998

This is the final issue of *London Student* for the year. Thank you for visiting.
In the meantime, if you have any queries contact the Web Editor.

Issue 13
Election scandal rocks UCL Union
Additional Film and Arts Pages

Issue 12
Speaker Scam men kidnap IC student

Issue 11
KCL Union silence as auditors report 'irregularities'

Oxford University
http://www.ox.ac.uk
Prospective students will find lots of information about the university, student lifestyle, students and courses, as well as a guide to the city of Oxford itself – informative and entertaining. You can search the university by colleges and halls, by departments or by associated institutions. Resources on the site include the OLIG (Oxford Libraries Internet Gateway) which gives you access to many free library services.

Student UK
http://www.studentuk.com
There are few good online student's magazines on the net – this site may qualify as one of them; it is certainly popular. There are sections on welfare, money, accommodation, health and even an academic area for those who can't remember why they went to university in the first place.

UK Map of Universities
http://scitsc.wlv.ac.uk/ukinfo/uk.map.html
This site, hosted by the University of Wolverhampton, will give you access to all of the universities, colleges and research facilities of the UK via clickable maps. Each facility is indicated by a small symbol on the maps with the name next to the symbol. But it does not end there – you can select which type of information to look at whether it is an undergraduate prospectus, postgraduate prospectus, the library, students' union the list goes on. This is a great site, and a must for students and their families.

WEA
http://www.wea.org.uk
The Workers' Educational Association performs a great service,

Fig. 19. To be a student in London has its pitfalls and advantages. London Student will help you out once you are there so you won't get too overwhelmed or bored.

Work: business and education

offering affordable courses all over the country. From creative writing to Advanced-level Spanish, there is probably a course for you – if you live near enough to a centre. Whether you want to study one of the many subjects in their list or teach one yourself, you should go to the site. It doesn't contain course details but you can find details of your nearest branch and send for a free course programme. The WEA are always in need of volunteers, and not only teachers, so why not get involved?

Schools

Department for Education and Employment
http://www.dfee.gov.uk
The British government has excelled itself with this well-designed site. It is easy to use and contains lots of useful information. DfEE documents can be searched by title or topic and include school performance tables, adult education, a guide to finance for students and links to many other education-related sites.

Internet for Schools
http://www.internetforschools.co.uk
Finding the best school for your child is important to ensure a good start in life. The Internet for Schools site has a section, Wired Schools, which is an alphabetical list of links to school web pages. There are other sections such as the Global Forum, which is a chat room where teachers and students can discuss issues like power and respect in the classroom, and the Online Resources section which is a collection of resources related to education.

Fig. 20. The DfEE site is the place for authoritative reports covering all aspects of education and employment. Not a stuffy government site at all but well designed and quite cool.

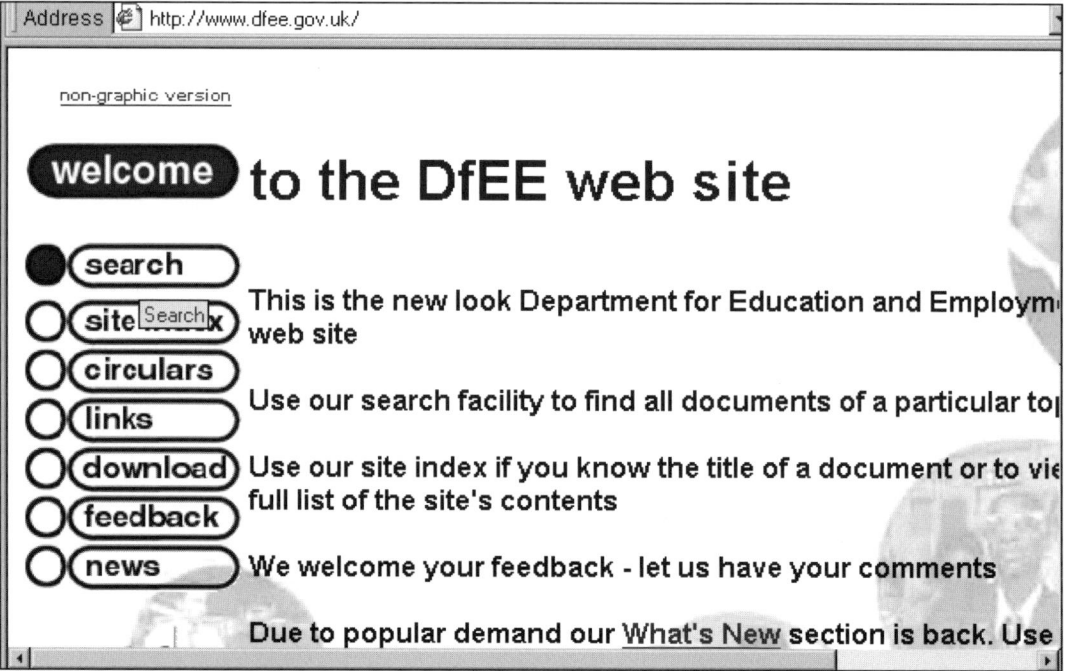

Politics

GOVERNMENT AND POLITICS

British Politics Page
http://www.ukpol.co.uk
There are links to more than 1,500 political sites in Britain and coverage of past and present political events. There is also plenty of opportunity to have your own voice heard by participating in an online chat or simply emailing your MP from the site. This is a good resource for anyone interested in politics, whether you want to run for prime minister or just learn a little more of what it's all about.

Customs and Excise
http://www.hmce.gov.uk
'HM Customs and Excise is responsible for collecting and administering Customs and Excise duties and Value Added Tax. The Department is also responsible for preventing and detecting the evasion of revenue laws and for enforcing a range of prohibitions and restrictions on the importation of certain classes of goods.' The site provides information and guidelines for companies and members of the public on issues such as travelling, VAT registration, and job opportunities.

Ministry of Agriculture, Fisheries and Food
http://www.maff.gov.uk
'MAFF is not simply about farming – its concerns go far wider. It does, naturally, cover production and processing but also food safety, the environmental impact of farming, and the wider contexts of the UK economy and the European Union. Essentially, MAFF's job is to help improve the economic performance of these industries, especially in the expanding markets of Europe and the wider world. At the same time, it has to protect our health and conserve our natural environment.'

NATO
http://www.nato.int
It is claimed that Serbian hackers managed to break into the site once or twice. Nevertheless, throughout most of the war with Serbia, NATO managed to release daily press briefings and a chronology of events. If you are unsure about how NATO was formed, or even what it is, check out the history section. NATO stands for the North Atlantic Treaty Organisation. There is also a comprehensive archive of official documents and NATO publications.

Number Ten
http://www.number-10.gov.uk/index.html
Downing Street, that is. You don't have to be a cat to take a look in Number Ten, this site admits everyone – well almost everyone: the site uses complicated JavaScript to achieve some flashy effects. The effects worked fine when online, but as soon as you start to view the page offline it gets a little complex. The site would be impossible for viewers with sight problems. Despite these drawbacks, however, there is plenty of interesting information on the site.

Political Links
E-mail Your MP
Political Books
History
News

Biographies of all M.P.s
Councils Page
Local Election Results Archive
uk.politics.* newsgroup
Add a Political Site
1997 Labour Cabinet
1997 Tory Leadership
Political Issues in Focus
British Politics Time-Line

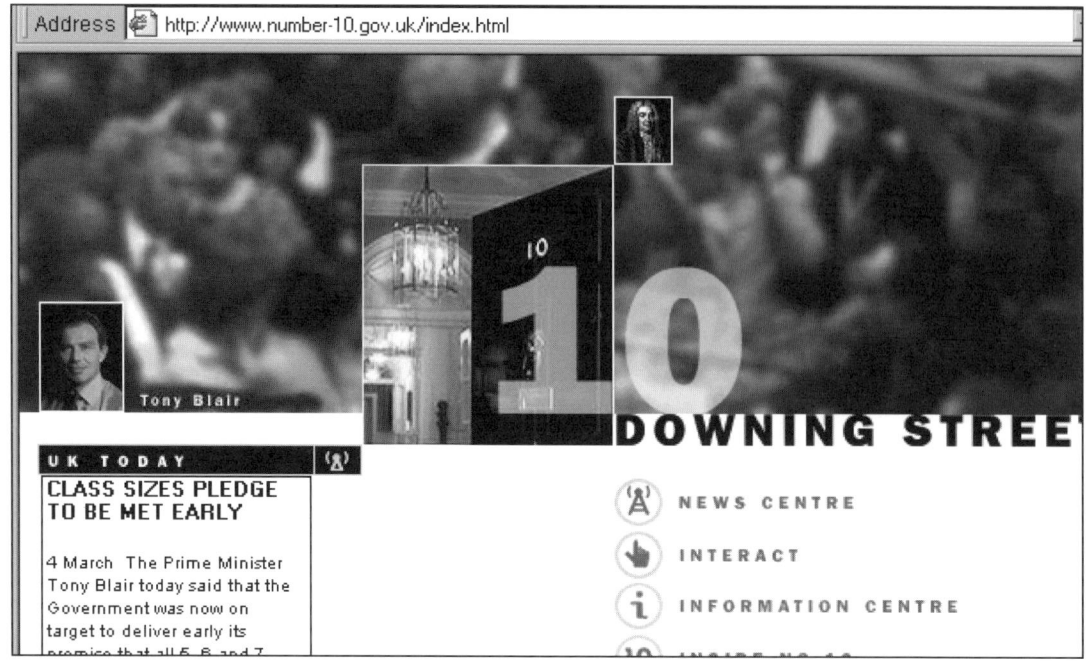

Fig. 21. If you want a say in what the British prime minister is doing, or if you only want to find out some further information then pop down to the Number Ten site.

Parliament
http://www.parliament.com
From the horse's mouth: information about the Parliament, the House of Commons and the House of Lords. There is a list of members and direct email links to those with email facilities. The site is plain and simple to navigate – no flashy designs, just functionality.

Richard Kimber
http://www.psr.keele.ac.uk
Richard's site contains more than 3,000 links to political and government sites all over the world. The site is updated regularly and contains plenty of other information such as articles on political theory and information on constitutions, treaties and declarations.

The Treasury
http://www.hm-treasury.gov.uk
Don't worry if you missed the budget speech, or if you fell asleep halfway through – it's all on this site. You can find the text of the speech and an index of all the budget news releases. There is also a section on job opportunities for people interested in a career in the financial sector. The Treasury is responsible for the Government's financial and economic policy and says its overall aim is 'to promote sustained growth and higher living standards.'

Western European Union
http://www.weu.int
The WEU is an association of European countries – Belgium, France, Germany, Greece, Italy, Luxembourg, The Netherlands, Portugal, Spain and the United Kingdom. It was set up to co-ordinate the control of security and defence. The WEU helped to create and works in co-operation with the North Atlantic Treaty Organisation (NATO).

.... **Human rights and ecology**

The White House
http://www.whitehouse.gov
The White House is the official residence of the president of the United States, located at 1600 Pennsylvania Avenue in Washington, DC – all 18 acres and more than 130 rooms. It has been the home of every US president since John Adams. The main building contains the presidential family's living quarters and is decorated in the style of the 18th and 19th centuries. Parts of it are open to the public on guided tours. The site gives you access to the archive of all White House documents such as press briefings, radio addresses, executive orders, and other publications. The following categories can be searched separately: press briefings, radio addresses and executive orders.

Human rights and ecology

Amnesty International
http://www.amnesty.org.uk
A British lawyer launched Amnesty International in 1961. His motivation was a news feature about Portuguese students who had been given a seven-year prison sentence for raising their glasses in a toast to freedom. 'His newspaper appeal, "The Forgotten Prisoners", was published world wide on 28th May 1961 and brought in more than 1,000 offers of support for the idea of an international campaign to protect human rights. Within 12 months the new organisation had sent delegations to four countries to make representations on behalf of prisoners, had taken up 210 cases, and had organised national branches in seven countries.' 'From the beginning, the principles of strict impartiality and independence were established. Amnesty members were to act on cases world wide, but not become involved in cases in their own countries and the emphasis was on the international protection of human rights.'

Friends of the Earth
http://www.foe.co.uk
Some issues can have direct or indirect effects on the environment and thus on our future survival as a human race. Friends of the Earth and Greenpeace aim to bring the sometimes complex environmental effects of current issues to the attention of the general public and put pressure on the government to implement change. Issues such as genetically modified foods continue to be covered on the site.

FreeSpeech
http://www.freespeech.org
FreeSpeech Internet Television was the first audio-video site created entirely by its members. Using the site, you can join the organisation and begin broadcasting your own internet 'television channel' or 'talk radio' show. This is internet freedom at its best – videos available at the time of writing included an interview of Noam Chomsky in which he explains 'the American propaganda model: "necessary illusions" that the corporate-owned media creates to diverge the public and protect the interest of the élite.' The site says, 'Democratic media can and will change society for the better. We will accept no lesser outcome.'

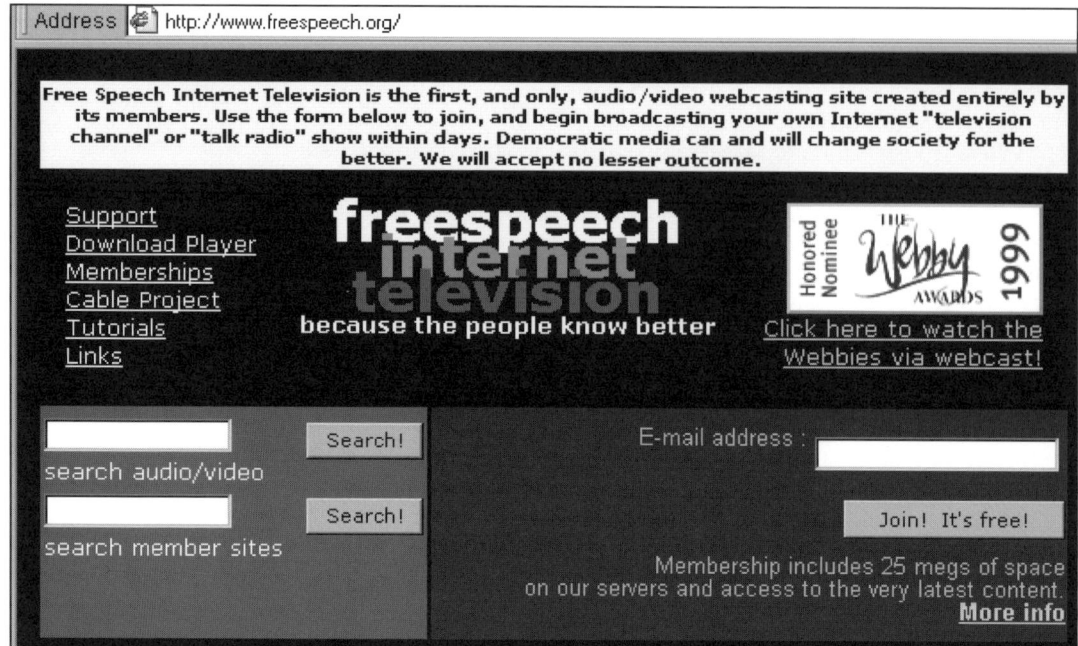

Fig. 22. Freespeech is a site offering a novel way of expressing your opinions – internet television. You'd better get your makeup

Going for Green
http://www.gfg.iclnet.co.uk
British environmental awareness campaign, with case studies and suggestions for how to make changes in business or lifestyles to help improve and preserve the environment. On the award-winning site, visitors can take a virtual tour of the *Rainbow Warrior*, the Greenpeace flagship.

GreenNet
http://www.greennet.net
GreenNet is an ISP and is 'part of the only global computer network specifically designed for environment, peace, human rights and development groups.' They offer email, hosted conferences, and dial-up Internet services. The site is easy and quick to use. GreenNet hosts the sites of many smaller human-rights and environmental groups such as the Campaign Against Arms (campaign working to eliminate nuclear weapons by the year 2000), Peace Pledge Union, and SaferWorld (campaigners against the small-arms trade).

Greenpeace
http://www.greenpeace.org
There are reports on the latest environmental issues, updates on Greenpeace activities, free access to Greenpeace Business and Campaign Report, and details of your local groups.

Statewatch
http://www.statewatch.org
This is another good site for those who want to keep abreast of human rights issues in the European Union. The site is essentially an archive of Statewatch's work. It contains over 24,000 entries of news, features, books, pamphlets, reports, EU resolutions and agreements, debates in

Statewatch covers -

- Policing and Europol
- Security and intelligence
- The Schengen acquis
- European databases: S
- Prisons
- Military
- Immigration and asylum
- Racism and fascism
- Openness and secrecy
- EU-FBI surveillance sy
- Northern Ireland
- Civil liberties
- The law and the Europ
- The Council of Justice

Politics

the UK House of Commons, House of Lords and the European Parliament. There are reports on cases in the European courts, and the Institute of Race Relations European Race Audit. The archive covers topics such as policing and Europol, security and intelligence agencies, prisons, immigration, asylum, racism, Northern Ireland, and civil liberties in general.

United Nations
http://www.un.org
The United Nations (UN) is the successor to the League of Nations, which was disbanded in 1946. The main purpose of the UN is to help find solutions to international problems or disputes. Each of the member countries has the chance to have their views heard and to vote on the policy issues of the international community. The UN has six main organs, including the General Assembly, the Security Council and the International Court of Justice, and fourteen more specialised agencies such as health, finance, agriculture, civil aviation and telecommunications. The site informs you of news related to the UN and access to UN documents in their database.

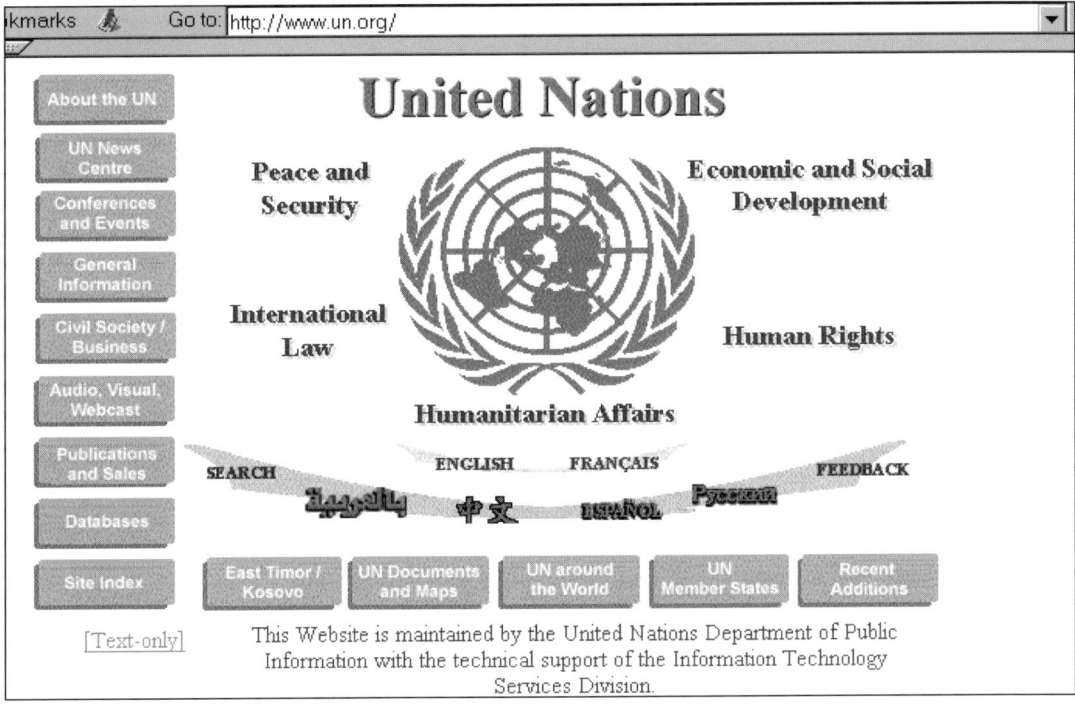

3 Rest

In this chapter we will explore:

▶ *Family and health*
▶ *Hobbies and interests*
▶ *Religion and spirituality*
▶ *Buying products and services*
▶ *Food and drink*
▶ *Travel and holidays*
▶ *National and international information*

FAMILY AND HEALTH

General health and fitness

4colds
http://www.4colds.com
The common cold is responsible for more suffering than any other ailment except alcohol intoxication. This site contains lots of information on alternative treatments for colds. It is a directory that contains lots of sites from those selling cough sweets to specialist physicians and associations. The parent site also hosts similar sites such as 4coughs, and 4diet.

Achoo is sponsored in part by: Canada's premier permanent and contract recruitment specialists for the pharmaceutical, biotechnology and healthcare industries.

Achoo
http://www.achoo.com
Achoo is a directory that specialises in health-related issues. Just type in a question to use the extensive health database. You will be directed to a relevant site that could be anywhere in the world. Achoo include aspects of healthcare, such as clinical medicine, and alternate medicine. They aim to provide 'the meeting place for consumers, professionals as well as people involved with the business of healthcare.'

The British Stammering Association
http://www.stammer.demon.co.uk
Stammering is a condition common among thousands of people in the UK. The British Stammering Association hopes to provide help and guidance to people. The aims of the BSA are to: initiate and support research into stammering, identify and promote effective therapies, offer support for all whose lives are affected by stammering, and promote awareness of stammering. The site provides plenty of information for anyone who suffers from stammering or who has children that stammer. There is also a library and a bookshop, and you can apply to become a member of the BSA online.

Health & fitness

Fitness Online
http://www.fitnessonline.com
The key to fitness is choosing a regime that suits you. One that is tailored to your circumstances and, above all, is balanced. Sitting in front of a computer surfing may give your fingers a little exercise but little else. But the internet can help you to choose a plan. And what about dieting? Fitness online is a very useful resource that will help you make these decisions and answer your questions. Fitness Online has information on all aspects of fitness: nutrition, exercise, lifestyles, and more.

HEBS
http://www.hebs.org.uk
The Health Education Board of Scotland is 50,000 pages of useful information – hints on how to prevent illness, how to look after yourself and what organisation to contact if you need support of some kind. There are sections on heart disease, drugs, cancer, strokes, HIV and healthy eating. The fact that the site is geared towards Scotland should not put other English speakers off the site. It beats many other UK sites hands down.

Insomnia
http://www.sleepnet.com
Everybody suffers from insomnia occasionally, and so this site, SleepNet, aims to gather as much information on the subject of insomnia as they can. The site has a forum, where people can chat away their insomnia, and lots of links to sleep research sites.

New Century Nutrition Online
http://www.newcenturynutrition.com
New Century Nutrition Online is a newsletter containing articles, research, recipes, links to other sites and current news. Featured Sections include the Cornell-Oxford-China Diet and Health Project – a comprehensive study of the relationship between diet and the risk of developing disease, getting healthy at your own pace, new century nutrition, nutrition around the world and lots of healthy recipes. You will also find health news and links to health and nutrition articles from elsewhere on the internet.

Obesity.com
http://www.obesity.com
If you think your weight is a problem, then the exercise section on this site may be what you need or it may be that your weight is only a problem in your mind. Obesity.com discusses the many aspects of obesity and the side effects. The news updates will keep you up to date with research and happenings such as the effects of giving up smoking on weight and the latest state of diet drugs.

Patient Information
http://www.patient.co.uk
This is a nice and simple site with none of the flashy graphics or

Patient UK

SELF HELP
ILLNESS & DISEASE
HEALTH PROMOTION
MEDICINES / DRUGS
PHONE ADVICE
GP SERVICE
PHARMACY SERVICE
DENTAL HEALTH
EYE HEALTH
TRAVEL HEALTH
PRIVATE HEALTH
BOOKS / VIDEOS
NHS INFORMATION
CARERS
BENEFITS
ETHICAL
COMPLEMENTARY
SEARCHING
MISCELLANEOUS

Rest

animations of many other sites, just plenty of information and well-organised links. The aim of the site is to help non-medical people find information about health issues. Health professionals may also find the information useful. Sections on the site include self-help, medicines and drugs, travel health and much more.

PeakHealth.net
http://www.peakhealth.net
'Whether you're an Olympic athlete or a (reforming) couch potato, we are dedicated to helping you achieve your optimal health and fitness level,' says the founder. The site includes health and fitness features and interviews with health and fitness experts, and an 'ask the doctor' section where you can answer your nutrition and dietary supplement questions.

Samaritans
http://www.samaritans.org.uk
Some of us may only feel comfortable with people when we speak via the internet. At the Samaritans, there is always someone willing to listen and help should we need a little support by email. Or if you don't want to wait for email, phone them on 01753 216500.

Fig. 23. Sometimes, when you most need it, there is no one around for you to talk to. As a voluntary organisation, the Samaritans perform a valuable service and are always available to listen to your problems and offer help and advice.

Hospitals and medical organisations

MedicineNet
http://www.medicinenet.com
MedicineNet is a network of doctors producing comprehensive, up-to-date health information for the public. They 'strive to bring a doctor's perspective to important medical issues.' The site is very comprehensive, with information from everything from using Viagra effectively to interesting facts about fingernails.

Medscape Patient Information
http://www.medscape.com/homePatient/PatientInfo.html
'The online resource for better patient care' is what they say on the site.

Hospitals and medical organisations

Aimed more at the medical professional, this site will appeal to you if you want a more in-depth knowledge about medicine. The articles are much more to the forefront of knowledge with information about new medical research and conferences.

National Health Service (NHS)
http://www.nhs50.nhs.uk
With over 400 pages to browse, this site covers topics such as the history of health in the UK and the evolution of the NHS. It includes an overview of a career in the NHS and what kind of training you can expect once you are employed, and plenty of advice and information on healthy living.

The Virtual Medical Centre
http://www.mediconsult.com
A site for all people: from those with chronic health problems, to those looking to get the most out of life. The site has comprehensive information on around sixty medical topics. There are support groups for people with eating disorders and undergoing obesity surgery, you can ask questions or make comments, and search through a drug reference centre or take a squint at the Eye Care site for the latest advances in eye health care. If you are a dedicated healthy person, subscribe to the weekly newsletter to stay current with all the new diseases and cures.

Fig. 24. What is that word that your doctor used? Some doctors just don't seem to realise that they speak a different language to the rest of us. The Virtual Medical Center site just might translate for us and let us know what is really wrong with us.

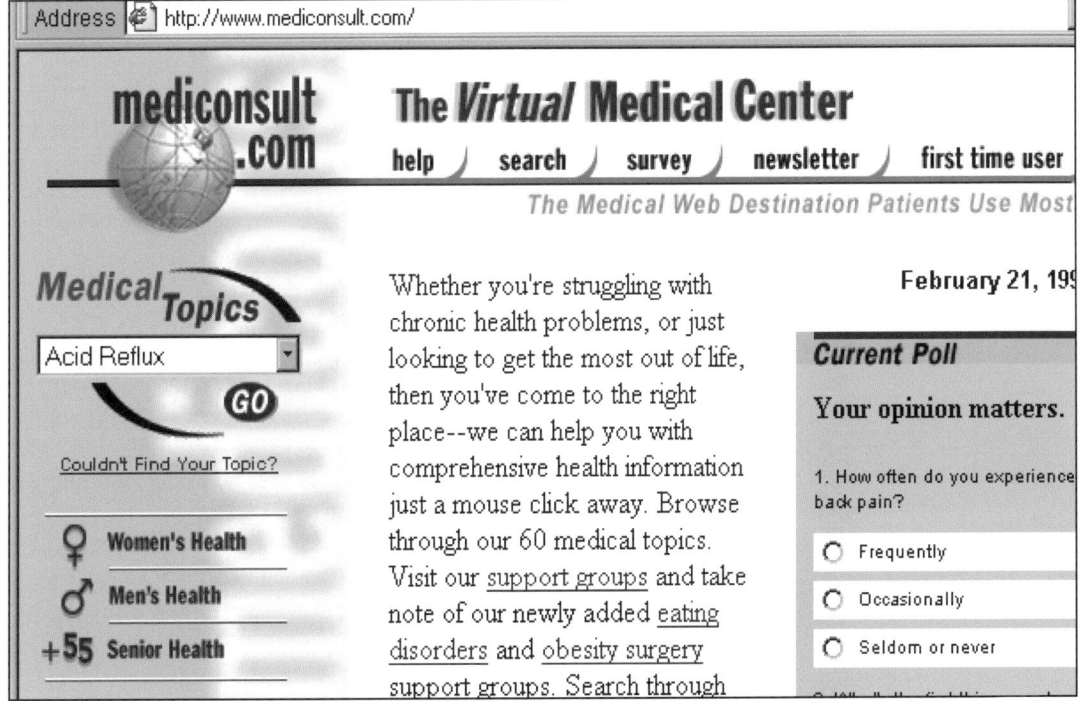

Rest

Addictions

ASH
http://www.ash.org.uk
ASH (Action on Smoking & Health) is an organisation of people who want to free the world of smoking and smoking-related deaths. The site reveals cover-ups by tobacco companies and offers advice on how to take legal action against them. There are also helpful hints and tips on giving up smoking for those who want to kick the habit.

Gamblers Anonymous
http://www.gamblersanonymous.org
GA is 'a fellowship of men and women who share their experience, strength and hope with each other that they may solve their common problem and help others to recover from a gambling problem.' GA resulted from a chance meeting between two obsessive gamblers during January 1957. After meeting regularly for a time, neither returned to gambling. They concluded, 'in order to prevent a relapse it was necessary to bring about certain character changes within themselves. In order to accomplish this, they used for a guide certain spiritual principles, which had been utilised by thousands of people who were recovering from other compulsive addictions.' The site goes on to say, 'Also, in order to maintain their own abstinence they felt that it was vitally important that they carry the message of hope to other compulsive gamblers.'

Online Interactive Alcoholics Anonymous
http://www.aa-intergroup.org
The aim of OIAA is to provide a site where alcoholics can interact with other alcoholics and is to carry its message to alcoholics who still suffer. They are dedicated to providing support for alcoholics and helping any groups or organisations that intend to support alcoholics. Their own site provides plenty of information and an online chat group where you can talk to others in your situation.

Disability and chronic illness

Many support groups and organisations maintain a presence on the net to inform people about news and activities and keep directories of resources. Some of the sites also offer a section where you can chat with other sufferers or their families. With most of the sites, further comment is not needed – the most important thing is to make contact with the organisation yourself. Some of them are:

Alzheimer's Association	http://www.alz.org
British Diabetic Association	http://www.diabetes.org.uk
British Heart Foundation	http://www.bhf.org.uk
Cancerhelp UK	http://medweb.bham.ac.uk/cancerhelp
The Insulin-Free World Foundation	http://www.insulin-free.org
Mental Health	http://mentalhealth.miningco.com
Internet Mental Health	http://www.mentalhealth.com

Children and young people

Multiple Sclerosis Foundation http://www.msfacts.org
Muscular Dystrophy
  Association   http://www.mda.org.au
National Kidney Foundation http://www.kidney.org
Royal National Institute
  for the Blind   http://www.rnib.org.uk
Medic-alert foundation   http://www.medicalert.co.uk

Children and young people

Babyworld
http://www.babyworld.co.uk
Babyworld is, as you would expect, about having babies – a place 'new and expectant parents can share experiences and support. Women can learn about their bodies, their baby, and childbirth, and parents can celebrate the joy of a new life.' Babyworld claims to be the first pregnancy advice service to go online. There are also product tests, offers, and regular features of the baby kind on the site. And men, don't feel left out, there is advice for you too such as the theory and practice of baby feeding, changing and transportation (i.e. you get to push the pram).

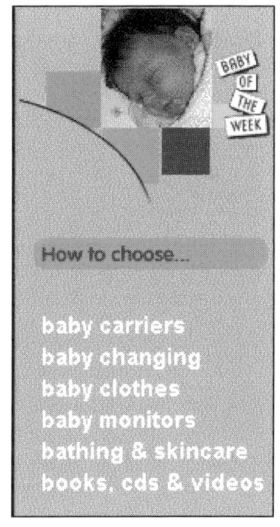

Eclectic
http://members.tripod.com/~Eclectic_Zine
Eclectic was started in July 1998 by Joanna Blackwell. She was tired of the e-zines on the internet at the time because they all focused on fashion, make-up and pop music. She wanted to write for teens like her who disliked all the teen hype and wanted something more real. Teenagers and young adults write most of the content of Eclectic, which features articles, essays, poetry, reviews, fiction, and bags more. Older people are welcome to voice their opinions too.

Headlice.org
http://www.headlice.org
Do you remember the days of the nit nurse coming into school? This site, American though it is, offers all the information you need to know about nits and scabies. You can even win a T-shirt.

Meningitis Research Foundation
http://www.meningitis.org
Here, you will have access to information on the symptoms of meningitis and septicaemia and how to identify the diseases. Meningitis and septicaemia are life-threatening diseases that can be fought with foreknowledge. For the information about these diseases and current scientific research, go to this site.

Need a Nanny
http://www.dfee.gov.uk/nanny
The Louise Woodward case underlined the need to be sure of the person you are hiring to look after your children. This site is British-government controlled and, if you are thinking of employing a nanny or

Rest

other types of childcare, has some useful pointers. The site is in five parts: what is a nanny, choosing a nanny, teamwork, factfile, and further information contacts.

Teen Talk
http://www.teentalk.com
Do you have problem parents? Here's another site dedicated to young people. 'Teens helping teens deal with issues like dating, break-ups, appearance, parents, depression and school.' There's a reference desk, cool links, and a free teen-talk mailbox. Go and have a look, you'll love the animated kids on the front page.

Trouble
http://www.trouble.co.uk
Trouble has almost everything a young adult would want such as gossip, advice, competitions, music and chat rooms. Examples of some of the things you might find are: pictures and information on your favourite TV shows, a 'fab new weird science game' (needs the Shockwave 7 plugin), and pop gossip.

Youth 2 Youth
http://www.youth2youth.co.uk
Are you fed up being misunderstood by adults? Go and talk to these people. Y2Y is a National telephone and e-mail helpline run by young people for young people under the age of 23. The service allows you to talk confidentially to young trained volunteers. Email them here for a confidential and supportive chat:

athelp@youth2youth.co.uk

The site says it all, 'Like to talk to someone your own age? Then contact us. We're young – we understand.'

Relationships, sex and health

Aidsmap
http://www.aids.map.com
This site is maintained by the National Aids Manual, the British HIV Association and St Stephen's Aids Trust and covers Aids, its prevention and treatment. The site also contains a weekly updated section containing fact sheets on anti-HIV drugs, infections, and viral load, and an extensive database of HIV treatment information.

Confetti.co.uk
http://www.confetti.co.uk
The site is not just for wedding accessories. Confetti is a useful tool for organising, planning and researching weddings. There are sections on the law, budgeting, online invitations, directions to the church and you can even have your own wedding web pages.

Sex & health

Condomania
http://www.condoms4u.com
This is a funny and light-hearted site that sells all kinds of condoms in all shades, shapes and flavours. Or, if you don't see anything to tickle your fancy, you can send someone a valentine's card or play a game or two.

Durex World
http://www.durex.com
Have you ever wondered about those strange bubble-gum machines in the pub toilets – with strange shapes and exotic flavours? It is rumoured that there is a bar somewhere in Britain that has a condom machine in the ladies toilet that is connected to a buzzer in the bar – when someone uses the machine, the buzzer sounds. Ladies be careful! The site is packed with interesting information about contraception; it offers advice and entertainment. Win a year's supply of condoms, talk to Doctor Dilemma in the clinic, find online lovers, or take a bath in the 'Tub of Love'.

Gay.com
http://www.gay.com
Gay people include individuals from all age groups, countries, social backgrounds and interests. No one site could hope to cater for them all but this one does, at least, touch the surface. Gay.com is a general interest site that covers political, health and religious issues surrounding homosexuality. There are articles on gay weddings, prejudice, medical news and advice. The site is divided into sections such as spirituality, shopping, and health and fitness.

Gingerbread
http://www.gingerbread.org.uk
Unfortunately, not all relationships end amicably. Gingerbread is perhaps the leading support organisation for single parents in the UK. The site includes a lot of information useful to single parents such as benefit rates and the location of, and contacts for local Gingerbread groups. There are over 160 Gingerbread groups in England and Wales; all of them are run voluntarily by members.

Hitched
http://www.hitched.co.uk
Stewardess: 'I'm sorry, Mr. Smith, but we left your wife behind in London.' Mr. Smith: 'Thank goodness! I thought I was going deaf!' That's one of the many jokes available on the Hitched site. They deal with everything to do with getting married – from the engagement to the honeymoon. There is information for brides, grooms, best men, bridesmaids, and ushers. Also tips for speeches, planning receptions, buying products and services, traditions and history, myths, wedding rings and lots more.

Fig. 25. A big part of getting married is the preparation, but don't worry, if there is a mistake to make, it's already been made by someone else. Hitched helps you to make that special day go without a hitch.

Viagra
http://www.viagra.com
This is the site from Pfizer, the makers of the drug Viagra. They answer questions such as what it is and what it does and the possible side effects. The site also provides some excellent information on sexual dysfunction and does not bombard you with too much advertising.

Alternative health and medicine

Healself Network
http://www.healself.com
This is a site for those who have lost faith in the NHS. It covers the more organic and natural forms of healing, political issues regarding such things as euthanasia, health matters like assessing and improving your energy balance, and a recipe exchange where you can offer your own remedies to other readers. The site also includes a health and healing bookstore.

International Federation of Aromatherapists
http://www.ifa.org.au/index.htm
The IFA site includes information on accredited schools, events and membership. Aromatherapy is a therapeutic treatment, using essential oils with a specialised massage, which enhances well-being, relieves stress and helps in the rejuvenation and regulation of the human body.

The Natural Health Guide
http://marches.county.net/health
Natural remedies and therapies are greatly undervalued in the West where cure is more important than prevention. Finding realistic information on natural health can be difficult, however. For those of you starting out, this site should be your first point of call. The site

Quizzes & games

provides information on the various types of complementary therapies and their practitioners.

Soil Association
http://www.soilassociation.org
The Soil Association is a charity dedicated (since 1946) to healthy food through organic farming. It exists 'to research, develop and promote sustainable relationships between the soil, plants, animals, people and the biosphere, in order to produce healthy food and other products while protecting and enhancing the environment'.

Whole Earth
http://www.earthfoods.co.uk
Warning to those of a nervous disposition – this site has some frightening information about 'food' such as sugar and fat. Quoted from their site: 'Refined sugar acts like a drug in our bodies. It contains fast-acting glucose, which goes straight into the bloodstream raising the blood sugar level and making us temporarily feel as if we have more energy. Your body reacts by flooding the bloodstream with insulin to bring the glucose level down to normal. After a while, the blood sugar level is safe, but the insulin is still there, taking the level below normal. Then, you feel tired, even depressed, and develop a hungry craving for more sugar. The addiction, which can be mild or severe, weakens the immune system and can lead to diabetes.'

HOBBIES AND INTERESTS

Quizzes and games

Computer games are plentiful on the internet – there are shareware games that allow you to play a limited number of levels and there are game servers where you play online against computer and human players. Be warned, though, before you run any program that has been downloaded from the internet, check it for viruses. See page 159.

▶ Server – a computer that is shared (accessed) by many users.

Anagram Fun
http://www.infobahn.com/pages/anagram.html
Ever wondered how many anagrams you can make from your name? Stop wondering and visit this site. The name of the author, Kye Valongo, was transformed into 'go yank love' and 'van key logo'. A simple site for a little simple fun.

Bizarre Stuff You Can Make in Your Kitchen
http://freeweb.pdq.net/headstrong
Did you know you probably have everything you need to build a radio, or a small volcano in your home? This site details some simple science projects that you can build with your children. There are several hundred sets of easy to understand instructions and illustrations. Most of the projects are harmless but some can cause injury and others can be messy so don't let your children attempt a project without supervision.

Rest

Christianity Online Games
http://www.christianity.net/fun/games
Check out this collection of 35 games online and ready to play! The games can be played right in your browser but some games require a Java-based browser or the Shockwave plug-in. There are the classic games such as Tetris, Checkers and Hangman, and there are some more exotic games such as Moo Maze where you help a cow out of a maze, and a build a Snowmobile puzzle. If you are a Christian, the rest of the site may also be of interest.

Crime Scene
http://www.crimesceme.com
Put on your detective hat and get your magnifying glass polished before you view the various cases on this site. Membership is free but be prepared for a challenge. You can view details of solved crimes to accustom yourself with the way the site works, then have a go at the unsolved crimes. Read witness accounts, view photos of the crime scene and review the evidence. Good luck, detective.

FunTrivia.com
http://FunTrivia.com
'Web-Today tends to focus on sites that offer deep content but every now and again we like to put edification aside and bask in sheer entertainment. FunTrivia.com is a compilation of little known facts and interesting info bites that are sure to put a smile on your face and make you a hit around the office or at the next party you attend.' The facts are arranged in a cool Yahoo!-like subject directory that makes for easy browsing. The facts are fully documented and you can even add to the database by filling out a request form.

Millions2000
http://www.milions2000.com
A brother site to Plus Lotto, Millions was launched by the Red Cross to raise four billion dollars by the millennium.

Playsite
http://www.playsite.com
Playsite offers old-fashioned games based on skill and luck, such as backgammon, chess and bridge. What's more, they're free.

Plus Lotto
http://www.pluslotto.com
With a credit card and an internet connection, you can gamble almost anywhere in the world. Plus Lotto is based in Liechtenstein, with all kinds of prizes to be won, including cash.

Puzzability
http://www.puzzability.com
Why not while away the winter with a hot-water bottle on your knee and you browser pointing towards Puzzability. If your browser is Java-enabled, you can spend your time having fun solving puzzles (and

Sites for children

increase your telephone bill at the same time). There are lots of free puzzles and brainteasers on this site. You'll find crosswords, word searches, and plenty of other clever games to tease and entertain you.

Trivia Treasure Trove
http://www.thirdage.com/news/archive/990120-06.html
Ever wonder why the sky is blue or bees buzz or what tatterdemalion means? Are you fascinated by the fact that the Eiffel Tower can grow taller or shrink by six inches, depending on the weather? If so, the Trivia Treasure Trove is ready made for you.

UselessKnowledge.com
http://www.uselessknowledge.com
Did you know that, 'If the head of a cockroach is removed carefully, so as to prevent it from bleeding to death, the cockroach can survive for several weeks? When it dies, it is from starvation.' Pretty incredible stuff, huh? But some of us thrive on this kind of irrelevant titbit to get us through boring or uneasy conversations. Where do we get them? UselessKnowledge.com is a site dedicated to trivia, quotes, quizzes, and useless facts.

WirePlay
http://www.wireplay.co.uk
One of the more popular multiplayer gaming sites is British Telecom's WirePlay. For the price of a local phone call, you can challenge unseen opponents to battles galore. The WirePlay service is free with 'no subscription and no commitment. In fact the only obligation is that they guarantee you a great time!' You can be up and fighting in minutes after you download their special software. There are two gaming arenas, Power Play and Open Play. Power Play is for players in the UK only and supports over 100 games. Open Play allows you to play against thousands of gamers worldwide regardless of how you access the internet. 'If you're not resident in the UK or want to connect via an office network then this is the arena for you.'

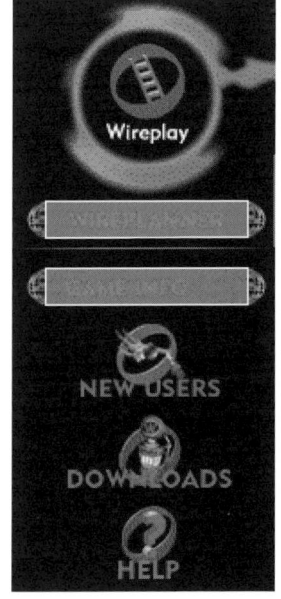

Sites for children

ArgoSphere
http://www.argosphere.net
ArgoSphere is an educational software company. Their site is not only an advertisement but also contains lots of games and quizzes. Most of the games on the site are Java based so you'll need one of the more recent versions of Netscape Navigator or Internet Explorer.

Children's Candlelight Stories
http://CandlelightStories.com/default.asp
Reading a story online is not easy but you can print out stories to be read later. Many of the best loved and most frequently read stories are on this site – and there are a lot of them. Most of the stories also contain colourful artwork. The site encourages any young storytellers out there to send in their own stories for publication on the site.

Rest

KidsFun
http://kidsfun.co.uk

National Association of Youth Theatres
http://www.nayt.org.uk
Meeting other young performers may not be easy where you live but this web site can act as a first point of contact and you can have fun at the same time. Members of the site are drawn from all over the UK to share new ideas, learn new skills and just chat and make friends. The site has very up-to-date information on current performances, workshops, success strategies and young theatre groups.

SafeKids
http://www.safekids.com
SafeKids.com is a site that helps parents, teachers and children to learn ways to stay safe when browsing the internet. The site explains the risks to children on the internet and offers guidelines for parents and children. SafeKids.com has links to sites containing safety information and to search engines that have special features for young people.

TheSite
http://www.thesite.org.uk
TheSite is produced and managed by YouthNet UK, a small registered charity founded in 1995, and is designed to connect young people in the UK. It aims to be the best source of information, help and advice on the internet and 'to enable people to make informed decisions for themselves and to be the best they can.' Sections include lounge, health and sex, drugs, money, education and work, housing, sport and action, and advice.

Thomas the Tank Engine
http://www.thomasthetankengine.com
Here, you'll find perhaps the only train company to run on time and have complete customer satisfaction. It's a great educational resource for young children but may need adult supervision due to the complexity.

Topmarks
http://www.topmarks.co.uk
Topmarks is a site with classified links to lots of child-friendly sites elsewhere on the internet. Many school subjects are covered as well as more general links to sites such as reference sites. The aims of Topmarks are: to provide easy access to the best educational web sites, to help teachers use the web in the classroom, and to publish articles for parents to help their children.

The Junction
http://www.the-junction.com
One of the many Virgin sites on the net, The Junction has loads of stuff for teenagers. There's sounds, games, a list of universities, celebrity news, love tips, and a chat area. The Junction is the UK's biggest teen and student orientated community and resource. You can search the

---

Resources

<u>Links and Safe Searching</u>
Great sites for kids, parents and teachers

<u>Child Safe Search Engines</u>
Search engines that are filtered or limited to sites that contain appropriate material

<u>Directory of Parental Control Software</u>
Filtering programs

<u>Other Sites with Internet advice for kids, parents and teachers</u>

.... **Younger children**

web, find out about night clubs around the UK, and chat to other teenagers online.

Younger children

Colouring
http://www.coloring.com
You, or your children, can colour in drawings for hours online or print them out for later use. What more can be said about this site – it is simple, colourful and fun for younger children. There are many different pictures to choose from and new ones being added regularly. You can choose from pictures such as apples, centipedes and racing cars.

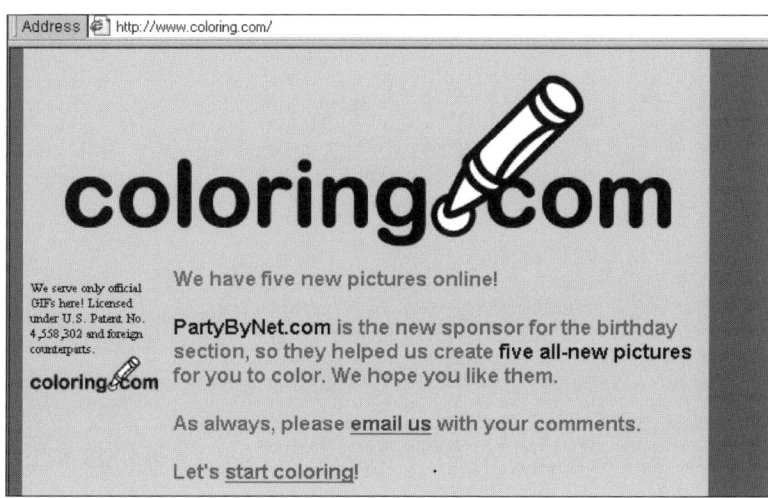

Fig. 26. Coloring.com. Give your child a flying start on the internet by colouring in pictures of cats and dogs. A mouse click here and there and what have you? A purple poodle.

Infant Explorer
http://www.naturegrid.org.uk/infant
This site is a good site to help your child with reading. The theme and the environment are both nature and your child will be guided through the site by Sebastian – a swan. Sebastian tells your child some stories about swans, nesting, and other similar things. If you or your child have comments or questions, you can email Sebastian or put a notice on the noticeboard for others to see.

Kids @ National Geographic
http://www.nationalgeographic.com/kids
This is a special section of the main National Geographic site that has features just for children such as a pen-pal section, a games area, a cartoon factory, and links to a mini encyclopaedia. Some of the things you can do on the site are: search an index of publications or visit the library, visit the museum, learn how to win a National Geography Bee, put a question to the staff, or check the mini-encyclopaedia.

Teletubbies
http://www.bbc.co.uk/education/teletubbies
Your toddler will be entertained for hours with the Shockwaved Teletubbies.

Rest

Home and garden DIY

Garden Web
http://www.gardenweb.com
The Garden Web is full of gardening resources. There is a directory of garden related businesses, a European gardening forum, and interactive weather maps. There is also a gardening dictionary and a selection of general gardening tips. A section of the Garden Web called The Seed Guild specialises in unusual and rare seeds:

http://www.uk.gardenweb.com/seedgd

Fig. 27. When you want a rest from weeding, what better than to read up on the best way to store those bulbs so that you will get a wonderful bloom next year. Follow the advice of the gardening experts on Garden Web and you can't go wrong.

Greenfingers
http://www.greenfingers.co.uk
You can never have too much compost, can you? Wrong – you can. Think of all those harmful insects that it encourages – cutworms, carrot worms to name just two. Look here for garden planning tips, advice on how to deal with different soil types, and shopping recommendations.

The History of Plumbing
http://www.theplumber.com/H_index.html
For those of you who want to know more about plumbing than how to repair a ball cock valve, this site is essential. What we now take for granted was once the latest technology. It all started thousands of years ago in Babylon when... well visit the site yourself – you will be fascinated. The home page is basic if not boring, but the well-written articles more than make up for it.

Internet Garden
http://www.internetgarden.co.uk
The Internet Garden provides a useful starting point for gardening enthusiasts. It has a clean and simple interface, free of large image files, and easy to navigate. There is a search facility, so you can explore the world wide web from within the site, and a chat facility is being planned.

Food & drink

The Natural Handyman
http://www.naturalhandyman.com/index.shtm
'A feast of home repair help, information, humour, and encouragement.' Most DIY sites are little more than an advert for books but this one is an exception. This site covers many DIY topics with step by step instructions. The articles are easy to follow and humorous. Also on the site are an online bookstore and instructions for submitting questions to the Ask the Natural Handyman section of the site.

The Virtual Garden
http://www.vg.com
One way to become a great gardener is to keep the company of other plant lovers. The Virtual Garden holds a vast amount of information on gardening, from beginners' tips to in-depth botanical information and advice. Other sections include gardening projects, ideas for children, and a seasonal planting calendar. It also hosts a forum that includes discussions on almost every gardening topic.

Cinema and theatre

Film Finder
http://www.yell.co.uk/yell/ff
To find a film in your area, you need go no further than the Yell Film Finder. Simply choose your region, then your nearest town, and there you go. At the time of writing there were links to individual cinemas, film summaries and a 'what's on stage' section.

First Call
http://www.firstcalltickets.com
First Call is a great resource for online theatre bookings. They also offer booking facilities for music, sports, ballet, opera and other events. If an event is not on one of the main pages, you might find it if you perform a search. The site also contains events in other countries in the selection of overseas events and destinations. Most events can be booked online by clicking on the name and filing in one or two forms.

Food and drink

For places that sell food and drink, see page 113.

ACATS
http://www.epact.se/acats/
ACATS internet bar pages puts a database of 1,100 drinks at your disposal. Now you can find the perfect drink for your taste and submit your own favourite recipe. Look up the latest new recipe on the Ultimate Drink List, or look for a job in the business. If you need to learn how to use all of that equipment you see in a bar – the site will help you with that, too.

Beer.com
http://www.beer.com
Everything you could want from a beer site is here – from free beer

Rest

contests to pictures of beer guts. There are, of course, many recipes for home brew and other sections such as the history of beer, terminology, beer humour and beer games.

Beer Info
http://www.beerinfo.com
Beer Info is a site for information about beer. That may seem obvious from the name but the site owners discourage the use of beer to become rowdy, aggressive and abusive. Instead, you will find information on the enjoyment of beer and related activities such as homebrew, festivals, breweries, world beer guides and more.

FEATURES

Wok Talk
Share recipes, discover great restaurants and get your Chinese cooking queries answered.

Eating Out
Need a Chinese restaurant? Check our guide to the best!

Recipes
Looking for a recipe? The Chopstix database stores the details of over 4000!

Chopstix
http://www.chopstix.co.uk
Do you know you can use chopsticks to eat soup? You can – as long as at least one of them is hollow (hint: use it as a straw). The Chopstix site has a database containing the details of over 4000 Chinese recipes and highlights the ten most popular recipes. You can also learn how to use woks and other oriental kitchenware, with hints and tips such as the random cookery hint, and how to get started with your first Chinese meal.

Epicurious Food
http://www.epicurious.com
Check the latest recipes from the 9,000 or so on the list. There is food for every taste which you can search for by keyword or category or just look through the latest additions. There are sections on eating, drinking, and playing with food, as well as articles, tips, video cookery classes, a dictionary of cooking, and, of course, lots of recipes.

IDrink
http://www.idrink.com
The next time you forget the recipe for your favourite cocktail or when you want to try something a little more exotic, go over to IDrink and have your mixer ready. IDrink is designed to 'allow partygoers to have more variety in their mixed drinks. You enter all the ingredients that you have around the house (or at the party), then our database of 5m464 alcoholic and non-alcoholic recipes is compared against your selections and a list of all the recipes you can make is provided.'

International Vegetarian Union
http://www.ivu.org
Vegetarianism often means much more than just eating nut cutlets and avoiding meat – there are heaps of political issues surrounding the meat industry. Find out what the point really is at this site. You will also find more light-hearted articles and lots of recipes.

Internet Chef
http://www.ichef.com
This is a great site if you haven't quite got all of the ingredients needed for your favourite recipe. The Cook's Thesaurus gives you suggestions

Food & drink

for substitutions for thousands of ingredients. So if you can't find kangaroo steak in the shops, you can look up a substitute.

International Vegetarian Union
http://www.ivu.org
The IVU is the successor to the Vegetarian Federal Union which was established in 1889 with the aim of bringing together vegetarian societies from all parts of the world. The major aim of IVU is 'to further vegetarianism world wide by promoting knowledge of vegetarianism as a means of advancing the spiritual, moral, mental, physical and economic well being of mankind.' The main page contains news, articles and links to other vegetarian and animal welfare sites.

La Cuisine de Veronique
http://www.cooking-french.com
This site has lots of delicious and delightful recipes from France. There are a wide variety of free recipes as well as a food/wine links database, which allows visitors to submit their favourite food/wine link.

TeaTime
http://www.teatime.com
The food and drink section would be lacking without a site dealing with tea. Have you ever wanted to know more about the history of tea? This site has it, plus a glossary of tea terminology, links to sites selling teas, books, recipes and even a tea quote of the day.

Vegweb
http://www.vegweb.com
Do you cook vegetarian food? Why not submit your favourite recipes to this site, you will find lots of tips from other people including how to grow and cook your own food.

Where To Eat
http://www.where-to-eat.co.uk
Making a choice between the medieval restaurant down by the river and that cosy little Greek place that offers a free glass of ouzo after the meal can be a nightmare in London – unless you look at this site first. The site gives you access to a clear and informative restaurant database. The database uses a form like a search engine: type in your fancy, such as 'Indonesian in SW1', click 'search', then order the taxi.

Wine Pages
http://www.wine-pages.com
This site is perhaps one of the best wine sites for enthusiasts in the world. You will find non-commercial information on almost a thousand wines including tasting notes, advice on the cheaper wines, which wines are the sexiest, and so on. There is an online wine course for the beginning wine taster to teach you the history of wine and how to buy and taste wine.

Rest

Music

Bignote
http://www.bignote.com
Bignote lets you customise a search to give you the type of music that it thinks you will like. You answer a questionnaire by giving ratings to music that you have listened to; Bignote uses those ratings to calculate the type of music you like and then creates a list of potential favourite albums for you. While you are there, you can check to see if anyone else is online who is interested in the same range of music as you.

CDnow
http://www.cdnow.com
American sites can sometimes be accessible to UK customers if, like CDnow, they have a European base. Price of delivery is reasonable and the site concentrates on the traditional way of selling music – on tapes and CDs. There is a built-in search engine and a categorised index of titles in the database. Simply select the titles you like, place them into your shopping trolley and pay when you have finished.

Dotmusic
http://www.dotmusic.com
Dotmusic was launched in 1995 by a traditional music magazine publishing company and claims to be the insider's guide to music that is 'able to access music stories that no-other magazine can,' the site says proudly, 'We break the latest stories and give fans a behind-the-scenes angle on music.' The site is produced by Miller Freeman Entertainment, the publishers of *Music Week*.

Fig. 28. What's the inside line on music? If your subject is music, the Dotmusic site will give you lots of insider news from the experts in the field.

MP3

Interactive Music and Video Shop
http://www.imvs.com
There is plenty of choice on this site: almost 250,000 titles including videos and computer games. Once you have ordered your CD or whatever, the order-tracking feature will let you check on the progress of your CD through the delivery process. While you are waiting for delivery, you can browse the iMVS sampler magazine, which has interviews, reviews and other features on music for you to read.

Live Online
http://www.live-online.com
No need to rush to Wembley or to push through the crush; put on your headphones and link up to Live online. The site provides a huge listing of online concerts. Don't expect the quality to be the same as if you were at a live concert but at least you can hear them from your own home.

Music Rough Guide
http://www-2.roughguides.com/music
Rough Guides have put details of over a thousand rock artists on the site in what is more like an encyclopaedia than a guide. There are other types of music, but none of them as detailed as the rock section. Classical, jazz, reggae, opera are featured but only highlights from the Rough Guidebooks and links to online bookshops.

Timewarp Records
http://www.tunes.co.uk/timewarp
Jazz and soul enthusiasts will like Timewarp, whose selection is specially compiled with those buyers in mind. You will find the originals like James Brown and Miles Davis but the site mainly consists of underground artists.

MP3

The internet is becoming a common source of free music, most of it is from new musicians who distribute their music to enthusiasts but there is still a large percentage of the music that is illegally copied. In common with other types of business, many artists and music companies are planning to cut out the middlemen – large manufacturers and distributors – by selling their music online in MP3 format. MP3 files need special software to play them such as the free WinAmp or Windows Multimedia Player.

▶ *MP3 (MPEG Audio Layer 3)* – an audio format that compresses music. It creates files that are small yet whose quality is almost as good as CD music. See http://mpeg.org for further technical information. At the time of writing, MP4, even faster to download, was being developed.

Lycos Music Search
http://mp3.lycos.com
The new music site from Lycos allows users to search through more

Rest

than 500,000 music CDs and download MP3 files. At time of writing, there was no way to ensure that the downloaded music was legal and not a pirate copy. This site should still be around but expect things to change as the legal situation tightens on piracy.

MP3.com
http://www.mp3.com
This site probably has the largest collection of legal MP3 files on the internet. Most of the music is from musicians wanting exposure but much of it is great listening anyway. The site also follows the legal situation regarding mp3 files and the music industry.

Fig. 29. Many say that MP3 is the future of music, and that vinyl records, tapes and CDs will fade into the background. Take a look at MP3.com to find out more to help you make up your own mind. There's lots of free music on the site, too.

MusicMatch
http://www.musicmatch.com
If you have a favourite CD, how can you get it onto your computer so you can listen to it without the CD? Download MusicMatch, which is a 'ripper' that will convert the music on a music CD into your computer into an MP3 file. Apparently, this is perfectly legal as long as you do not distribute the file to other people.

Techtronics
http://www.techtronics.com
Some say that MP3 is the future of music; Techtronics is one of these. They have manufactured a portable MP3 player similar to a Walkman for about £145, which you can order from this site. Instead of carrying tapes or CDs with you, you just download your favourite MP3 files into the player and off you go.

Religion

Music publications and news sites

NME
http://www.nme.com
Probably the number one magazine for people interested in the music industry, *New Musical Express* is online. You will not find the full text of the magazine but there is a news archive, lots of reviews, gigs listed by town, bands and dates. There are also, of course, the charts (present and past).

Rolling Stone
http://www.rollingstone.com
Here, you'll find plenty of RealAudio Radio stations with pop and new wave stations and the latest MP3 downloads. There is also lots of free stuff, contests and news of the music world.

Top Magazine
http://www.topmag.co.uk
Here is yet another music site with lots of news, reviews and articles – the internet equivalent of the free printed version. The full *Top Magazine* is available free from a Tower Records shop near you.

▶ *RealPlayer* – technology that allows you to listen to audio and watch video over the internet.

Billboard Online
http://www.billboard.com
Are you still looking for music news? Want to know what music is on its way to your local music store or when and where artists will be performing? Billboard is a source you might consider. It covers most popular types of music: country, R&B, latin music and pop. There is a classifieds section for notices about anything in the music industry. And you can find jobs, get CDs duplicated and packaged, or outfit a retail store.

New Stars Wanted
Attention, unsigned artists: Here's your chance to upload your music straight to the ears of Rolling Stone's critics
Show us your stuff

New Downloads

RELIGION AND SPIRITUALITY

There are hundreds of thousands of religious sites on the internet. The following list includes something of interest for everyone.

Western religions

The Catholic Encyclopaedia
http://www.knight.org/advent/cathen
With an answer for almost every question, the Catholic Encyclopaedia is certainly comprehensive. Everything from freemasonry to witchcraft, and altar carpets to holy water – it's in there, treated from a Catholic standpoint.

Chapter and Verse Online
http://bible.gospelcom.net
The Gospel Communications Network has developed Bible Gateway, a

Rest

search tool that lets you search online Bibles for particular passages or words. You can, if you want, restrict your search to one of six English versions of the Bible by selecting from a drop-down list. Bible Gateway even lets you search the Bible in nine languages other than English, including German, French, Spanish, and Tagalog (Philippines).

Church of England
http://www.church-of-england.org
The Church of England is the 'mother church' of the Anglican communion, which covers 160 countries. It claims to be experiencing a resurgence of interest at the moment. They say on their site: 'Calls to the ministry are up, giving for the church's work is up and the church is confident that, with and by God's grace, it can make an increasingly valuable contribution to the life of the nation, its people, and do so far beyond its borders as well.' The site features the latest C of E news, today's service, and details of the Church's views on various matters.

Christianity Today
http://www.christianitytoday.net
This is the online version of the printed magazine *Christianity Today*. Features on the site at time of writing included: It's a Small Church – how globalisation is changing Christian ministry; Sri Lanka: A Light in Buddha's Shadow; and Vietnam: Jesus can still mean jail – the plight of Vietnam's 700,000 evangelical Christians.

The Vatican
http://www.vatican.va
The Vatican City is the home of the Pope and the centre of the Roman Catholic church. Tourists flock to the museums, the Sistine Chapel, and the Borgia Apartment. The site provides comprehensive details of all public aspects of the Vatican. The city itself has its own telephone system, post office, radio station, an army of more than 100 Swiss Guards, its own banking system, stores, and a pharmacy. There is no income tax and no restriction on the import or export of funds, and the banking organisations in the Vatican are veiled in secrecy. Sadly, they do not accept many immigrants.

Eastern religions

The Hindu Universe
http://www.hindunet.org
The Hindu Universe is the web site for GHEN (Global Hindu Electronic Networks). This site is full of information relating to Hinduism and Hindu society. It is a directory containing links to events, culture, arts, customs, philosophy and much more. If you want to know anything at all relating to Hinduism, start here.

The Islamic Digest
http://www.islamicdigest.org
This is an Islamic and cultural e-zine, with articles, focus articles on issues, general articles, poems, a complete greeting card section, a subscription-based mailing list, and much more.

Religion

The Muslim News
http://www.muslimnews.co.uk
This is a good site for news and views of Muslims in the United Kingdom. The Muslim News is known for its objectivity and its independent views – it features many reports that mainstream media refuses to cover. On the site, you can read about domestic and international issues – both Muslim and non-Muslim.

Tibetan Buddhism
http://www.diamondway-buddhism.org
China may be suffocating Tibetan culture, but Tibetan Buddhism is alive and thriving. It is probably the most popular form of Buddhism in the west. Perhaps it is the belief of the possibility of reaching enlightenment in this lifetime that fits best with our materialistic outlook, or it might be that Tibetan Buddhism stresses benefits to all beings on the planet. You can, as the site says, 'discover and develop our inner richness for the benefit of all beings as well as ourselves.'

Others

Artwell's Oracula
http://www.artwells.com/newwings
The I Ching, or Book of Changes, is the Chinese method of divination. You throw coins or sticks. The I Ching itself is a classic piece of literature that some take to an incredible philosophical depth. The I Ching is intended to open the mind to broaden one's outlook and discover the meaning underneath a situation. This site has an interactive version of the I Ching – you can make a query on the site and get a short reading.

Astrology.net
http://www.astrology.net
Whether you believe in horoscopes or not, you can't deny that they are popular. With this site, all you need is to know where you were born, and on what date and what time and the site will help you to plot a chart. Astrology.net has daily and monthly readings, an interactive horoscope charting application and charts of various celebrities. The site also includes a history of astrology and information on how horoscopes are made. The site says, 'Astrology.Net is published by Kelli Fox, the internet's foremost astrologer. Kelli enjoys a global following, and has numerous memberships in professional astrological associations around the world. Kelli's mission is to bring astrology to the widest possible audience and help people use astrology as a tool for all aspects of life.'

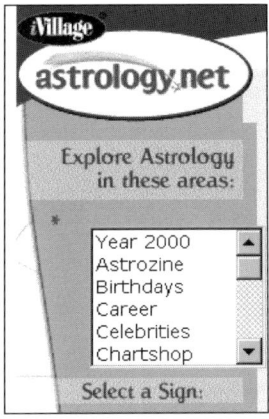

Astrology – Astrodienst Atlas Database
http://www.astro.com/atlas
Almost everyone knows what zodiac sign they were born under. Astrodienst expands on that by helping you obtain further astrological information. Select the city where you were born (the database contains over 250,000 cities) and Astrodienst looks up the latitude and longitude for you. Enter your date and time of birth, and you'll get back

Rest

an in-depth astrological chart showing you all of the information about the planets in your chart and what your rising sign is.

ParaScope
http://www.parascope.com/index.htm
ParaScope is a huge interactive archive of paranormal and alternative information. Sections cover UFOs, black ops, government cover-ups and Fortean phenomena. Whether you believe in UFOs or not you can enjoy the site's light-hearted and professional design.

Religious Freedom
http://www.relfreedom.org
Religious cults seem to be a safety valve of the young, or at least that is the belief that Professor Hadden's site seems to be putting out. Do you remember the American cult whose members committed suicide in March 1997? They believed that there was a spaceship in the tail of a passing comet that had come to collect them – that is just one of the hundred or so cults documented on the site. 'Religion is the final line of defence against every form of tyranny.' Says the professor. Well, judge for yourself.

The Runic Journey
http://www.tarahill.com/runes
One of the earliest forms of divination was the simple throwing of stones or bones. Later, with the invention of the alphabet, these stones were engraved with runic characters to make them easier to identify. The Runic Journey provides an interesting history, a chart of rune meanings and an essay on the magic of rune stones. Are your bones aching now?

Salem Tarot
http://www.salemtarot.com
Don't be a fool or a tower of strength – both are destined to fall. Well, according to the Tarot, they are. Filled with archetypal meanings the Tarot images are 'iconic in nature and extremely refined in execution.'

Fig. 30. Tarot cards have many uses besides fortune telling. Many people use the cards as a kind of psychotherapy, others use them in magical rituals. The Salem Tarot page is biased more towards their use in magic.

Buying goods over the internet

Of course, throwing cards to predict the future is only one way to use the Tarot – some use the cards as more of a spiritual or even psychological tool. However, the Salem Tarot page was written by a group of witches who take the art very seriously. Try out the CGI script that gives you a reading with three cards.

BUYING PRODUCTS AND SERVICES

Buying products on the internet is easy but can be risky – there are many less-than-honest web sites out there. It is so easy for anyone to construct a professional looking site now, and it is becoming harder to know for sure whether a site is reliable. You can trust big name sites such as Tesco or Waterstones, but what about the thousands of smaller specialised sites such as one advertising secretarial or family tree tracing services?

How to avoid being conned

Here are eight ways to avoid being conned when buying products on the internet:

1. Only give your credit card details over a secure server. You can tell if the connection is secure in a number of ways. You should notice that the URL begins with https:// rather than just http:// and your browser should warn you that you are entering a secure web site.

2. Check the phone number on the web site if possible to make sure it is genuine.

3. Fax your order. You can never really be sure that your credit card details are not being read by any number of people: fax is safer. Any serious online business will also have a fax number on its web site. If it has not – be suspicious.

4. Print copies of your order. It is too easy to forget the vital details, which may be needed if it comes to a dispute.

5. If the offer is too good to be true, it probably is – especially if it is claiming a miraculous cure. Wherever possible check the facts and ask or read about the returns policy.

6. Check your next credit card statement. If you see a problem, inform your credit card company immediately – they can wield a lot of power.

7. Consult the Advertising Standards Agency and Office of Fair Trading (see below) – search for any complaints about the company that you are thinking of paying.

8. Be extra careful when buying from overseas companies – UK laws may not apply and you may not have any protection.

Office of Fair Trading
http://www.open.gov.uk/oft/frames/consumer.htm
This may be another site of use to a prospective internet consumer. The site is not spectacular but if you want to know your rights, this is the

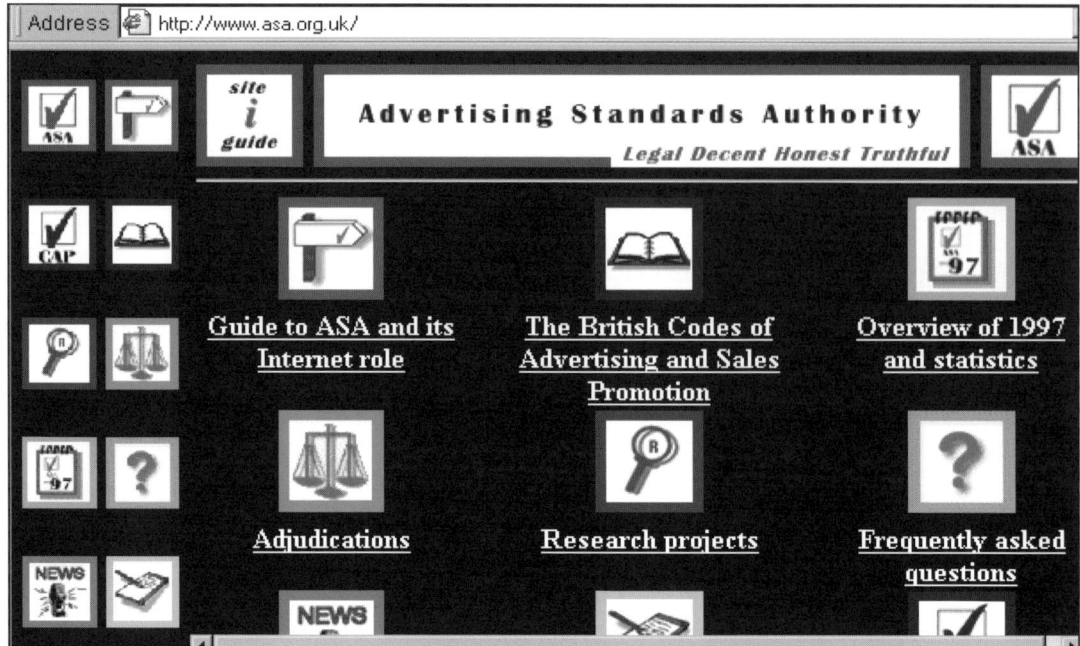

Fig. 31. Looking through the Advertising Standards Agency site will open your eyes to the many occurrences where even the most respected companies will try to pull the wool over your eyes.

site. There are also explanations of arbitration schemes, small courts claims, and tips for buyers.

Shopping directories and malls

Enterprise City
http://www.enterprisecity.co.uk
When you are confident or courageous enough to try some online shopping, have a look at Enterprise City – a directory that reviews hundreds of UK shopping sites. You might get some surprises.

Lastminute
http://www.lastminute.com
The internet was almost tailor-made for specialist markets such as Lastminute, which offers last-minute deals on anything from flights to flowers. Lastminute wants to encourage 'spontaneous, romantic and sometimes-adventurous behaviour by offering users the chance to live their dreams at unbeatable prices.' For more information on the flights for sale, see the entry on page 125.

MyTaxi
http://www.mytaxi.co.uk
Not a taxi-booking service but a free shopping assistant comprising a collection of over two thousand retail and information sites. Taxi was the first to compare prices of the many outlets in its database. This price comparison will let you search for the best price for the item or service you want. Prices will include such extras as local taxes and delivery charges.

Shopping City
http://www.ukshops.co.uk
The site says, 'Space is currently available in most areas for medium to

Shopping directories

long term lease, and all relevant details in respect of available rental units, and the cost of them is available on request.' You can walk into a shop by first clicking on a little cartoon village representing a group of buildings such as a sports centre, science park, and travel area. Once you have 'entered' a building, you come to a floor plan and can select the shop you want to enter. Clicking on a 'shop' opens their page. Everything seems a little strange and cumbersome but at least there is a games section to keep you entertained. The search facility is the saving feature of the site. With hundreds of 'shops' on the site, this is a must. You can search for company or keyword; 'Shoes' brought up five shop names.

Shopguide
http://www.shopguide.co.uk
A useful directory of hundreds of shopping sites – one of the few that seems to be on the shoppers' side. There are no fancy advertising gimmicks and none of the shops pay to be on the site. The stores are ranked and rated with, for instance, the prices of goods compared. The range of products available runs into thousands, from music to flowers.

Priceline
http://www.priceline.com
Wouldn't it be nice if we could set the price when we want to buy something? You could walk into a travel agency and say 'I want a flight to Bangkok for £100'. Priceline lets you do just that – almost. You name a price that you are willing to pay. If Priceline finds a company prepared to match or beat that price, they take the offer and pass it to you. They aim to make a profit from cashing in the difference in price or charging a commission. Services and products that you can 'bid' for include flights, hotels, cars and mortgages.

Fig. 32. Reserve a week in the year for a holiday but don't plan anything. When that week approaches, go to Lastminute.com and see what kind of last minute bargains are available – you may never plan a holiday again.

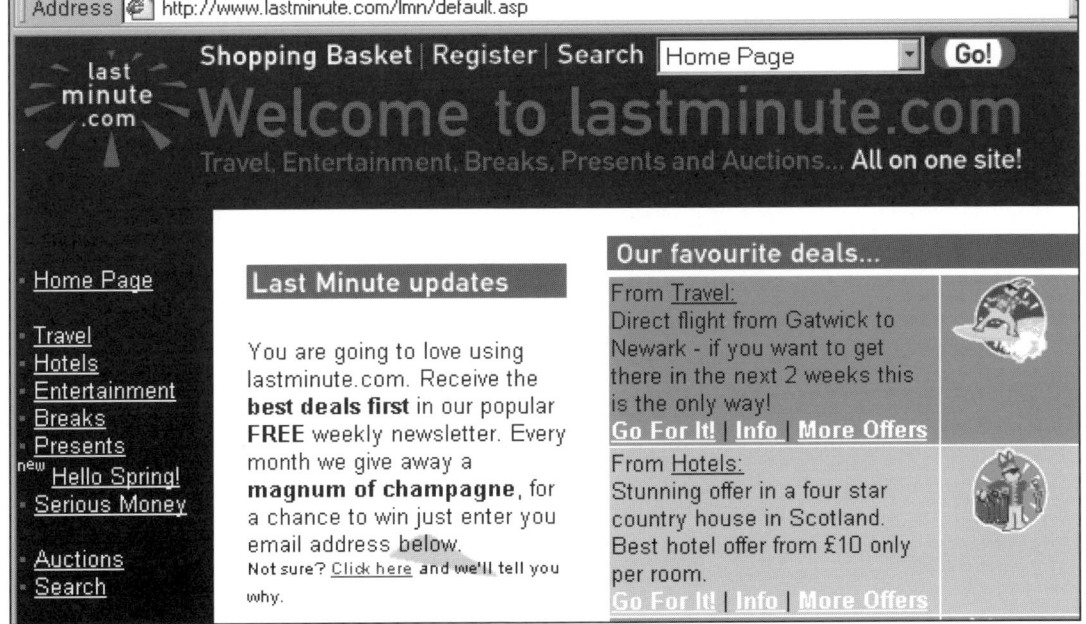

Rest

categories
- Antiques
- Books, Movies, Music
- Coins & Stamps
- Collectables
- Computers
- Dolls, Figures
- Jewellery, Gemstones
- Photo & Electronics
- Pottery & Glass
- Sports Memorabilia
- Toys & Bean Bag Plush
- Miscellaneous

All Auctions
- All Auctions
- Antiques
- Automotive
- Beanie Babies
- Books & Magazines
- Clothing
- Collectibles
- Computer Hardware
- Computer Software
- Electrical
- Household Goods
- Internet
- Jewelery
- Movies
- Music
- Office Goods
- Sporting Goods
- Tickets
- Toys & Games

Auctions

Online auctions account for around two-thirds of customer complaints regarding buying online so be careful with auction sites — especially new ones. Warning given, you can buy and sell almost anything you can imagine in an auction. Items are open to bids until a specified time or date, and the highest bidder at that time wins.

eBay
http://www.ebay.com/uk
This service started in 1995 with trading candy dispensers and, within a few days, it was making money. Now is has developed into a huge business selling millions of items in over a thousand categories. Although the site is US biased, the UK section is worth a visit to see how it is developing. You can buy or sell almost anything from here.

eBid
http://www.ebid.co.uk
eBid is probably the most lifelike of the auction sites. You see the time left on an item and can wait till the last minute before placing your bid.

Morgans
http://www.morgan-auctions.co.uk
Morgans is one of the high street favourites for buying end-of-line computer items at very cheap prices. An auction takes place every few days or so and you can see the action on several items at the same time so if you are beaten on one product you can try for another.

QXL
http://www.qxl.com
An established name like QXL ('Quick Sell') is a safe place to buy and sell. There can be great rewards if you do things right. Auctions are one of the fastest growing areas of online commerce and QXL is probably the biggest and most popular, with hundreds of auctions going on simultaneously. All you need to do to take part is to register on the site, find the product you are interested in, and start bidding. You can set an upper limit and let the site increase your bid until either the other parties stop bidding or you reach the limit. There are no hidden charges – V.A.T. is included and a small charge is made for delivery.

Books and magazines

Will internet bookshops ever replace those in the high street? Internet booksellers may be more efficient and often cheaper, but will prospective customers want to give up handling the real thing? If you know what you want, take a look at these sites.

Amazon Books
http://www.amazon.com
The pioneer of internet book selling, Amazon is now a multi-million dollar business. It has the biggest selection of books for sale on the internet, and many of them cheaper than in the high street stores.

....**Cars & bikes**

Amazon added a UK site in 1998 at http://www.amazon.co.uk. Many of the books in the database have a review, and if one doesn't, you can write one for them. The site also has author interviews and excerpts from books.

Barnes and Noble
http://www.barnesandnoble.com
Breadth of choice is the advantage that Barnes and Noble have over Amazon – there are around five million titles available on the site and over six million in a rare and out-of-print database. Delivery charges (around five dollars per order and six dollars per item) are high, as you would expect from a company based in the USA with no depot in Europe.

Bibliofind
http://www.bibliofind.com
The supreme source of rare and out-of-print books must be Bibliofind with over ten million books in its database. Bibliofind is a free service that searches for the book you require with booksellers all over the world. It then links you directly to the vendor to find more information and complete the sale.

Blackwell's
http://www.bookshop.blackwells.co.uk
Even the huge lists of books that Amazon and Barnes and Noble hold may not list the academic book you want. Blackwell's, however, specialises in academic books. Based in Oxford, it has access to over 1.5 million academic titles. You can search for a book or just browse by subject area. Delivery takes a couple of days if the book is in stock and carries a charge of a pound or two per book. There is also an express service which costs around six pounds.

Waterstones
http://www.waterstones.co.uk
One of Britain's favourite high street bookshops is also getting in on the internet bookselling act and offers a free ISP service. Waterstones seems to cater for more upmarket customers than Amazon. Are you a book collector? The site lets you search for out-of-print books in the secondhand market.

Cars and bikes

Buying a car can bring nightmares of salesmen saying 'She's a good runner, guv, I'm cutting my own throat at that price', but not on the internet – if you feel the price is not right, just click the disconnect button or try a different site. The internet is having a big impact on the secondhand and classic car markets. Buyers can often get a better bargain online and dealers are starting to recognise this as well. The power and choice you have is a big bargaining chip. If you don't like the price at one dealer, simply show a printout of the web results and threaten to go elsewhere. Most sites usually allow a user to specify the type of car, the price range, and postcode. The site then produces a list

Rest

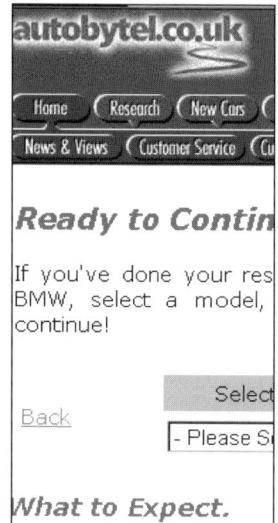

of all the cars that match the specifications.

Used cars

Autobytel
http://www.autobytel.co.uk
A revolutionary site in the motor industry, Autobytel is big in the USA. The site provides lots of information about many models and makes of car – specifications, prices and links to reviews. Once you have decided on the type of car you move to the car-builder where you can customise some items of your dream car. You can add or remove extras such as power steering, a sunroof, and manual gear-change.

Autotrader
http://www.autotrader.co.uk
Autotrader is perhaps the first magazine that people turn to when they want to buy a car. The online version is likely to become just as popular. It includes colour photos, price guides, online finance quotes from Alliance & Leicester, insurance quotes from Screentrade, books from Haynes and more.

Loot
http://www.loot.co.uk
Loot has almost acquired cult status because of the breadth and amount of its free ads. Loot online allows you to browse sub-sections such as cars for sale in the northwest, and refine the search even further. Loot can also save your search requirements and send you an email message as soon as something comes in matching your needs.

New cars

Freeway
http://www.freeway.ltd.uk
Buying a car has never been easier, and that is what the salesmen like. Buying a new car over the internet is less risky than buying a secondhand one: there are no previous owners who may have mistreated it or swapped good parts for bad, and you get guarantees. If you want to pay by instalments, you will like the design of this site, which gives you an instant quote on one of their top twenty cars. There are thousands of cars to look at and you can find out more about them by selecting the make and model from drop-down menus.

New Car Net
http://www.newcar.net
This is an award-winning site that aims to make buying a car a pleasure by using a clear and accessible design. Choose the cars that catch your interest and the site will compare them to one another. It will offer you details such as boot size, seating capacity, torque, fuel consumption and so on. Fill your details into a form and you can request a brochure of the vehicles you like.

> # The NewCar.Network
> *The best place in the world to buy your next new car.*
>
> **Ready to Buy New?**
> Select a make: Bentley   Zip code: [ ]   Go
> powered by autoweb.com
>
> **Search Used Cars**
> Select a make: All Makes   Zip code: 95008   Go
> powered by autoweb.com
>
> NewCar.Net recommends the following resources for your car buying needs.
> Autoweb a new and used car buying service.
> Autoworld The accurate vehicle pricing source
> Carfax Get a complete vehicle history by VIN number online.
> Usedcar.com Everything you need for buying or selling a used car
>
> Welcome to the New Car Network. With all the automotive decisions you have to make, you will

Classic and special cars

Car Lounge
http://www.carlounge.com
The Car Lounge provides lots of information for car enthusiasts and plenty of links to other interesting sites. It is 'the largest independent library of links to all the best web resources for both the motor industry professional and more importantly, the car enthusiast.' The site adds, 'Every make of car. Every racing sport. Every magazine on the web. And every piece of breaking news from all over the world.'

Carsource
http://www.carsource.co.uk
What is your dream car? Are your fingers ink-stained from searching the papers? Carsource will notify you when a car matching your description becomes available in your area. Their database contains tens of thousands of used cars. Carsource promises to contact up to seven dealers in an effort to find your car and the service is free for private buyers. Their new car service includes comprehensive specifications, photos and contract hire prices and, should you wish to take your interest to the next step, you can obtain quotes or book a test drive.

Classic Cars World
http://www.classiccarsworld.co.uk
Experts bring you reviews and previews of auctions around the country and let you know the going auction rates for thousands of classics. There is also a comprehensive directory of classic events from rallies to exhibitions. Need a club to join? Find one on the site's database of information on all the UK's classic clubs.

Fig. 33. Buying a new car is often quite a gamble. You rarely know whether you are getting the best deal you can. Check with The New Car Network and you will be far better able to know a bargain when you see it.

Rest

Homes and property

A growing number of properties are being offered for sale on the internet, including a growing number of private sales. Estate agencies may say that they help in the process of buying and selling a house but many who have sold their own houses would disagree.

Castle Search
http://www.castle-search.co.uk
Castle search is a property search agency that offers a list of services including details of special offers and a property of the week section. There is also plenty of advice and information in the online newsletter. Castle Search covers the whole of the UK so let them know where you want to buy a house and they'll help.

Home Directory
http://www.homedirectory.com
Buying a house is almost inevitably going to be difficult but finding the best agency need not be so painful – on the internet. Home Directory is a 'super site' listing agents throughout the country. The key is the search engine – select the area, price range, type of property and number of rooms, and inspect the details of the matching properties. If nothing takes your fancy, save your search and Home Directory will email you as soon as a match comes in.

The House Directory
http://www.house-directory.co.uk
This site advertises houses for sale in various areas of the UK listed by district and by price. There are very brief property details on the site (e.g. 'Burnage, Manchester, Errwood Road, £99,500, 6 bedrooms, 3 reception, semi, garage') but you can request full details of up to 20 properties. The company can also organise other property-related services such as solicitors, mortgage providers, surveyors and builders.

Property Live
http://www.propertylive.co.uk
One of the most stressful activities for most people is moving house. Here is a site which gives you access to approved estate agents from all over the country. The National Association of Estate Agents is behind this site so there is some assurance of quality.

PropertySight
http://www.property-sight.co.uk
PropertySight features thousands of properties from hundreds of estate agents. The information is updated daily direct from the agents' computers. Therefore, properties are often submitted before they feature in local newspapers or agents' mailings.

UK Property Register
http://www.property-realestate-uk.com/index
If you want to buy or lease a new shop or office, then the agencies

Homes & property

listed here may be your answer – they deal solely with commercial properties. There are sections for city centre premises, business parks and out of town areas, production and distribution sites, and retail and shopping centres.

UK Property Gold
http://www.ukpg.co.uk
Serving both the corporate and individual homeowner, this site lets you place a free ad for your property including a picture if you have one. The site contains access to over 40,000 UK homes for sale or for rent. You can search in the normal way or by using a map to pick the location. A very useful addition to this site is the section with local guides to schools and colleges, recruitment agencies, railway stations, and airports in the area you specify.

UpMyStreet
http://www.upmystreet.com
To quote their site, 'UpMyStreet.com is Europe's first web site that helps you pick and probe at the latest published statistics about where you live today or might live tomorrow.' You will be amazed at how little you know about the area where you live – this site is shocking in its revelations. You can see reports on schools and colleges, environmental pollution (companies and chemicals are named), house prices, MPs, maps and environment, unemployment rates, council tax, and local crime statistics.

Fig. 34. Have you ever wondered how your neighbourhood compares to others in terms of schooling or policing or council tax? Find out in detail just how you do compare to others with the help of the UpMyStreet site – unmissable.

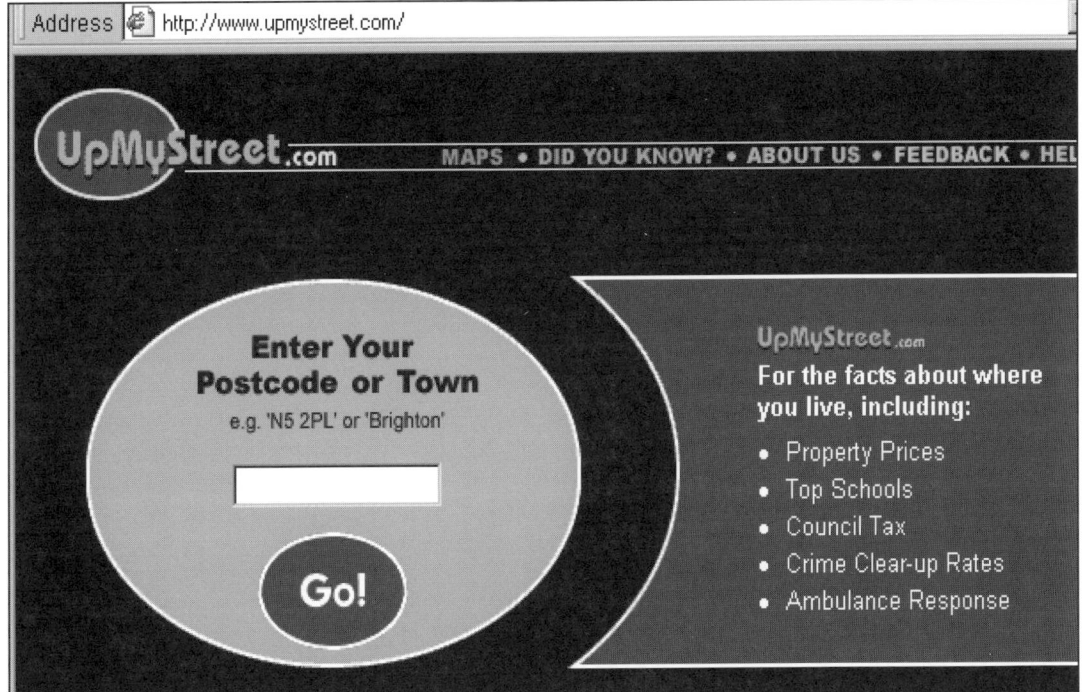

Rest

Small goods

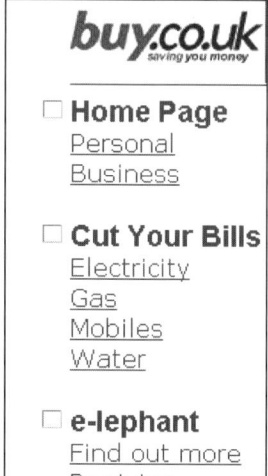

Buy.co.uk
http://www.buy.co.uk
This site has calculators for gas, electricity and mobile phone tariffs that compare the different companies and finds the best deal for your circumstances. With the phone calculator, for example, you enter your average call times per month, and a screen pops up with a typical breakdown of phone usage. If your details differ, simply alter the form and the calculator will find the best deals. Further clicking will reveal the prices and other details about mobile phones for example.

Exchange and Mart
http://exchangeandmart.co.uk
Is it about time you got rid of that old washing machine? At *Exchange & Mart,* you can buy and sell secondhand goods from cars to cushions. The site is updated weekly like the paper. There are thousands of vehicles for sale, a home and leisure section, and a business section. The site asks you to register, free, but thinks people will be prepared to do so because of the benefits of the site.

Flowers Direct
http://www.flowersdirect.co.uk/home.htm
Here's another flower delivery site. Delivery is next day by courier. Let the site send you reminders for those important dates you tend to forget like anniversaries and mother's day. Flowers Direct site includes a provision to select and make up your own bouquet, or a hand tied arrangement. Prices and flower variety are updated daily. Products are designed by 'the best consultant floral designers, to give the most aesthetic ambience and pleasing designs. We also provide sufficient cut flower food for two weeks with each delivery.'

Gift Store
http://www.giftstore.co.uk
'One of the largest selections of quality greeting cards and giftware available anywhere,' they say. The perfect site for a parent or partner working away from home for any length of time – just order your gift here and it will be delivered to your home, or someone else's home. The Gift Store uses a secure online ordering system and guarantee all their products and services. The selection of gifts includes toys, music, computer games, jewellery and (if you fancy a gift with a difference) juggling equipment. You can even choose the gift-wrapping.

Interflora
http://www.interflora.barclaysquare.com
'Say it with flowers'... and a message. Interflora are the traditional company to handle these flowery messages, and they do it quite well. Now they are on the internet, they are better.

Staples
http://www.staples.com
Staples hit on a winner when they offered free delivery to the home for

Tickets

orders over thirty pounds, now they have introduced stationery by internet. Staples has thousands of products available from the site and next (working) day delivery can be free depending on how much you spend and whether you live near a warehouse. There is a loyalty discount scheme, product matchmaker, and readymade lists for the more common requirements.

Tariff On Line
http://www.toll.co.uk
Similar to Buy.co.uk but also can calculate which normal telephone company will be cheapest for your circumstances.

Tickets

Global Tickets
http://www.globaltickets.com
'Your source for theatre and entertainment around the world.' Booking tickets for an event is becoming easier. Global Tickets specialises in theatre, opera, dance, exhibitions, sightseeing, and other special events. Tickets and bookings can be instantly confirmed via the 'live and continuously online' network. Venues are mainly in European countries as well as Canada and the USA.

Ticket Links
http://www.ticketlinks.com
Ticket Links is the latest arrival on the ticket selling stage – and their site looks good. You can search the extensive listing of events then, once you have found something of interest, buy the tickets online very easily. The search page is excellent; you can search using many different

Fig. 35. Where do you want to go today? A festival, puppet show, or the theatre? Ticket Links may brighten up your day by offering tickets for loads of events that are happening all over the country, and you can buy online.

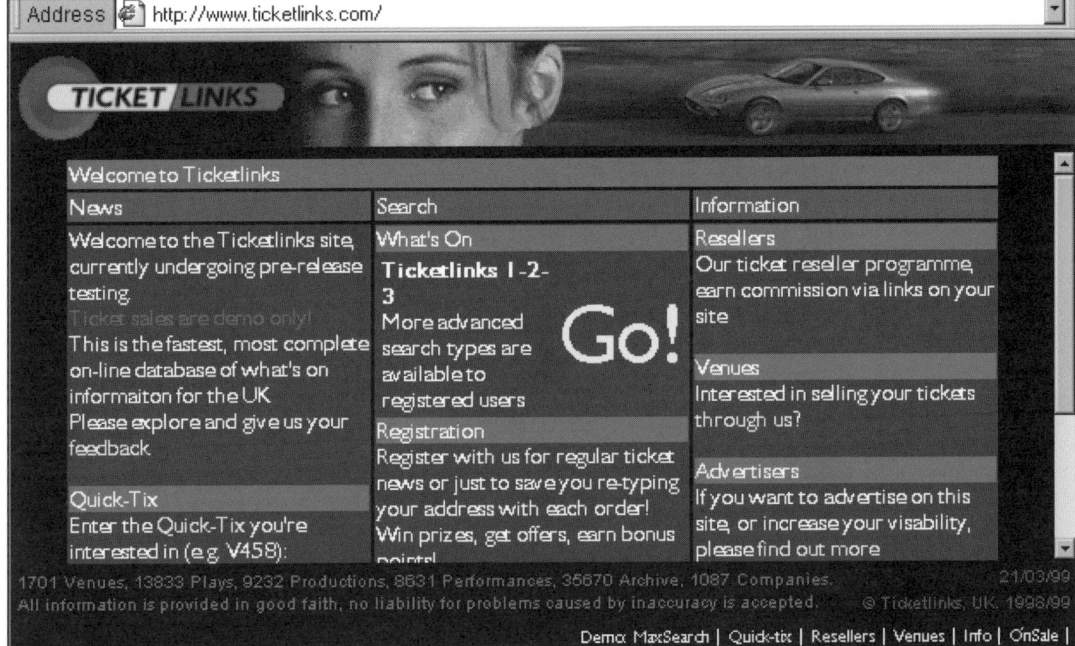

Rest

criteria such as venue, city, play and dates. It does not end there, you can also instruct the search to look only for the types of show you are interested in such as concert, opera, puppet show, kid's event and more. This site is essential for anyone seeking a good night at a show.

Electrical goods

At the time of writing, the latest computer chip was the Pentium III, but by the time you are reading this, it may be the Pentium V chip. The speed at which technology is advancing means that in the time you take to read this book, the computer you are using will probably be obsolete. Buying a computer online may make it easier to keep up because you can design one using your own preferences and see the resulting price in seconds. You can then order the computer or redesign it at your leisure without an annoying salesman sitting on your shoulder. Elonex and Dell, for example, allow you to design your own system online.

Dell
http://www.dell.co.uk
Dell allows you to play around with the design of your computer before you order it. Start off with the type of use you will put the computer to such as home use, small business, large business, or public sector, then you can move onto the finer details of the system. Once you have designed and ordered your system, you can follow the order as it progresses through the assembly and delivery process.

Dixons
http://www.dixons.co.uk
Dixons is one of the many UK companies to offer free internet access, in fact the one that started the gold rush. Claiming well over a million members, Dixons' FreeServe is a success. The site itself holds a plethora of PCs and other gadgets for you to drool over. You can navigate the headings until you get to the product you are interested in or, if you know the brand or model, you can perform a search and go directly to it. If you prefer to pop into a store, click your area on the store location map and you have no further excuse to hold on to your savings.

Elonex
http://www.elonex.co.uk
Once you have selected the specifications and peripherals for your computer, you can save the quoted prices for your designs, go away to compare prices at other sites or shops and later return to the Elonex site and place your order without having to repeat the selection process. The prices are reasonable so you may indeed return.

MacWarehouse
http://www.macwarehouse.co.uk
The only place you need to know about if you insist on buying an Apple computer. It is a site with lots of special offers, great prices and a good search capability. There is even a section for PCs. Whether that says anything about for their confidence in the future of Macs you'll have to judge for yourself. See: http://www.microwarehouse.co.uk.

Dell News

▸ Empower Your Business through the Internet with Dell
▸ DELL OFFERS "MEGA"-EXPANDIBILITY ON INSPIRON NOTEBOOK
▸ Dell® Launches Online Business in Israel
▸ Expandability and lower prices brings benefits of Dell Precision within reach

▸ Free internet access with DellNet

.... **Fashion**

Software Warehouse
http://www.software-warehouse.co.uk
Yet another free ISP, the Software Warehouse has oodles of software and some hardware too. Prices are good and delivery is quick; customer care is very good. The site is difficult to browse – you have to know what you want in advance to get the best from it.

Fashion

Coppernob
http://www.coppernob.co.uk
Most of us like to think we are young, stylish and fashionable. Coppernob have taken advantages of the visual aspect of the web and displays models on its virtual catwalk. You can change the model's angle and zoom in on a garment that interests you. The site uses Shockwave to good effect.

FashionMall
http://www.fashionmall.com
Fashion shops for men and women line both sides of this shopping centre. There are also several guides and some popular fashion-related magazines of interest to both fashion experts and casual shoppers. Some of the top fashion names include Axis, Diesel and Sunglass International.

FashionUK
http://www.widemedia.com/fashionuk
Also known as FUK, Fashion UK covers the fashionable in the UK. Readers can write in and ask questions about various fashion matters in the clinic. The site contains fashion news, beauty news and a message board.

La Redoutte
http://www.redoutte.co.uk
This site is worth a mention not least because of its returns policy: there is free postage and packing on returns and exchanges. The collections are stylish in the French way and concentrate on modern classics and daywear. As with all of the internet fashion sites, there is no changing room but UK sizes are used and you can return clothes if they don't fit.

FOOD AND DRINK

Most of the sites selling food and drink also contain interesting articles such as the usual 'how to cure a hangover' tips and the histories of the various drinks. An advantage of buying food and drink online is that you can find something for a special occasion at short notice.

Food

Brits Abroad
http://www.britsabroad.co.uk
It is strange what you miss when you are in another country for any

Rest

length of time. It is usually the little things like a certain type of teabag or a bar of chocolate. If you are so desperate that you are willing to pay for a box of cheese and onion crisps to be posted to you, contact Brits Abroad. They stock hundreds of typically British items and will send them anywhere in the world; delivery to some countries may take some time , so order early.

Fromages
http://www.fromages.com
France's most visited and best loved cheese web site contains recipes, articles, an encyclopaedia, books, notice of cheese festivals, cheesy links, and a 'treasure trove' of information on cheeses. An order of cheese from the UK will take about 24 hours to deliver.

Fresh Food
http://www.freshfood.co.uk
The Fresh Food Company will deliver organic food and, refreshingly, a range of organic beers regularly to your door. The site also contains an online version of the weekly newsletter, *Fresh News*, and a section called the CookBook, which contains recipes and tips.

MacDonalds
http://www.smokedproduce.co.uk
This is not the fast food giant, but a Scottish smoked food specialist. You can order smoked ostrich or alligator for under a fiver or salmon, game and cheese for more. They also sell the more traditional Scottish foods such as haggis.

Sainsburys
http://www.sainsburys.co.uk
At time of writing, Sainsburys had a reputation for not always delivering what was ordered. A small muesli would transform into a large packet, and a French lager would change into a Belgian one. Some shoppers would play 'guess the meal' if they ordered food from an online supermarket. Since groceries are ordered using barcodes, the difference between pencils and oranges may only be slight – a slightly dirty or damaged barcode and you would receive the wrong product. Hopefully by the time you read this book the problems will have been solved.

Somerfield
http://www.somerfield.co.uk
For one of the smaller players, Somerfield is doing quite well on the internet. There is a section for in-store offers and promotions to try to pull you away from your computer, and a recruitment section to try to get you to stay in the shop and work.

Tesco
http://www.tesco.co.uk
Tesco are now offering free internet access to anybody with a loyalty card; if you are near enough to a store, you can also order products

---

Online ordering
Take part in the internet vegetable revolution by ordering on-line. Browse our website catalogue, make your selection, and send it to us at the touch of a button. Of course, fax, post and phone are fine, too. Here we tell you how.

About the company
Frequently asked questions about the fresh food co. What, where, when, who and why?

Customers
Customer care, testimonials, and your opportunity to tell us what you think.

Beers & wines

online. Go to the site and type in your postcode to see if you are near enough.

Beers and wines

Beers Direct
http://www.beersdirect.com
This site sells quality British and foreign beers. There is a good selection of real ales and some pretty strong European beers too. It's a pity the site is not easy to use – to place an order you have to remember the product number and description while you go to another page to fill in the order form.

Berry Bros
http://www.berry-bros.co.uk
There's nothing like a colourful shop and a friendly shopkeeper to whet your appetite for a fine wine or two; the quaint old-fashioned style of the Berry Bros home page is appealing in that simple, no-nonsense way that is so lacking in the high street shops. If you order one or more of the thousands of wines before noon, the shop promises to deliver the next day.

FinestWine
http://www.finestwine.com
There is also a warehouse full of wines in Bordeaux waiting to send you the best of the best. It boasts the finest and largest collection of rare wines and champagnes in the world.

Fig. 36. One of the biggest advantages of the internet is that you can find almost anything. In the world of wine, this means any kind of wine. At the FinestWine site you can buy wine one day and sometimes drink it the next.

Rest

French Wines
http://www.frenchwine.co.uk
This site has a cute little map of France that you can click on to take a closer look at wines from that region. The wines are kept in a warehouse in London so delivery should be relatively quick and cheap.

The Virtual Bar
http://www.thevirtualbar.com
This site offers information on all things alcoholic, such as tempting cocktail recipes, tips on preventing or curing the morning after feeling. Searching through the 3,000-plus drink recipes is easy and can be done in a variety of ways. In addition to an alphabetical listing, you can search by name or string, by ingredients you have on hand, search by category (like shots), by particular ingredient or pull out a Random Drink. Soon you will be mixing drinks like an expert.

The Wine Cellar
http://www.winecellar.co.uk
The Wine Cellar holds over 500 of the world's best wines in stock together with spirits and beers. The site also has a good selection of crates and will deliver orders over £50. At time of writing the site was undergoing a complete redesign so watch out for new features and offers.

WineNet
http://orders.mkn.co.uk/wine/.en
Order before one-thirty and you will get your order by the next day. WineNet also delivers single bottles in a wood gift box such as a 1996 Chardonnay Marquis De Goulaine for £12.93 + £6.99 for UK delivery.

Spirits

The Whisky Shop
http://www.whiskyshop.com
This store has perhaps the most extensive collection of whiskies on the web, organised into categories and regions. You can read about the history of the whisky trade whilst indulging in an online tasting session.

TRAVEL AND HOLIDAYS

General travel information

A2B Travel
http://www.a2btravel.com
Book a holiday in France, or calculate the distance from your home to your holiday destination with this site. You can also check flight arrivals at British airports and book a hotel room using the database of over 30,000 hotels and other types of accommodation or follow the link to Travelocity (see page 125) to book a hotel room almost anywhere in the world. If a fully planned holiday is what you are after, use the search engine provided.

Travel & holidays

Balesworld
http://www.balesworld.com
Even more exotic holidays can be booked at Balesworld who organise cultural holidays, often escorted, to countries like Peru, India and China. Online reservation is possible.

Coral Cay Conservation
http://www.coralcay.org
Do you want to help the environment while you have a holiday? Coral Cay is an organisation that co-ordinates conservation expeditions in places such as the Honduran rainforest and coral reefs in the Mediterranean. The 'holiday' is not free, but can cost upwards of £600, plus the cost of the flights.

Ecovolunteer
http://www.ecovolunteer.org
Why not give something back to the earth by combining your holiday with helping nature? You can specify what type of ecology you would prefer and the site will try to match you to a holiday in that area.

Fodor's Travel Online
http://www.fodors.com
A good starter site with general information about most aspects of travelling with tips on planning your journey, forums for people wanting to share journeys and ideas with other travellers, and a mini-guide. The mini-guide is a personalised travel plan, which the site compiles for you as you select the many options for your journey. Pick a destination, price ranges, hotel types, type of restaurants, travel plans at your destination, and your interests, etc and the site gives you an itinerary for the trip, which you print out.

Package Holidays
http://www.packageholidays.co.uk
Over 100 tour operators have contributed to this site and holidays are listed by type: cruises, packages, self-drive, etc.

Travel Resources
http://www.travel-resources.com
You may want a holiday with a little more substance than most, such as a language course while in Spain or a holiday with inclusive history lessons. Take a look at this site, if that sounds like you. Whether you want to try a little angling in Alaska or trekking in Tibet, you will probably find a link or information here.

TripSpot
http://www.tripspot.com
TripSpot has some of the best travel-related resources on the web. Find the best fares, tips, guides, accommodation, destination ideas, maps, currency exchanges, airport directories, travel news and much more.

Must-See Sites
TravelZoo
Fodor's Travel
TheTrip.com
Excite Travel
Travelocity
Travlang

Hot Deals
Amtrak Fall Fares NEW
4-Day Europe Getaways
Unlimited Asia Travel

Fig. 37. London is a huge city and finding sights of interest is an equally huge task. Planning your tour with the help of Virtual London, however, lightens the load and lets you spend your time doing what you really want to do once you get to the capital.

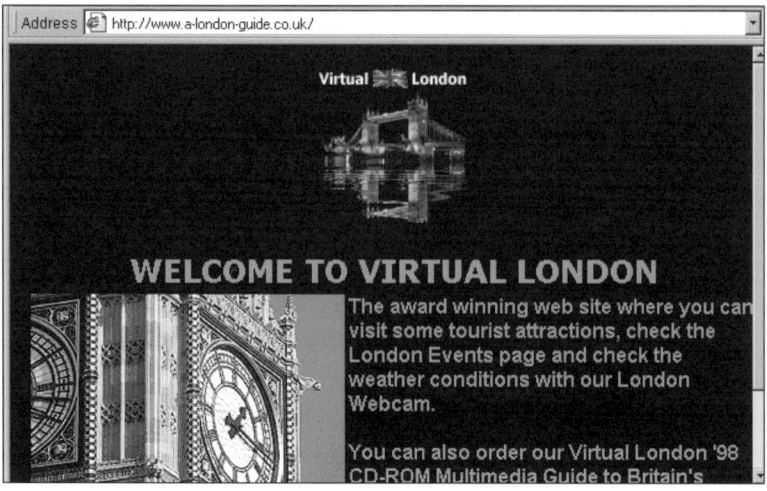

Virtual London
http://www.a-london-guide.co.uk
The information for this site is supplied by the London Tourist Board. It includes a calendar of events, theatre listings, and a web-cam showing a typical London suburban scene.

What's New
http://www.whatsnew.com/id
This comprehensive listing of current travel and entertainment news and tickets is sorted by category. The site makes buying a ticket easier by collecting the resources of 1Ski.com, A2bAirports.com, A2bTravel.com (see below), Aloud.com, Bargainholidays.com and Whatsonstage.com (all part of EMAP Online Ltd) in one place.

Worldwide Directory of Tourism Offices
http://www.towd.com
If you are looking to go on a holiday but have not decided on a country yet, take a look at the Tourism Office Worldwide Directory, which has a surprising amount of information on many different countries. The site links you to the official tourist authority of the country or the most relevant site.

Fig. 38. The web site of the Tourism Office Worldwide Directory. Holidays abroad can all too easily become a matter of habit, but once you know a little about another country, you may find a better resort or tourist attraction.

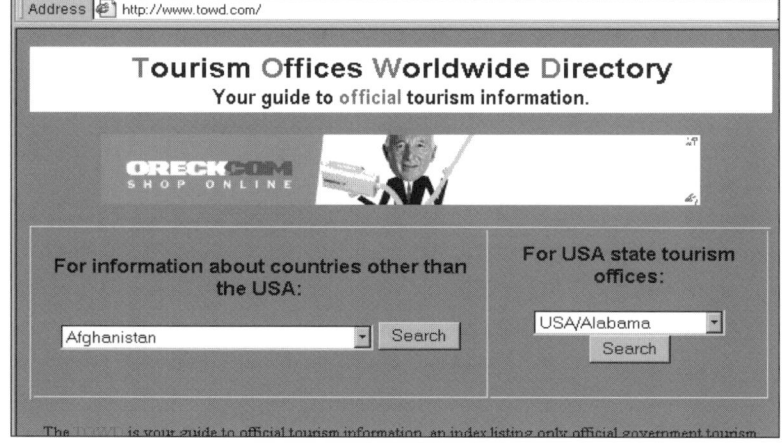

.... **Transport**

Health and safety abroad

British Foreign Office Warnings
http://www.fco.gov.uk/travel
Some of the more interesting countries also happen to be some of the most politically unstable. Before travelling to a suspect country, check this Foreign Office site for warnings.

Travel Health Online
http://www.tripprep.com
Visit this site first to find out what jabs you will need for any particular country. American forces use it to find out about the health risks in a particular country. There is also daily news and advice on diseases.

UK Department of Health
http://www.doh.gov.uk/hat/emerg.htm
Health advice for travellers is presented on this site using bulletins containing the latest health news in various countries. You will find out which vaccinations are necessary, whether you are allowed to take food items into the country, and where any epidemics are spreading.

Transport

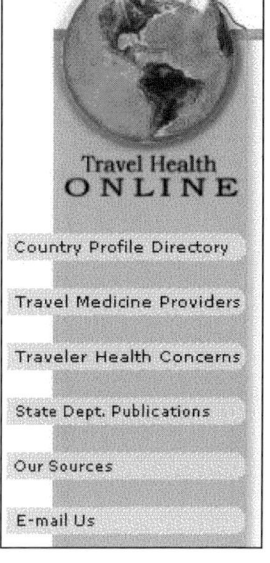

London Transport
http://www.londontransport.co.uk
Besides the normal things you expect from the London Transport site, you can download maps of the underground and bus routes and read about route changes and line extensions. Most of the information is provided in fifteen languages. One section is devoted to the London Transport Museum.

National Express
http://www.nationalexpress.co.uk
Although trains are usually a more comfortable way of travelling than car, coaches can be much less expensive. National Express gives you a site where you can find coach times and fares using an interactive form. You can also book seats when you have found the correct service, and take advantage of any special offers that are advertised.

RailTrack Travel Information
http://www.railtrack.co.uk/travel.index.html
Travel information call centres have been known to give confused answers, but websites are usually clearer. Railtrack's site cuts out the middlemen and gives you access to the railway timetables. Just enter your journey start point and destination, the date, the approximate time and you'll receive all the details within seconds. You will also be given details of any stations where you need to change trains. Unfortunately, you can't book a seat online.

Subway Navigator
http://metro.ratp.fr:10001/bin/cities/english
This French site is one of the best places to go for information on the

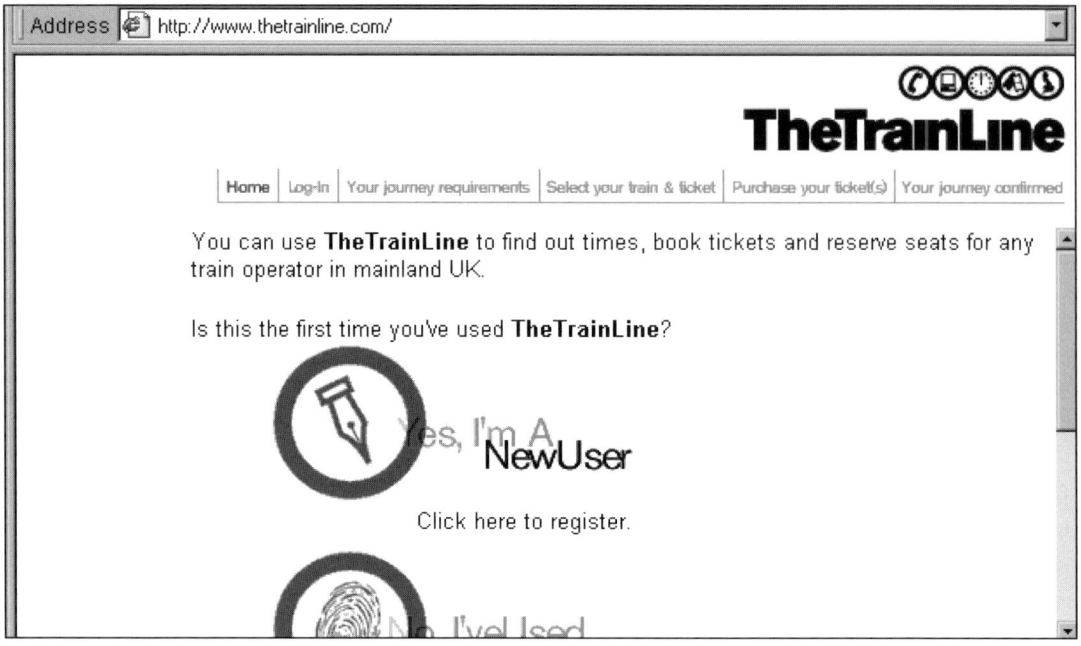

Fig. 39. Virgin have done a great job with their TrainLine site. This is one of the few sites where you can find reliable information about trains and buy tickets in advance.

London underground. The Subway Navigator has underground routes world wide and includes a planner that finds the quickest route between stations.

Trainline
http://www.thetrainline.com
You may not trust the times of the trains but the journey is almost always more comfortable than by car, and always better than coach. Getting the best ticket price has just got better – with Virgin. Even if the best ticket price for the journey is not via Virgin trains, you can still buy the ticket on this site – Virgin don't mind. The site aims to offer the cheapest fare for any train journey in the UK.

Motoring

DVLA
http://www.open.gov.uk/dvla/dvla.htm
The primary aims of the Driver and Vehicle Licensing Agency (DVLA) are 'to aid general law enforcement by maintaining registers of drivers and vehicles, collect taxation and assist the road safety objectives of the Department.' The FAQ section is extremely useful with answers to most of the questions you might want to ask such as 'How do I apply for an international driving permit?' or 'I have lost my driving licence. How do I apply for a duplicate copy?'

Off-Road.com
http://www.off-road.com/toc
There is much more to off-road driving than just point and drive. What if you have a default on the rise (an uphill stall), or have to descend a steep slope with a turn half way down? Find out on this site, it's a must.

Driving

Top Gear
http://www.topgear.com
This immensely popular site may not satisfy your desire to drive an F1 car but it gets you as near to it as you can on the internet. The site features a database of over 4,000 new and used cars, a loan calculator for when you want to upgrade your wheels, and a fantasy Grand Prix league. The intention is to provide a specially animated site to enable you to do things like click on the bonnet of a car and it opens showing you what's under it.

Driving

The AA
http://www.theaa.co.uk
The AA site is very yellow, and very useful. You can, of course, join the AA online but there's more. A comprehensive guide to buying a used car will take you step by step through every stage from planning to servicing; a hotel and restaurant guide will take your reservations online and an insurance section will give you a quote in a minute or two.

British School of Motoring
http://www.bsm.co.uk
The internet highway takes on a different meaning at the BSM site where you can learn all about the art of driving, short of how to make an examiner smile. You can also take a Highway Code quiz in the 'But Theriously' section.

RAC
http://www.rac.co.uk
The RAC site looks good – professional and classy. It covers motor maintenance, car health checks, and accommodation. You can plan a journey using the site's planner page and even buy RAC products and membership to cover you on your journey.

Royal Society for the Prevention of Accidents (RoSPA)
http://www.rospa.co.uk
If you habitually break the speed limit, check the RoSPA site which demonstrate the dangers and the most likely causes of road deaths.

Fig. 40. RoSPA is not as well known as it deserves to be. Many accidents are totally avoidable, and, by taking note of the tips and warnings on their site, you will be able to avoid those future accidents that are just waiting to happen.

Rest

The site is a gold mine of information, but, like a gold mine, some of the riches are buried quite deeply. Persevere, though, and you will find important and up-to-date information on many aspects of safety in all areas of life.

Classic cars

Classic Car Source
http://www.classicar.com
Classic Car Source is the online community for the enthusiast. CCS features over 90 chat and forum areas, classified advertising, museums, events, club and link listings, plus great new articles each month.

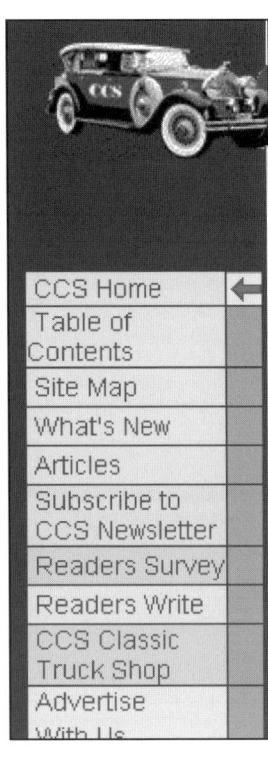

Harley-Davidson
http://www.harley-davidson-london.co.uk
This is the web site of Warr's, one of the oldest Harley dealers in Europe and famous amongst HOGs (Harley Davidson owners). The site provides a history of the company accompanied by the realistic growl of a Harley. Warr's has an extensive vintage parts database and a 'babe' section showing some of the fairer members of the HOG community.

MG, The Classic Marque
http://www.mgcars.org.uk
MG enthusiasts can find almost all the information they could ever want – news, motor sport, history, events, insurance, pictures. Log on to the net and take a virtual spin round this site where you will run into links to MG owners' clubs from countries such as Denmark and Thailand. Those who have other cars in mind might be interested in the links to many pages about other, mainly British, marques.

The Mini Site
http://www.mini.co.uk
Another popular car, the Mini, has a site that cannot be described as 'mini' at all. The site uses ActiveX to produce exceptional interactive effects. One part of the site allows you to design your own mini.

▶ *ActiveX* – a piece of software that allows effects such as animations, games and other interactive features to be included in a web page.

Travel agencies and airlines

It is probably safe to start your holiday plans with one of the larger organisations such as Deckchair, Microsoft Expedia, or Bargain Holidays. A company with an established reputation is not likely to ruin its business by offering poor service. Buying an air ticket over the internet is easy – no need to phone round and be left on hold for ten minutes. Expedia, for example, searches for the cheapest scheduled flights and is updated every few minutes. The internet offers great advantages for those planning a holiday – with the sites listed below, you can find ideas for a holiday, find the cheapest flight and the best

Travel agencies

accommodation, book a seat and a room and plan the activities you are interested in once you arrive.

Air Sickness Bag Virtual Museum
http://www.airsicknessbags.com
Just when you thought you'd seen it all, this site comes up. Do you suffer from airsickness? Here you will find a large collection of photos of airsickness bags arranged by issuing airline. You could even print a picture and take it on holiday with you!

Bargain Holidays
http://www.bargainholidays.com
There's nothing better than flying to the Bahamas in a seat which you paid peanuts for. The last-minute bargains that spring up in travel agents are often worth the daily traipsing round the city centre. But, even better, the internet takes much of the walking out of the hunt and brings the bargains to your desktop. Bargain Holidays has been registered with ABTA so if you buy a holiday from the site, you are given the same level of protection as those who buy from normal high street travel agents. On the down side, information such as flight times, operators, airlines, and hotels, seems lacking from the travel information.

Cheap Flights
http://www.cheapflights.co.uk
Before you plan any overseas journey, check the prices on this site. You can search by destination or airline. Information is collected from a number of airlines and travel agents and analysed to find the cheapest flights and packages. Not all the airlines and travel agencies allow booking online but a quick phone call and you could be booked on a holiday of a lifetime.

Deckchair
http://www.deckchair.com
Bob Geldof, after being driven mad trying to find a cheap flight to Florida, decided to set up his own site – Deckchair. He wanted a site

Fig. 41. Deckchair is one of those sites that has filled a gaping hole in the online travel market. It will independently give you information on the cheapest flights and let you pay for a ticket in no time at all.

Rest

where you can 'go and find the cheapest flight, enter your credit number and have the ticket arrive a day or two later.' The site lives up to expectations and is well designed and user friendly. The site searches for discounted fares and orders them according to price.

Epicurious Travel
http://travel.epicurious.com
This site has a section (The Beach and Island Concièrge) where you fill in a questionnaire and it will try to find your ideal resort. The resulting information contains maps and recommended hotels. Epicurious also has a section called Terminally Hip, detailing how to get from an airport to the nearest city by the easiest method.

Fig. 42. As an alternative to high street travel agents, the online service of Epicurious is great – and the information you receive is more likely to be impartial and perhaps even more accurate.

Excite
http://www.excite.com/weather/airport_delays
If you're travelling by air, you can quickly check Excite Weather's Airport Delays section to see whether any delays may affect your trip. Just enter the airport code or city name and you get information on any weather problems affecting the airport. The site also includes links to weather maps and other forecasts. If you scroll down the page, you can find even more links to handy travel-related sites.

Flight Bookers
http://www.flightbookers.co.uk
Don't chase your tail trying to find cheap flights, Flight Bookers negotiate special deals with airlines and therefore often offer the best prices for scheduled flights. It offers full online flight booking facilities as well as car hire services, charter flights, hotel bookings and insurance.

Travel agencies

Flightline
http://www.flightline.co.uk
Flightline is similar to Bargain Holidays – it lets you search all the tour-operator's databases. The information refreshes every 20 minutes, and when you fill in the form it is sent to a team of people who will get back to you.

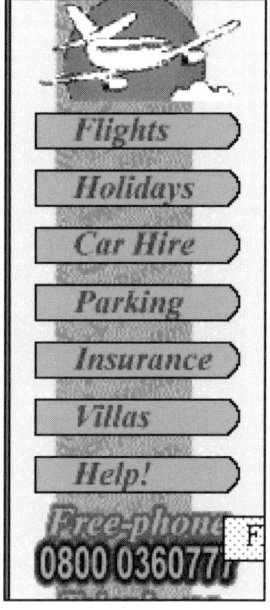

Lastminute
http://www.lastminute.com
If you are adventurous or always leave things until the last minute, this site is for you. Here you will find cheap flights and holidays. Lastminute will refund the difference if you can find a cheaper deal for the same destination and date. At time of writing, there was Incredible Easter offer for a weekend in Bilbao with flights, accommodation and transfers included for only £179, and a stunning offer of a room in a four-star country house in Scotland for £10. There is also an auction section, which is in the planning stages, to enable you to bid for holidays.

Microsoft Expedia
http://www.expedia.co.uk
This is the UK version of Microsoft's successful American site. It aims to become a one-stop travel shop where you can research your holiday, finalise the details and book it. You find a holiday by filling in your choice of dates, length of stay, destinations, and preferred airport. At the time of writing, though, the site asks for your credit-card details before telling you whether seats are available for the flight that interests you. The flight details are obtained from its partner, Thomas Cook, so it is still worthwhile shopping around other sites.

Thomas Cook
http://www.thomascook.co.uk
From this site, you can order travellers' cheques and money and have it delivered within two working days. There were no pages where you could buy charter flights online, but Thomas Cook give information about late deals on flights and allow you to look up around 15,000 scheduled fares. By the end of 1999, it is hoped that the site will allow more facilities.

Travelocity
http://www.travelocity.co.uk
Travelocity uses the Sabre electronic ticketing network to find discounted fares. On the site, you'll find information on scheduled flights with diagrams of the aircraft to help you to book your preferred seat. As well as flights, you can book holidays, car hire and read details on more than 200 hotels world wide. To find out more about the place you want to visit, you can consult the guides on the site which will describe the area including theatres and other places of interest. In common with many travel sites, there is also a currency converter.

Rest

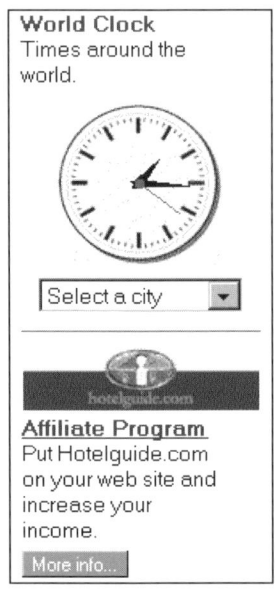

World Clock
Times around the world.

Select a city

Affiliate Program
Put Hotelguide.com on your web site and increase your income.

More info...

Hotels and other accommodation

The Hotel Guide
http://www.hotelguide.com
At The Hotel Guide, you can search for a hotel by name or location or just browse the information on more than 60,000 hotels, resorts, motels, B&Bs, and other accommodation. There is also a section called Hotel Talk that acts as a chat area for travellers to swap tips and comments, and a currency converter.

Hotel Reservation Service
http://www.hrs.com
Whether you want a room for a holiday, or a whole conference service, you can make a reservation from one of over 30,000 hotels in Europe. The site also has 23,000 photos, street maps and hotel reports to help you choose and find a suitable hotel.

Lodging.com
http://www.lodging.com
Travellers to the States should not book accommodation until they see this site. The site lists more than 35,000 places to stay in 2500 US cities. It also has one of the web's most thorough listings of off-the-beaten track guesthouses. The system allows online reservations at about 25,000 places, many of which reportedly offer discounts only through Lodging.com.

Travlang
http://www.travlang.com
Travlang lists over 30,000 hotels and offers discounts on many of those. If you are going to hire a car, this site is a must because of the details of road signs and traffic information covering the country you are going to.

Youth Hostel Association
http://www.yha.org.uk
Youth hostels are cheaper and friendlier than a hotel. You can find information on all UK hostels at this site and even plan a journey using the interactive map.

Maps and guides

When you travel to a new city, one of the most useful things you can buy is a map. Why not save some money and get the map in advance from the internet? There are plenty of sources of maps and guides and, if you have a colour printer, there can be no need to carry round a large guidebook or map in a foreign language. Just print out the information and size of map you need.

Britain

British Tourist Authority
http://www.visitbritain.com
Whether you want to find a hotel for a few days, take a trip to the

Britain

seaside or find an interesting stately home to see, it is worth looking at this site first. It has interactive maps of the UK, library of photos of Britain, suggestions for activities, and a shop that sells maps and guides online. The 50,000-page site is designed to bring tourists to Britain from abroad, but it is also useful to people already living here.

National Trust
http://www.nationaltrust.org.uk
Whether you want a working holiday in the countryside or just some information on the National Trust, visit this site. The NT 'cares for over 240,000 hectares of beautiful countryside in England, Wales and Northern Ireland, plus 575 miles of outstanding coastline and more than 200 buildings and gardens of outstanding interest and importance.'

Fig. 43. There is an immense amount of beautiful countryside in the UK, much of it maintained by the National Trust. You can learn lots about Britain's heritage and natural history by taking in this site.

Ordnance Survey
http://www.ordsvy.gov.uk
You can buy almost any kind of UK map you can imagine from the Ordnance Survey site, from atlases to wall maps. There are also sections for computerised maps, an interactive tour of the national grid, jobs, education and one for research.

Ramblers' Association
http://www.ramblers.org.uk
One of the more relaxed outdoor activities is walking. The Ramblers Association promotes rambling, protects rights of way, campaigns for access to open country and defends the beauty of the countryside in England, Scotland and Wales. The site gives you an introduction to rambling, a guide to membership and much more.

Rest

Strolling.com
http://www.strolling.com
Strolling in London, Paris and other cities can quickly tire even the most seasoned traveller. Why not take a tour while sat at your computer instead? Strolling.com is packed with high quality pictures that you access by clicking on a map.

UK Travel
http://www.uktravel.com
Another useful site with plenty of information – in fact you could probably plan a whole holiday in the UK from this site. There is information on airports, hotels, car hire, bicycles, customs, education, ferries, food and drink, government, visas, etc.

UK Street Map Page
http://www.streetmap.co.uk
When you enter a postcode, you are presented with a colour-coded map of the area, with hills shown in relief and all the other features that are normally shown on a map. You can search by postcode, UK place name, London streets or grid reference. There are street maps of Greater London and road atlas maps of the rest of mainland Britain.

Westminster Abbey
http://www.westminster-abbey.org
Alhough this site is not extensive, it provides some fasinating historical information, including a list of the kings and queens of England entombed within the Abbey's walls. There are some lovely audio files including the choir link, where you can hear recordings of two of the songs that the Abbey choir sang at the funeral of Diana, Princess of Wales.

Other countries

Atlapedia
http://www.atlapedia.com
Atlapedia contains all the maps you'd expect to in a traditional atlas and an A to Z option that takes you to an encyclopaedic index. The entries include basic information such as ethnic, language, and religious background of the people, physical geography and climate, economy, educational system, and history of the country. Select the World Maps option to see physical or political maps of a nation.

Excite City Net
http://www.city.net
This is another site that tries to give you everything to do with travel, and it pretty well does just that. There are guides to cities and restaurants, travel information, lists of embassies, language guides, and so on. Like other Excite sites, you can customise the content by adding anything that is of interest to you and excluding the rest.

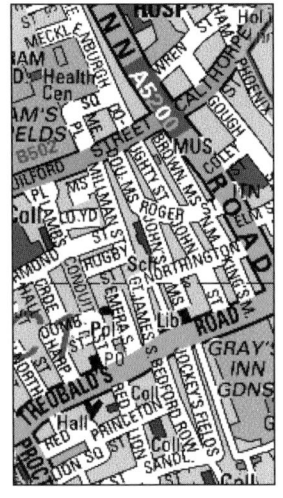

Other countries

MapQuest
http://www.mapquest.som
This is a US site but coverage of major cities in other countries is surprisingly good. You can zoom down to street level and choose whether to include different features on the map such as banks, ATMs etc, or you can zoom out so you have a large-scale map of a greater area.

Multi Media Mapping
http://www.multimap.com
Just enter the name of a city, town or village, or postcode to get a detailed map of the area. You can then zoom in on any part of that or you can look at a different area. A scale indicator at the bottom of the map lets you know what size the map represents. You can also search by London streets, post codes, phone numbers or grid references. You can pick out your favourite town, find the street and even the fastest route.

National Map Centre
http://www.mapsworld.com
The National Map Centre contains over 800 maps from all over the world and if the map you want is not made, they will make one especially for you. The site also invites regular users of the site to join the Explorer Club. This offers a number of benefits such as a complete map image library catalogue with each page showing a single image of over 800 available maps, regular map library updates, priority treatment, and the Explorer Club newsletter, with special offers and competitions.

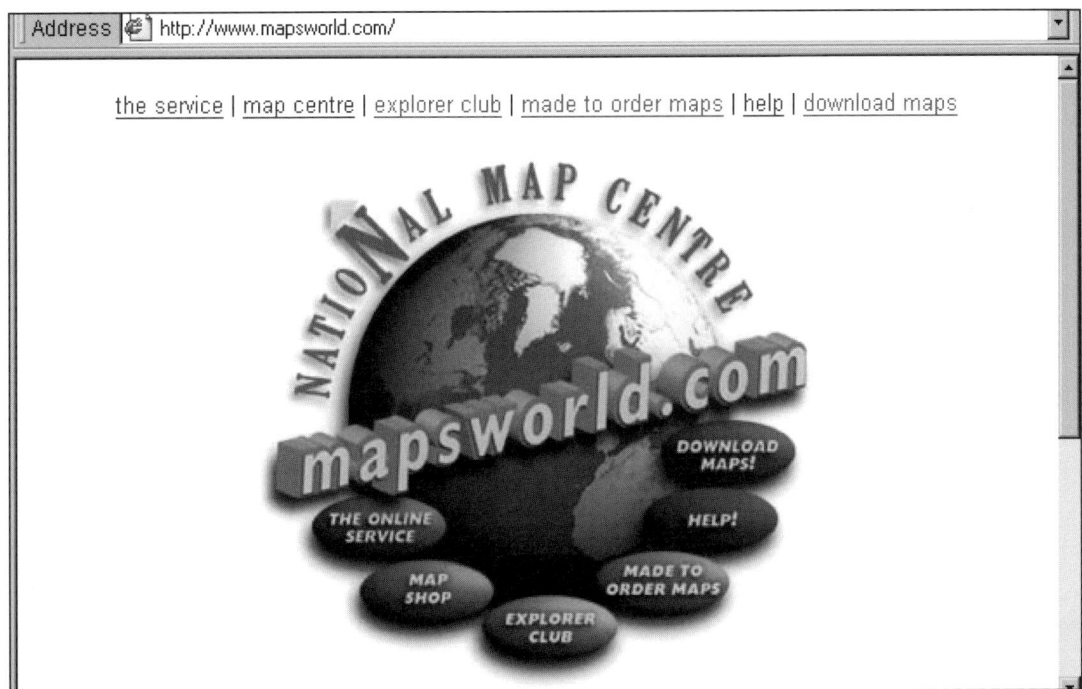

Fig. 44. When planning a holiday, it often helps if you have a map of the area you are thinking of visiting. Where are you going to start looking for that map, though? National Map Centre, of course.

Rest

Travel Guides
http://www.travel-guides.com
The World Travel Guide provides some of the most comprehensive and objective information about the countries of the world available online. 'Every country is presented in a highly detailed and structured format and includes essential information for business travellers, holiday-makers and travel agents alike.'

Currency and other necessities

Euro calculator
http://www.eurocalculator.com
What can be better than having your own calculator on your own PC? This site has just that – a computer program that will calculate currency conversions for you, and it's free! You can download the software and use it with no limitations and no annoying registration messages, except you need to register the program (for $29.99) if you want professional features such as online collection of exchange rates, but even without that it is still a good program.

O & A Converter
http://www.oanda.com/converter/classic
This site will calculate the exchange rate and let you print a neat little conversion chart to take with you.

NATIONAL AND INTERNATIONAL INFORMATION

Towns and cities

Go Edinburgh
http://www.Go-Edinburgh.co.uk
There are plans for this site to sell tickets for the Edinburgh festival online and synchronise the sales with a What's On guide to the festival. The festival has traditionally been a confusing affair with so many events going on and not enough information on where those events are taking place. Hopefully, when the site is ready, things will be much clearer.

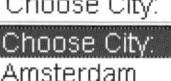

Time Out
http://www.timeout.com
This is the internet counterpart of the printed *Time Out* magazine. You'll find weekly updates, arts and entertainment listings and coverage of over twenty cities. Each city guide is divided into ten sections: living guide, accommodation, sightseeing, essential information, entertainment, eating and drinking, shopping, kids, gay and lesbian, and web links. Plans are in hand to include holiday and flight bookings.

Government and national organisations

British Council
http://www.britcoun.org
Their site says, 'The British Council promotes educational, cultural and

Fig. 45. Time Out is the definitive source for information on what's happening in London – for residents and visitors alike. If you want a good time, look at the Time Out site.

technical co-operation between Britain and other countries. The Council's work is designed to establish long-term and worldwide partnerships and to improve international understanding.' This site is a good source of news and information on events in Britain.

CCTA Government Information Service
http://www.open.gov.uk
Information at this site is easy to find and is organised around two main indexes: a functional one (consumer protection, Inland Revenue, foreign affairs, etc.) and an organisational one (Greater Manchester police, Bank of England, cabinet office, etc). From these two indexes, you can access most government information.

Ministry of Defence
http://www.mod.uk
The MOD undertakes a variety of tasks connected with the defence interests of the UK. In 1964 five departments integrated almost completely to form the MOD as it is now: the Admiralty, the War Office, the Air Ministry, the Ministry of Aviation and the Ministry of Defence itself. On its site, the MOD releases the official information on any conflicts the country is engaged in and details of which of Britain's armed units are involved, why they are there, and who are they fighting.

Royalty

British Monarchy
http://www.royal.gov.uk
Ever wondered whether the Queen has a passport, or what her 'beasts' are? Take a look at her web site, which has a FAQ – they call it 'Your questions answered'. The site is presented in a polite and formal manner, as you would expect, with information on many aspects of the royal family. This would be a good starting point for either tourism or a

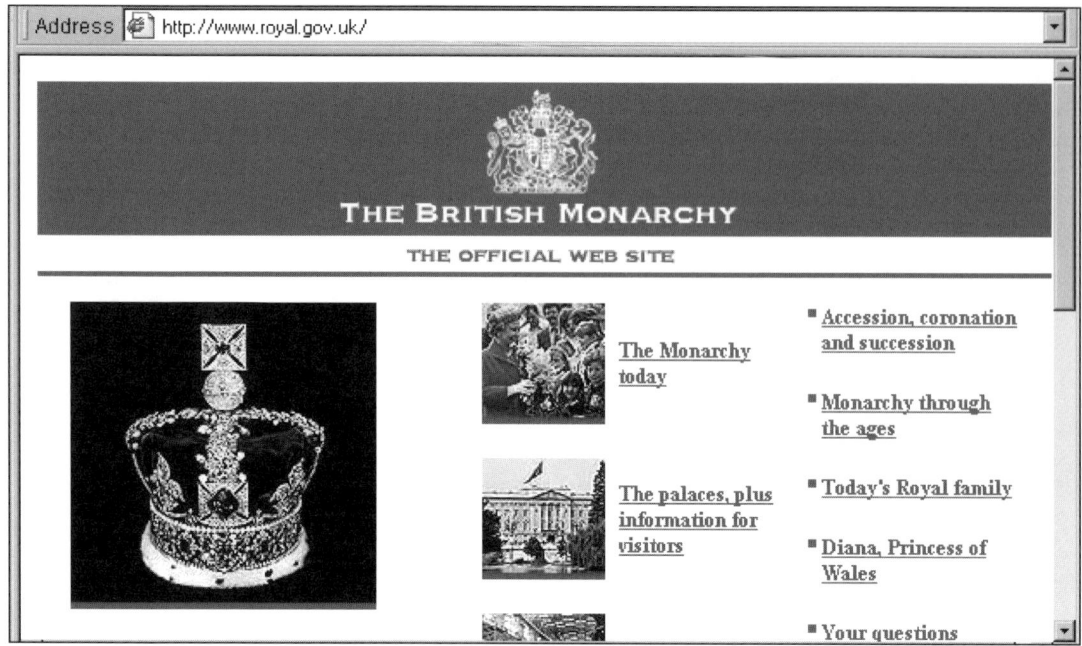

Fig. 46. The monarchy has always been much more than just a tourist attraction. to find out just who they are, what they do and what their history is, take a tour of the British Monarchy site.

more in-depth study of the monarchy. Read about the crown jewels, memorabilia, history, traditions and much more.

Royal Insight
http://www.royalinsight.gov.uk
The Queen is obviously trying to get closer to her people with this informal monthly magazine style site that reports and announces royal engagements, and other more interactive features. People can email questions to the family and a selection is published in the next issue.

Royalty Magazine
http://www.royalty-magazine.com
Royalty Magazine was launched in June 1981, the month before the marriage of the Lady Diana and the Prince of Wales. It now claims a reputation as 'the most colourful, the most perceptive and the best-informed magazine in its field.' There is news, interviews and pictorial coverage of the UK and other royal families.

World information

The CIA World Fact Book
http://www.odci.gov/cia/publications/factbook
Despite its name, this site is nothing to do with world secrets or the techniques of spying, but it is one of the best and most comprehensive sources of international information on the internet. It is a valuable general research tool that should make a nice addition to any bookmark file. The site contains information about the people, economy, climate and culture of nearly every nation in the world.

Disaster Relief
http://www.disasterrelief.org
Human tragedy often accompanies an earthquake, especially when

World information

one hits a major city. Disaster Relief helps by allowing people from all over the world to make contributions to a variety of charitable institutions. The site lists 14 institutions with explanations of what they do. Other features of the site include earthquake news, a library of articles and an earthquake forum where people can share ideas.

The E-Conflict World Encyclopaedia
http://www.emulateme.com
'Conflict' is what politicians call wars when they are the ones waging them. This site profiles the nations of the world, including maps, flags, world weather and national anthems. There are over 1,400 pages of written text on the nations.

Global Earthquake Response Centre
http://www.earthquake.com
Are you on shaky ground? Here, you will find a list of recent quakes with links to in-depth information on each, a directory of links to other earthquake pages and an earthquake specific search engine. If you think you are susceptible to earthquakes, you may want to buy some of the products advertised here that are designed to earthquake-proof your home.

InfoNation
http://www.un.org/Pubs/CyberSchoolBus/infonation/e_infonation.htm
The United Nations has created InfoNation – an extensive archive of data on the geography, economy and culture of the entire set of UN member nations. From the main page you select up to seven countries then move onto a second page where you choose the type of information you want to retrieve.

Paper Currency
http://aes.iupui.edu/rwise
The creator of this site, Ron Wise, reassures me that he is not a money forger. He just wanted to make a site that was interesting and educational. The bank notes section of his site has over 4,000 scanned images of bank notes – both sides. Warning: If you are thinking of forging a note or two, you will need a better printer than a colour inkjet!

TerraServer
http://www.terraserver.microsoft.com
TerraServer is a great reference work by Microsoft – an interactive collection of aerial and satellite images covering North America and most of Western Europe. Click on a map to zoom in or simply go to a specific location by entering keywords in a search form.

World Flag Database
http://www.flags.net
Much more than just flags, the site has over 260 pages with information on countries and international organisations. Information includes formal name, capital city, area, population, currency, languages, and religions, national and state flags, ensigns, and sub-national flags.

Rest

Where countries have changed their flags in the last few years the old flag is also shown. Flags are updated when the Flag Institute receives confirmation of the new flag. Even the index includes miniature national flag for each country.

HUMOUR AND GENERAL KNOWLEDGE

Cartoon Network
http://www.cartoon-network.co.uk
Scooby Doo, where are you? Cartoons are not only for children – how many of you can honestly say that you pass by the cartoons in a newspaper with out a glance? Scooby Doo, Tom and Jerry, many others make an animated appearance on this site. Yes, that's not just cartoon stills but animations with sound, and games to play besides. Cartoon Network makes itself out to be the world cartoon headquarters – the 'literal and virtual home of some of the world's best-loved characters.' The game is a parody of dungeons and dragon style games but with cartoon characters instead of the usual dragons and goblins. There are dossiers on more than seventy cartoon characters, so whoever is your hero, you will probably find the character here.

Hitch Hiker's Guide to the Galaxy
http://www.h2g2.com
Fans of The Hitch Hiker's Guide to the Galaxy will be familiar with the writings of Douglas Adams but may not be so familiar with the web site. This site gives every person who signs up a page where they can upload any piece of information they wish. Any user can compose a web page with information on anything that they think would belong in the guide.

Fig. 47. The Douglas Adams Hitch-Hiker's Guide to the Galaxy site promises to be one of the internet's greatest collaborative projects – why not add your own contribution and become part of a legend.

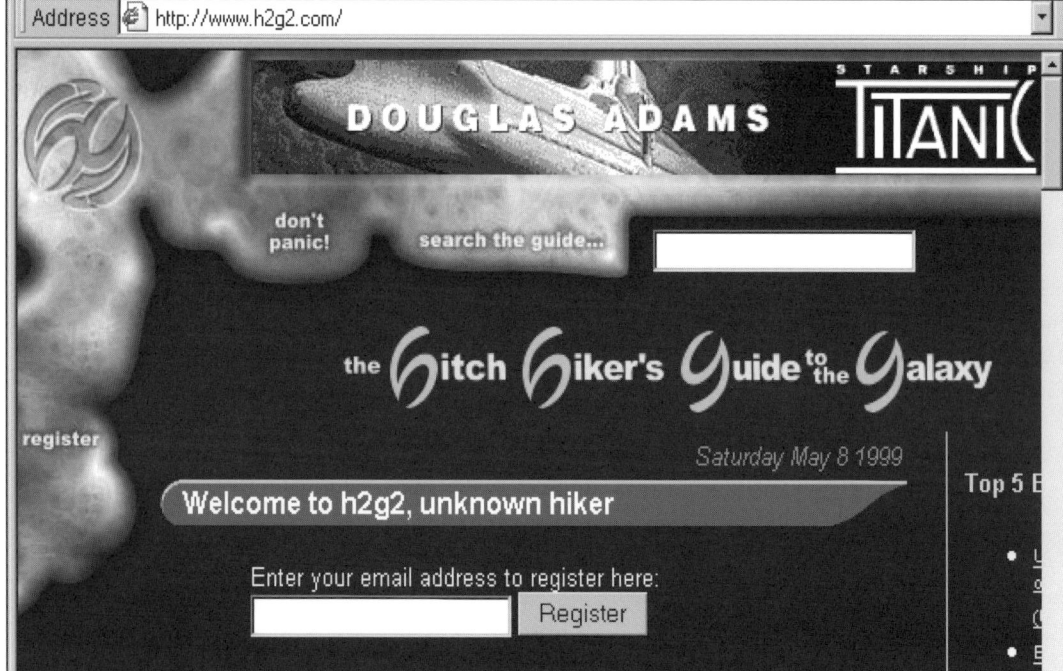

General knowledge

How Stuff Works
http://www.howstuffworks.com
Author and former teacher Marshall Brain has developed this site which has a lot of information on how things work. At How Stuff Works, you can find easy-to-understand explanations and pictures of everything from rocket engines to toilets. This site is a great resource for students and anyone else who's curious about the technology around us. You can browse a list of all How Stuff Works articles or search by keyword. You can also ask and read questions of the day or sign up for the site's newsletter. If you know how things work, why not write for them?

HumourNet
http://www.humournet.com
If life gets too serious, lighten up by reading some of the jokes, anecdotes and funny stories on this site. If you are stuck for a witty comment or two for your wedding speech, you will find plenty of ideas.

WhatIs
http://www.whatis.com
WhatIs contains over 2,000 individual encyclopaedic definition/topics and a number of quick-reference pages. The topics contain about 10,000 hyperlinks between definition-topics and other sites for further information. The entries are arranged in alphabetical order on a 'wall of words' – just find something of interest and click. If you have ever asked 'What is that?' then you will like this site.

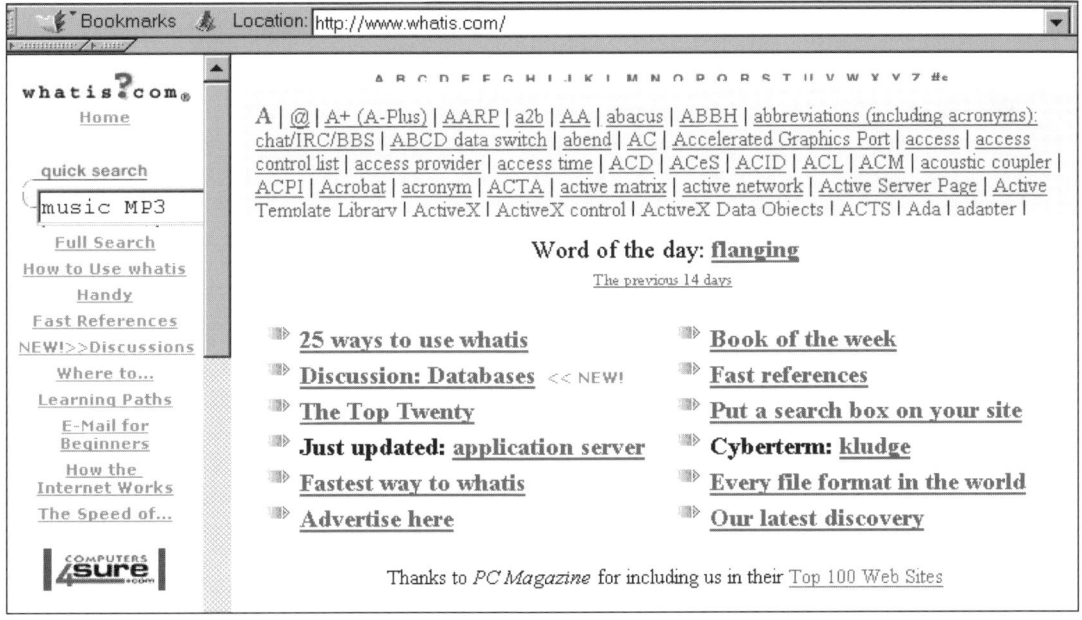

4 Play: social life

In this chapter we will explore:

▶ *Sport and recreation*
▶ *People*
▶ *Animals*
▶ *News and entertainment*
▶ *Computer games and software*

SPORT AND RECREATION

FitnessLinks
http://www.fitnesslink.com/links.htm
FitnessLinks provides a multitude of links to sites on everything from yoga to football and it directs you to the best sites by rating them on the basis of content, credibility, and ease of navigation. You can look for links by browsing categories (bodybuilding or footwear, for example) or by entering a topic in the search engine.

SportsWeb
http://www.sportsweb.com
There is a wealth of sports information (supplied by Reuters) on this site. The main sporting events of the moment are featured prominently and other areas are accessible from the rest of the site together with a diary of events and up-to-the minute coverage of events in progress. There are also games you can play on the site itself, such as an F1 racing and skiing games, and a daily sports quiz. If you want to buy some fashionable sports clothes, you can visit the shopping mall on the site.

Soccer

Fantasy League
http://www.fantasyleague.co.uk
If you dream of making the national team, you don't have to dream any more, you can play out your fantasy – pick, manage and coach a team to success or failure. There are over two thousand teams in the league and more than twenty thousand people playing each week. Players have comprehensive statistics available on their teams. The site also has a newspaper called the Fantasy Pink that is updated daily.

FIFA Online
http://www.fifa.com
From youth teams to the international teams, this should be your first stop to find out what's on in the football world. Here, you'll find information on football around the world. The site also has details about the rules of football, a calendar of events, reports, rankings and a history of Fifa itself.

Football News
http://www.footballnews.co.uk
This is probably the finest football site on the internet. Football News covers over 60 leagues and 4,500 clubs and more than 5,000 players. Not just football, either – you can read betting advice and take part in an online auction.

Football 365
http://www.football365.co.uk
You like football so why not have the latest news delivered to your email inbox? Here, you will find a personalised daily news service that brings you news, features and opinions – ten to fifteen pages of it. Scores are up on the page within minutes of the action and the site is easy on the eye, and mouse.

Matchfacts
http://www.matchfacts.com
Matchfacts starts life as a feature in the printed Match magazine. It covers every game played featuring an English or Scottish League club and is recognised by football statisticians as the most accurate and comprehensive guide to the UK football scene. It scores the players' performance, the quality of the match and other information.

SoccerNet
http://www.soccernet.com
The British SoccerNet site has lots to read and to do if you're a footy fan. Besides the gigantic news coverage, you can make your voice heard in the forum and participate in polls. There are results, reports, statistics and tables. There are also features, which analyse, criticise and predict the performance of teams from all over the world.

Fig. 48. How is your team doing this year? Not too well? Think you can do better? Why not start your own with the help of the Fantasy League? You won't even need a football.

Play: social life

Cricket

CricInfo
http://www-uk.cricket.org
'The home of cricket on the internet'. CricInfo offers news and information on cricket, as well as features and in-depth reports and interviews. There is also a beginner's introduction to the sport explaining the rules of play. The news coverage is said to be second to none.

Lords
http://www.lords.org
CricInfo claims to be the home of cricket on the internet but Lords definitely upstages it in looks, and is a strong challenger for content, too. Lords claims to bring you 'the best of English cricket on the internet – at every level'. Walk into the Lord's shop for leisurewear, memorabilia and other items of interest; browse the extensive news archive with stories and press releases; or Join their free mailing list. Send an email to editor@lords.org with 'subscribe' in the subject field.

Rugby

RFU
http://www.rfu.com
Sweat and tears and lots of mud – that's what this site has got, and you can enjoy some special animations if you have one of the later browsers. There is almost everything a rugby fan could want, from a history of rugby, rules of the game, biographies of players, club details and fixtures, and more.

Scrum.com
http://www.scrum.com
The 'Premier Rugby Web site' gives you the latest news about rugby-related happenings and events from the Press Association. You can keep up to date with the internationals, sevens and women's rugby.

Fig. 49. No need to worry about poor television coverage any more, just wander over to Scrum.com for no-nonsense up-to-date news and information on the world of rugby.

Sports

There are also heaps of statistics, games, quizzes, features and more.

Planet Rugby
http://www.planet-rugby.com
Whatever your interest is in rugby, you should visit this site which has comprehensive figures, scores, facts and previews.

Rugby Club
http://www.rugbyclub.co.uk
Mainly an advert? Allied Dunbar hope that this will become the number one site for rugby enthusiasts. They give you plenty of information, and there is a chat room, message area and more to come.

Golf

GolfWeb
http://www.golfweb.com
Get in a little virtual practice on the GolfWeb. If it's golf, it's on this site, somewhere – professional and amateur, news and results, in a combination of text, pictures and RealAudio. There is also information on over 20,000 courses all over the world. When you get tired of browsing, go over to the shop to lighten your wallet a little with golf accessories galore.

Royal & Ancient Golf Club of St Andrews
http://www.RandA.org
Here you will find the complete rules of golf, in seven languages; if you have golfing friends that can't speak English show them this site, which has details of championships past and present, future venues and conditions of entry.

Outdoor sports

1st Ski
http://www.1ski.com
Wondering whether the conditions are right for skiing in Europe? Weather reports, equipment guides and travel bargains will ease your next trip and help you to decide where to go for your next holiday.

Bonnington.com
http://www.bonington.com
Here you will find 'fantastic voyages and adventures' undertaken by Chris Bonnington. The latest involves a millennium trip to Nepal to climb a virgin peak and later that year a trip to Greenland. Motivation and drive are essential if you are going to be a climber, and Chris can help with his motivational presentations.

British Athletics
http://www.british-athletics.co.uk
Where is your nearest club? You can find out here, and learn about the events in the rest of the country. 'The British Athletics Home Pages are undergoing a restructure to allow many other contributors to upload to

Play: social life

the site directly, thereby enabling the diverse elements within the sport to be maintained by the enthusiasts.' If you think you can contribute a section, get in contact.

British Watersports
http://www.waterski-uk.com
A site mainly for water-skiing but it also covers wake boarding and knee-boarding. The site is bulging with news, features, and tips from experts in the field, and once you are tempted to give it a try, there's a chat area where you can ask the experts and a history of the sport so you can find out where it came from.

COLA
http://www.cola.org.uk
COLA (Camping and Outdoor Leisure Association) acts as a centre of information on outdoor leisure and sports products, and where to buy them. You can find out about organisations involved in outdoor activities. 'For anyone interested in outdoor activities and clothing and equipment designed to ensure an enjoyable, active, outdoor experience.'

Fishing World
http://www.fishing.org
Fishing is probably one of the most practised sport in the country, and this site is an excellent resource packed with information and hosting chats with some celebrity anglers.

Horse Racing
http://www.timeform.com
Timeform has been in the business (offline) for fifty years, and it is now the online venue for racing information. Once a member, you can download race cards and get good odds at the racecourse.

International Amateur Athletic Federation
http://www.iaaf.org
The IAAF site gives you the latest news and competition results in the amateur athletics field. A week by week calendar keeps you informed of what is happening and where, and video clips give you an extra dimension with interviews and clips of various events. The site also offers training tips to give 'an idea of what it is all about and, to those who practise actively, practical assistance to develop their skills.'

International Olympic Committee
http://www.olympic.org
There's much more to the Olympics than what is usually featured on television – did you know that there is a separate Olympics for the veteran (older) athlete, and another for disabled athletes? The site also has a museum where you can read about the history of the Olympic Games.

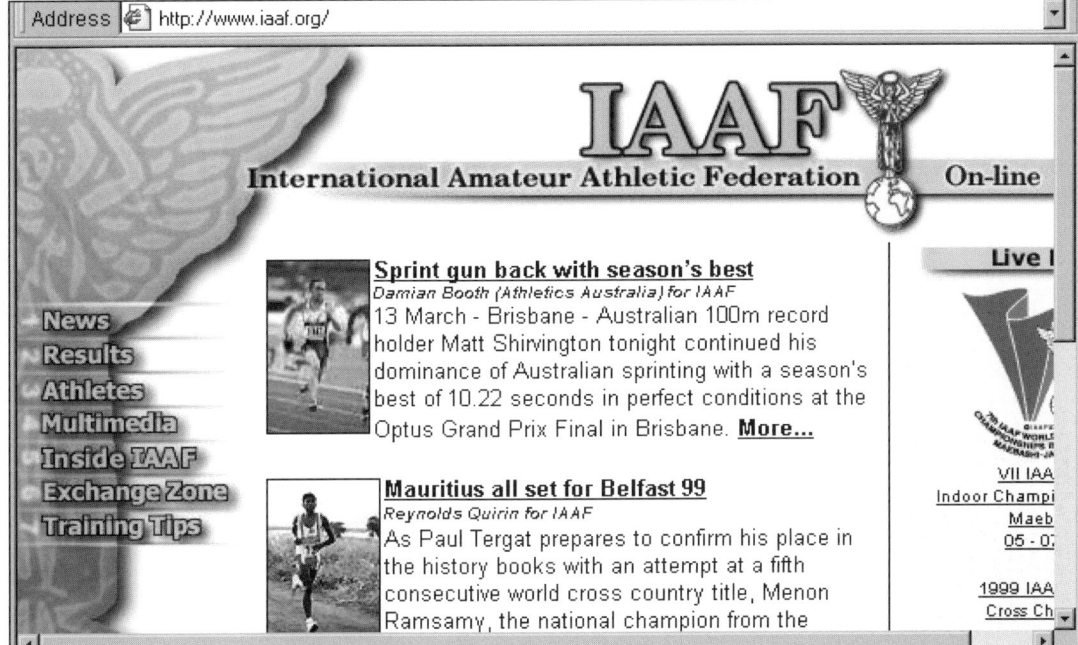

Racenews
http://www.racenews.co.uk
Another site dealing with horse racing, there are sections about British horse racing and information on many racecourses. Racenews specialises in a range of services such as supplying *The Racing Post* and other outlets with news stories and features, providing media information packs and press releases, and more.

Resort Sports Network
http://www.rsn.com
The weather is one of the most important factors when choosing a skiing destination and this site covers a large number of ski resorts. Weather reports at the sites are updated daily and shown via photographs and relevant information such as amount of snowfall. The site also has information for the summer traveller, competitions, and previews of winter sports videos.

Fig. 50. Athletics is perhaps the most international of sports. The IAAF well know this and have developed a fully featured athletics site. No second place for the IAAF!

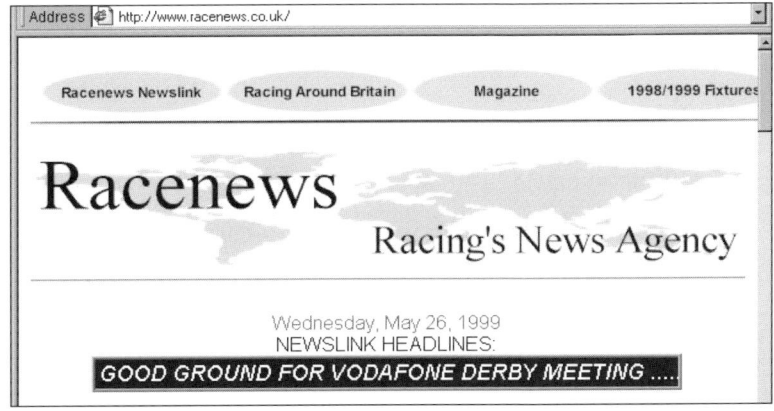

Fig. 51. Racenews is a serious site for all those who are serious about horse racing. Here, you will find top news for one of the top spectator sports.

Play: social life

Runnersworld
http://www.runnersworld.ltd.uk
Running is one of the most popular methods of keeping fit, but also one of the biggest causes of foot injury. This site has features on choosing the correct shoes, and other equipment, to reduce the likelihood of injuries to feet, knees and backs. There's also a nutrition expert to answer your questions on the best diets for runners and a list of upcoming events.

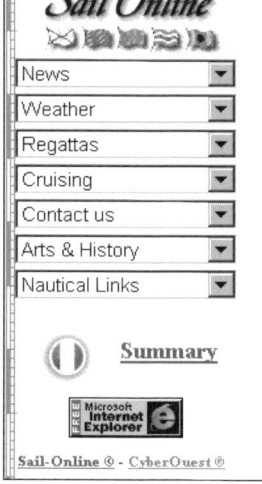

Sail Online
http://www.sail-online.com
If you enjoy events such as America's Cup or the Whitbread Round the World, you will like this site. The site features the sporting aspects of yachting and includes weather forecasts, images and a history of ships, boats and lighthouses, and full coverage most of the famous races.

Snowboarding
http://www.isf.ch
The International Snowboarding Federation site is the place to find information on the professionals in the sport. The site is crammed full of competitions and events in many countries.

Motor sports

Demolition Derby
http://www.brophy.simplenet.com
'My other car's a wreck'. If you are bored with your current car why not enter it into a demolition derby? In a Demolition Derby the participants buy cars to intentionally destroy them. You buy an old, hard top automobile, gut it, chain the doors shut, put on a helmet, and ram into other cars until only one is left running. The winner is the one that made last contact, and can move at least 12 inches in any direction.

Formula 1
http://www.formula1.com
Here, you get a chance to vote for the best 'starting-grid babe', and you can enter a competition to put a caption to a picture – you can also read the latest racing news and take in the various UK circuits and other racing information.

FOTA
http://www.fota.co.uk
A Formula 3 car is a single-seat racer powered by a two-litre engine. They are capable of around 165 mph and need a 'clean, precise, committed driving style.' The site has a driving game as well as the usual news, history and team information.

Others

Boxing Monthly
http://www.boxing-monthly.co.uk/home.htm
Get a free T-shirt when you order a subscription to the magazine or just

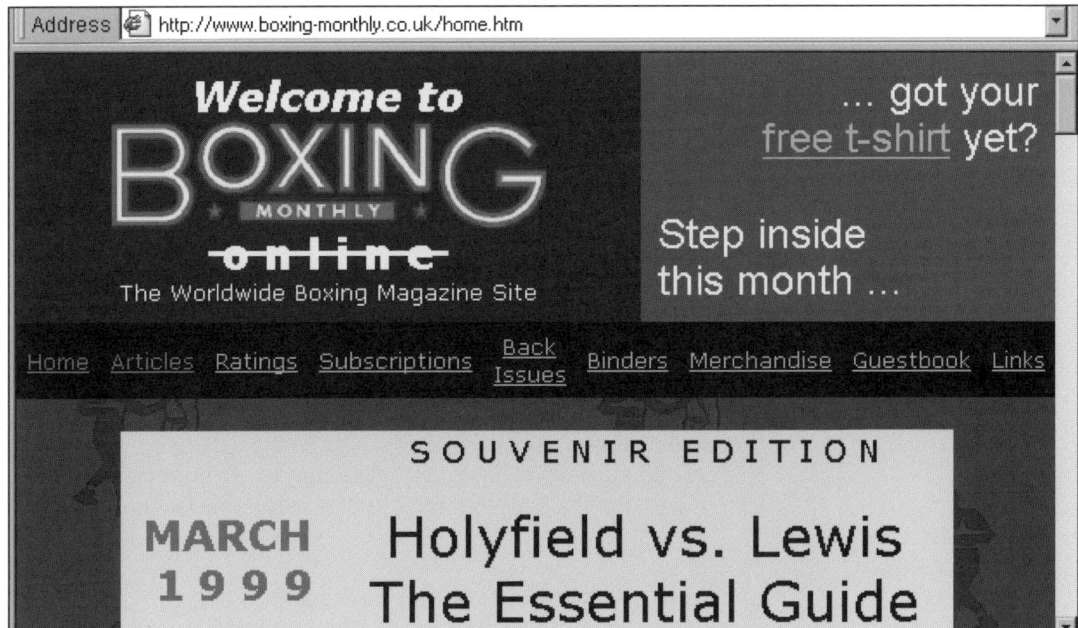

Fig. 52. Punching through the pages on this web site will reward you with great news and plenty of information on the sport of boxing.

browse the site. Boxing Monthly has interviews, profiles, previews and opinion polls of the fights. The editor of the magazine gives tips and predictions on the upcoming fights.

Cheltenham Racecourse
http://www.cheltenham.co.uk
Every March, Cheltenham plays host to the 'annual Olympics of steeple-chasing'. The event, consisting of over 20 races, attracts people and horses from all over Britain and further afield. You will find the latest news of the season, information about the Cheltenham festival and the town itself.

Tennis
http://www.tennis.org.uk
This site is a resource and a search engine for tennis information and news. There is also a useful section with reviews of other tennis sites on the net. The site has been designed to help tennis enthusiasts world wide keep track of new web tennis developments and keep in touch with other enthusiasts. Check out the interactive messages page 'the club house', the web site announcement facility 'what's new in tennis' and the web site review section 'ace sites'.

World Snooker
http://www.embassysnooker.com
As with most good sports sites, this one has an introduction to the basics and the history of the game with a special section on how the game is televised. You can also test your knowledge of snooker in the quiz section and view pictures of snooker matches and personalities from around the world.

Play: social life

PEOPLE

Friendship and romance

The internet is very popular for romance and friendship. Perhaps it's because people are less reticent about chatting intimately via a keyboard, or because they don't know what the others look like. A New York professor, Joseph Walther, says the reason is that it is easier to lie on the internet. However, it does tend to draw people into special friendships, and many of them result in long-term relationships. Some of the sites that offer romance online are cashing in on people's loneliness; others are matchmaking for fun. An American study stated that 33 per cent of all online relationships led to a date; but be warned, most of the successful dates are those that result from pictures being exchanged and the people talking on the telephone before meeting.

5W
http://www.womenwelcomewomen.org.uk
Friendships can also be useful in non-romantic ways. Take the organisation Women Welcome Women World Wide (5W), for instance. They have over 2,000 members in 67 countries. You can contact any other member and arrange to stay with them, go for a meal or whatever you agree. There is also a newsletter in which you can place a notice. The arrangements are totally between the parties involved, 5W just maintains the list. The focus of the group is travelling – not just cheap accommodation but international co-operation between women and their families.

Blind Date
http://www.blinddate.co.uk
The site is not connected with the television programme *Blind Date*. It is a singles dating service aimed at 25 to 45-year-old professionals. IRC is the preferred method of contact, being real time and more informal than email and there is a fee to join. At time of writing, there was a free trial. Give it a try.

▶ *Internet relay chat (IRC)* - a popular method of chatting over the internet where you type your message instead of speaking into a microphone. The 'listener' then responds by typing a reply.

Club 18-30
http://www.club18-30.co.uk
For fun and romance join this club – as long as you are 18 to 30 years old. The risqué screensaver is a guide to what kind of relationship you can find here: not a site for the squeamish.

Dateline
http://www.dateline.uk.com
Dateline is perhaps the best-known and most respected of the dating agencies. It bases its matching on a questionnaire designed to analyse your personality.

Dateline

How it Works
Database Search
Register Online
F.A.Q.
Couples Stories
Members' Area
Dateline Magazine
Contact Details
Press Release

Friendship & romance

Experiment in International Living (EIL)
http://www.eiluk.org
Another site that encourages cross-cultural exchange is EIL. It is non-profit and encourages people to travel and learn about other countries through study abroad, au pair work, home stays, and group travel. Their purpose is 'to foster respect among people everywhere in the world regardless of race, creed or politics, as one means of furthering peace.' They add, 'we offer a unique and truly worthwhile opportunity. We provide unlimited opportunities to learn more about the world in a very personal way.'

Introduction
http://www.introduction.net/uk
Feeling romantic? This site is an introduction service with an anonymous emailer so, if you want to, you can advertise your hobbies and vital statistics without giving away your email address. At present the service is free but plans are under way to begin charging for the service. You fill in a short questionnaire, write a short description of the type of person you are interested in meeting, and, if you have one, send an electronic picture of yourself. It is not a sex-shop and at the time of writing there were over two thousand people on the database. If you are looking for someone in the database, you can narrow the list down by selecting according to sex, age range, and area of the country.

Fig. 53. Here is a personal introduction site where you can post a description of yourself and perhaps find the perfect partner – something which can be difficult in the rush of modern society.

Finding someone's email address

If you have someone's name but not their email address, you should try looking in an email directory. One of the best directories is Bigfoot at http://uk.bigfoot.com. All you need to do is enter the person's first and last name and click the 'Search' button. You will then be given a list of email addresses for people with that name. Try it yourself: Point your browser at Bigfoot and enter 'Kye Valongo'. See if Bigfoot will give you my email address. If it does, send me a short note.

Play: social life

Beware, though, if you search for a name like John Smith you will be overwhelmed by thousands of addresses, whereas 'Kye Valongo' will only give you my address and, perhaps, one other.

Yahoo People Search
http://people.yahoo.com/
This is another good site. On the Bigfoot and the Yahoo! sites, you can perform an advanced directory search. Advanced searching can fine-tune your search and reduce the number of entries returned by the search. If you know the town where that person lives or the organisation, or **node**, you can narrow down the list.

▶ *Node* – the part of an email address after the @ sign.

The email address of the author is: **admin@ukwriters.com**
The node is: ukwriters.com.

Some other sites

Telephone Directories on the Web
http://www.teldir.com
This may be the internet's most detailed index of online phone books, with links to yellow pages, white pages, business directories, email addresses and fax listings from all over the world.

The Ultimates
http://www.theultimates.com
Scott Martin has developed a handy site called The Ultimates to help you contact people and businesses. With it, you can search several different reference sources by filling out one online form. The site is

Fig. 54. Having the world's telephone directories within reach is a wonderful service made possible by the internet. Think of the fun you can have talking to people in all of those exotic countries – even better if you are able to call from work.

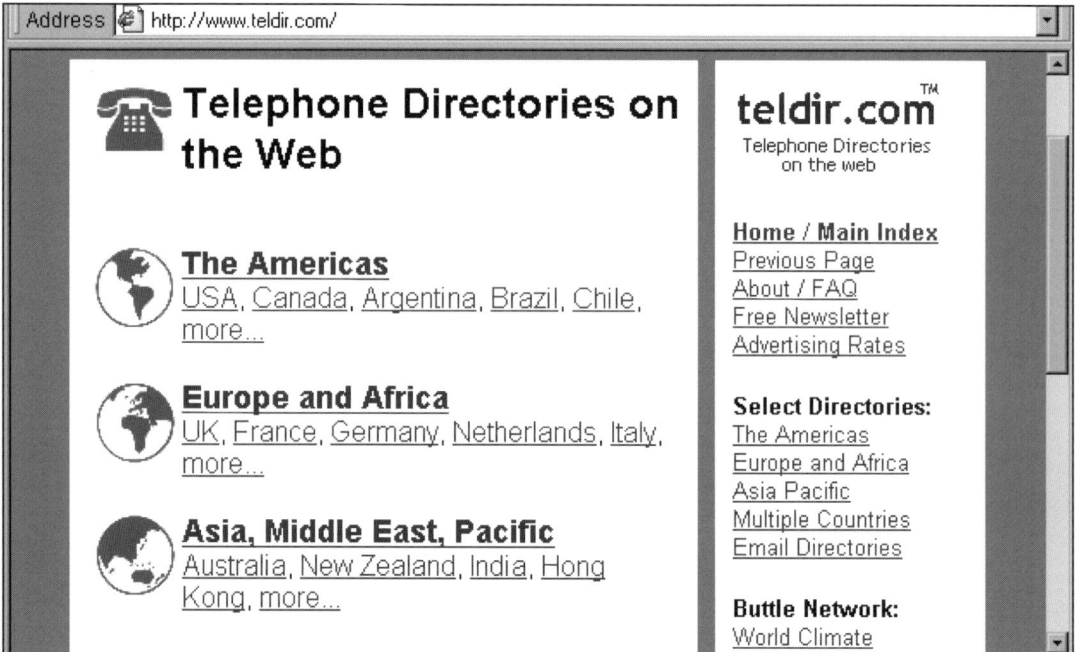

Animals

great for locating people or businesses because it enables you to search White Pages, Yellow Pages, or e-mail directories through a common interface. You can click the Ultimates Email Directory, for example, to search six different directory services, including BigFoot, WhoWhere, and Four11. Just fill out the first form and when you tab to the next field, scripts automatically copy your entry to the corresponding fields for the other services. Once you track down an address, you can even use the Ultimate Trip Planner to find maps and routes for getting there.

WhoWhere
http://www.whowhere.lycos.com
WhoWhere is operated by Lycos, one of the big search engines, and as such provides its service as a part of the search site as a whole. You can add and update your email address, add your homepage URL and include a phone number.

ANIMALS

Battersea Dog's Home
http://www.dogshome.org
Battersea Dog's Home has a site where you can meet the dogs and cats – you will probably fall in love and want to adopt one. You can also read about some of the stories of animals with character and what happened to them, or buy treats for your pet, read about pet first aid, or even apply for a job online.

Cat Fancy
http://www.catfancy.com
Cat Fancy is a great resource for cat owners that includes information on feline health and nutrition, discussion groups, a handy breed finder and lots of general articles. In addition there are a number of interactive cat forums (you do the talking) and a great selection of links to other cat resources.

Crufts
http://www.crufts.org.uk
From the tiniest to the largest , you'll see it at Crufts. Crufts is one of the greatest canine events in the world with tens of thousands of the world's top pedigree dogs competing for prizes. If you can't get to the show, the online results service will inform you about the competitions. There's also a history of the show, which was started in 1891 by Charlie Cruft.

Dog Breed Information Centre
http://www.dogbreedinfo.com
What kind of dog is your favourite? Not sure? Then flick through the thousands of pages on this site. They give information on almost every kind of dog you could imagine. The information is easy to find, with lots of useful tips and lots of cute images. Entries include details of temperament, grooming tips, common health problems, the breed's origins and the ideal living conditions for the dog.

> **More Lookups**
>
> Homepages
> Communities
> Celebrity
> Search
> 3D People
> Finder
>
> Find Ancestors
> Maps &
> Directions
> Yellow Pages

Alphabetical
(includes all breeds listed)

Photo or Size

Apartment Life

Child Companions

Lap Dogs

Jogging

Allergies

147

Play: social life

The Electronic Zoo
http://netvet.wustl.edu/e-zoo.htm
The goals of the Electronic Zoo are: 'To categorise and organise veterinary medical and animal-related information on the internet in a relevant, easy to use format for people interested in these topics.' The site is primarily intended to give information to veterinary surgeons but the information can be useful to anyone with an interest in animals.

FriskyPet
http://www.friskypet.com
Is your pet domesticated but quirky and irrational? This site answers dozens of questions about pets. It offers nutrition tips and pet care resources. You can even ask specific questions about your pet and FriskyPet will create a customised report with information, features, and promotions relevant to your pet problems.

Horse Planet
http://www.horseplanet.com/horselinks.htm
There are links to other good sites and information on tools, training, stables, ranches, tips, vets – in fact anything to do with horses. If you have a site, why not add a free link.

National Zoo Web Cams
http://www.si.edu/organiza/museums/zoo/hilights/webcams/webcams.htm
This is a webcam site that keeps its eye on various animals in the National Zoo in America. There are several cameras watching various animals such as a naked mole rat, the elephants, and a rhino calf. It is interesting to set the camera so you can see it while you are online – keep it updating on your desktop while you're browsing.

▶ *webcam* – a camera fitted to a computer that sends pictures to a web page every few seconds. The view you see on the site is what is currently happening.

RSPCA
http://www.rspca.org
The RSPCA is the champion of the animal world. It backs the fight against animal cruelty in its many forms: from convicting owners of badly run fur farms and battery farms, to dealing with private owners who injure pets and wildlife. The site contains the latest news on animal welfare work, re-homing appeals, coverage of a variety of RSPCA campaigns, information for pet owners or people thinking about getting a pet, and lots of other information including the history and present-day work of the RSPCA.

World Wildlife Fund
http://www.worldwildlife.org
There is much more at stake in the world than whether or not to give chimps 'human' rights. The World Wildlife Fund will open your eyes to some of the many painful truths about the state of the natural world.

Fig. 55. Protecting animals from the cruelty of human beings is the main aim of the RSPCA, and to this end, it does a good job. The organisation depends on help and support from the public, though. Visit the site to see if there is a way you can help.

NEWS AND ENTERTAINMENT

Television

All-Movie Guide
http://allmovie.com
Almost everything you need in order to find a decent film is on this site: search the database by movie, person, keyword or plot. For new films you can read reviews, news and read Barry Norman's views.

The Beeb
http://www.beeb.com
The Beeb describe their site as 'an *rse-kicking new web site'. In other words, a collection of webzines catering to almost every taste you can imagine. It tries to be everything to everybody but, with its roots in television, it has the feel of bouncy easygoing entertainment, which can be a nice change and contrasts with other more serious BBC sites. If you venture away from the home page, it gets a little gimmicky and you are bombarded with a series of smaller browser windows, which tend to get in the way. The site is split into a *Comedy Zone* for laughs, a *Top Gear* section for cars, and *The Score* for sport. You will find games, quizzes, gossip, competitions, video and audio clips, screensavers and humour. There is also useful information – from TV listings to holidays.

BBC News
http://news.bbc.com
One of the best sources of news – a 24-hours a day service with news updated as it comes in. The site is split into six main sections: UK, world business, science and technology, sport, despatches and world summary. There are RealAudio and RealVideo clips from the BBC World Service and archives of most major news items.

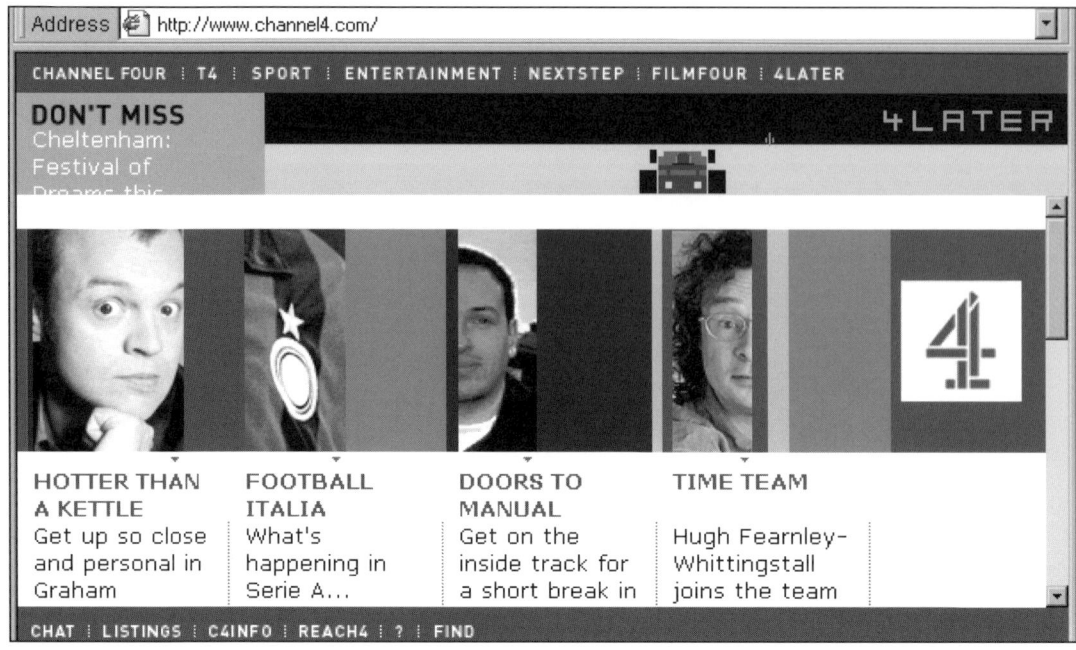

Fig. 56. The Channel Four web site is a nicely designed and simple site and serves well as an accompaniment to the television channel allowing you to follow up on your specific interests.

Channel 4
http://www.channel4.com
Do you want to get a close up view of Graham Norton? Besides that, the Channel 4 website gives you information about new shows and other items of interest on channel 4; if you need further information you can search the listings for the title you want. Channel 4's site is fun, informative and interesting and there is even a special download section where you can get hold of all sorts of tools. You can also search for Channel 4 shows by name or categories.

Channel 5
http://www.channel5.co.uk
You may not be able to get Channel 5 on your television set, but it's on the internet and you should be able to get their site from almost anywhere in the world. At the time of writing, the site was still under construction, though. Normal service will resume as soon as possible.

Coronation Street
http://www.coronationstreet.co.uk
Yes, your favourite soap is online! Follow the antics of Deirdre or read about the old days with Minnie Caldwell and Mrs Sharples.

ITN
http://www.itn.co.uk
It is a pity that the ITN site does not provide a no-frames version for those who have an older version of a browser. The use of videos, though, means you can watch a little picture of Daljeet reading the various news stories and, if you want to know more than just a summary, you can read a text report. The site is better looking than the BBC's in some ways but is harder to find your way around.

Films

Sky
http://www.sky.co.uk
This is Sky's portal to the other stations that make up the Sky satellite network: Sky Sports, Sky One, History Channel and many others. The British news section is well done, with up-to-the-minute news on all the major events and sports in the country.

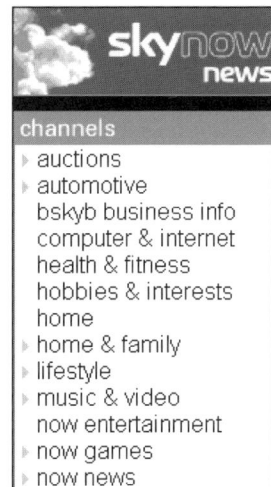

Time Machine
http://www.timemachine.co.uk
The time machine has a dial-shaped home page that you use to build specific television preferences according to your tastes. Once you have defined your area of interest – channel, type of film, time of day, dates – you are shown a list of programs matching your preferences.

Yearling's TV guides
http://www.yearling.co.uk
Are you fed up with trawling through lots of boring TV listings to find your favourites? Yearling's will give you a personalised schedule based on the type of program you like and the times you prefer to watch the TV. Being a couch potato has never been easier.

Films

Internet Movie Database (IMDb)
http://www.imdb.com
The IMDb claims to be the ultimate movie reference source. And indeed it does cover almost everything you would want to know about films and has thousands of links to other film sites. IMDb currently covers around 170,000 titles on the site. The database is extensive and includes reviews, plot summaries, character names, movie ratings, running times, quotes, filming locations, detailed technical data, direct purchase links, posters, and Academy Award information.

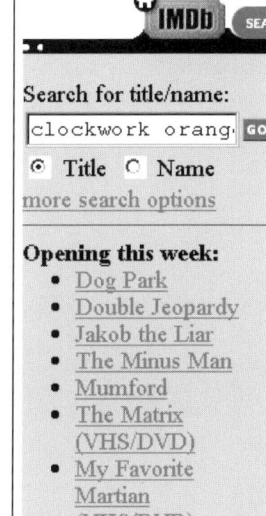

ScreenTalk
http://www.screentalk.org
If you like films, you'll love this site. ScreenTalk is designed to be the premier destination for screenwriters and film professionals but it includes a collection of downloadable scripts from dozens of movies

Radio

Radio deserves its own section because of the availability of streaming audio which enables many of the stations to broadcast live news and music over the internet.

▶ *Streaming audio* – a piece of music or voice transmission is converted into a digital signal. Just enough of the signal is sent to your computer for the RealPlayer (the software on your computer that plays the music or speech) to keep playing. If the internet is congested or the connection is slow, the player tells the site to reduce the quality or speed of transmission so that the music or voice sounds as normal as possible. See RealCom for more information and to download the software: http://www.real.com.

Fig. 57. Find out what's on the BBC radio channels in the coming days and never be caught unawares again. The site is clear, businesslike and uncluttered – a rarity on the web.

BBC Radio
http://www.bbc.co.uk/radio/
Live radio over the internet may not be the best quality but at least you can listen to the Archers or find out who is in the top ten from anywhere in the world as long as you have an internet connection. The BBC World Service excels at bringing top quality news to the world at large.

Capital Radio
http://www.capitalfm.co.uk
This is a quality site considering the limitations of live sound broadcasting over the internet. You can search for an artist or a particular song in the online database. Most of the songs also have a short video clip so you can see what you are listening to. The site also boasts coverage of lots of restaurants, a cinema guide, and a search engine.

Radio Tower
http://www.radiotower.com
RadioTower.Com is a public internet broadcast company and has been 'serving the world' since 1996. Their aim is to make it easy to find and tune in to audio on the internet and to be 'a top ranked audio portal, matching a diverse array of content with a world wide audience.' The site certainly is a good first point of call for anything audio on the web.

Virgin Radio
http://www.virginradio.co.uk
Virgin Radio's site is bright, jazzy and aimed at a young audience. You can join in the fun in the *Breakfast Show*, follow the football or wheels of steel, listen to new music from The Zoo or simply take advantage of the free software and other goodies on the site.

Newspapers online

The Economist
http://www.economist.com
Once you have registered, you can access articles published in *The*

Newspapers

Economist since January 1995. If you subscribe to *The Economist* either in print, or the web edition, you can retrieve the text of any article free of charge. If you are not a subscriber you must 'pay' one archive credit each time. Credits cost a dollar each and you must buy a minimum of ten. When you register, you get five free credits. Once you have registered, you can download *The Economist* screensaver (statistics of the world's leading economies – pretty). *The Economist* also offers two weekly email newsletters, business and politics.

The Electronic Telegraph
http://www.telegraph.co.uk
Online since 1994, the *Telegraph* site has had chance to mature into one of the most useful news sources on the internet. UK and international news, city and finance, reviews, interviews with personalities, and 'health on Tuesday, fashion on Wednesday; food and drink on Thursday, and motoring, gardening and horoscopes on Saturday.'

The European
http://www.the-european.com
The European gives very little away and what it does give away comes in Adobe Acrobat format, which means you need to download the Acrobat file to read the news on your computer. To access the full site content you must subscribe, at £26 for six months. If the rest of the site is as unwieldy, many people will be put off very quickly.

▶ *Adobe Acrobat* – a free program that makes it possible to view PDF (portable document format) files. PDF files are larger than the text equivalent but have far more features including different font styles, hyperlinks, forms and more. The .pdf format is read only, though text within documents can be searched or copied for inclusion in other documents.

The Financial Times
http://www.FT.com
FT.com offers a supplementary service to the printed version. There are commentaries on the markets of the day, summaries of the daily news, video news stories and more in depth news of the money world, including the stock market and other financial information. And, for really up-to-date news, you can receive personalised news by email.

The Guardian Network
http://www.guardianunlimited.co.uk
The Guardian Network attempts to be more than an online news source and it succeeds. It is 'a number of specialist sites, each of which sets out to be the best in its field.' The network includes the regular news site, four unlimited sites, football, cricket, and jobs. Planned for later in the year are a film and work unlimited.

The Independent
http://www.independent.co.uk
News is updated daily and top news headlines are placed on the home

Play: social life

page with links to articles on the rest of the site. A menu provides access to other sections of the paper such as sport, books and international. The site is easy to navigate but has no search feature for archived articles.

The Mirror
http://www.mirror.co.uk
The site offers mainly celebrity-based news presented in a bold and dramatic way. Perhaps the most unusual part of the site is the Mirror Dome Watch. A webcam provides a live image of the progress of the millennium dome:

> http://www.mirror.co.uk/cgi-bin/dome.htm

The New York Times
http://www.nyt.com
Almost up to the same standard as the MegaStar is that huge American paper the *New York Times*. The online version uses a little less paper. Despite its size, the news content is superb and, with the late breaking news from AP on its front page, it is current.

Private Eye
http://privateeye.uk.msn.com
Some say it is irreverent and libellous, others say it is healthily cynical. Either way this ever scurrilous site is worth a visit, for the comic animations, sound effects and satire.

Fig. 58. The Star newspaper needs no introduction; its theme is universally known and ridiculed, but it's a lively site and full of the kind of features you would expect such as MegaBabes, MegaPosters and Bagpus.

Newspapers

The Scotsman
http://www.scotsman.com
Scotland has produced a cracking newspaper in *The Scotsman,* and the online version is just as good. Some of the news is specific to Scotland but much of it is more general – and the quality of its English news reporting rivals that in the English newspapers.

The Star
http://www.megastar.co.uk
Where else but at *The Star*'s site, called Mega Star, can you grab a handful of news, enter competitions and admire girlie pictures? The headlines at the time of writing were 'Sun editor feels a right tit after he prints Royal boob pic' and 'United snatch Euro glory in dying seconds'. Because the site is very graphic, it takes a long time to download.

The Sunday Times
http://Sunday-times.co.uk
Registered users can retrieve articles in the *Sunday Times* and the Saturday *Times*.

The Times
http://www.the-times.co.uk
This site was launched early in 1996. You must register first, but it's free and worth it. The news is authoritative, comprehensive and plentiful.

Other news sources

The Drudge Report
http://www.drudgereport.com
This is hardly a good looking site, but it is probably the first site to break many of the big news stories. Matt Drudge uses a couple of televisions, a police scanner and the internet to chase news stories. Despite the meagre tools, the site often causes a storm by getting the gossip before any of the other news outlets, possibly because of his influential and knowledgeable contacts.

Fig. 59. The Drudge Report is a simple, no-nonsense, even boring-looking site, but don't underestimate the fresh hard-hitting news that often breaks here before any other news source even has the time to turn on the lights.

Play: social life

NewsNow
http://www.newsnow.co.uk
NewsNow is updated every five minutes with new UK and international headlines. NewsNow's aim is to supply the latest headlines from leading news sources. Categorised into general news, business and finance, information technology, sport, entertainment and computer gaming. There is a live newsfeed and, if you missed something the first time round, you can search the archive of the previous month's news.

One World
http://www.oneworld.org
The news on One World is presented from a human rights and global viewpoint. The information is arranged in sections such as news, media, and action. The news is updated daily and followed up by in-depth reports. The archive is searchable and is about four years old.

Press Association
http://www.pa.press.net
PA is the oldest and largest news agency operating exclusively in Britain. Founded in 1868, it supplies news to all the London daily and Sunday newspapers, provincial papers, and trade journals and other periodicals. If you want to read the unedited news before it reaches the newspapers, go to the PA and browse the site or, if you have a more specific interest, use StoryFinder. StoryFinder powers a search using the keywords you enter to find related news stories from up-to-date quality UK news and sport sites.

Reuters
http://www.reuters.com
Reuters gathers news from around the world and provides news services to the world's leading newspapers, reaching almost all of them and many thousands of others, as well as hundreds of radio and television stations around the world.

World in Action
http://www.world-in-action.co.uk
The hard-hitting investigative reporting of television's *World in Action* shows what is really happening in the world. The television programme only has a half-hour slot but the site has a 24-hour presence. It makes the information that has been gathered extremely useful because it is accessible. The site contains lots of useful information and contacts – from issues about airbags to breast implants.

Weather

CNN
http://cnn.com/weather
CNN has four-day coverage of over 6,000 cities world wide with details of current weather, satellite maps, radar maps, forecast movies and animations. Subsections include weather maps, a complete listing of all available weather maps, and the Storm Centre which contains background information about hurricanes, past storms and links.

Weather

The Met Office
http://www.meto.govt.uk
Climbing in the Cairngorms, or rafting on the River Wye? Check the weather at the Met Office's site. You can see today's weather (and a few other forecasts) for free or get a five day regional forecast if you pay. The site uses a ticket system where you pay for a number of tickets and each service you use, takes one or two tickets off you. Tickets cost fifty pence and entry to the site costs one ticket.

Fig. 60. The Met Office has a bright and sunny site with lots of information about one of the most unpredictable aspects of planet Earth – the weather.

Rain or Shine
http://www.rainorshine.com
Rain or Shine Weather is a weather service that offers a customised weather page with hourly forecasts for 800 cities world wide. There is also a five-day forecast updated twice daily for those cities. Also included are three national maps: a 24-hour forecast map, a satellite and a radar map.

Cartoons

Magixl
http://www.magixl.com
This is the European web site dedicated to caricature. Take a look at over 200 caricatures of international stars and explore the easy-to-use method of sketching faces with a few clicks of the mouse. You can browse the large gallery of famous people or create your own masterpiece.

The Simpsons
http://www.foxworld.com/simpsons/simpsons.htm
Bart gets up to his usual anarchistic activities on his own family site. 'Now the longest-running prime time animated series in television

Play: social life

history,' the site proclaims, 'The Simpsons has changed the face of the medium forever. Award-winning and critically acclaimed, the series delivers solid messages about family, society and the environment, without sacrificing the social and political satire or edgy humour for which it is heralded.'

COMPUTER GAMES AND SOFTWARE

Children's Software Review
http://zippy.tradenet.net/childrenssoftware
The Children's Software Review began as a newsletter in 1993 and has evolved into a nationally circulated magazine. Teachers, parents, and businesses engaged in developing children's software read it for the reviews and commentary. The highlight of CSR's web site is the children's software finder, which lets you search more than 3,000 reviews. You can specify the title, grade level, publisher, content, and rating of the software you're looking for. Review pages also include links to online sources for ordering the product.

PCgame search engine
http://www.pcgame.com
PCgame is one of the web's most comprehensive search engines for PC games with over 3,500 titles in its database. There are direct links to all of their reviews, cheats, demos, screen shots, FAQs, movies, music, and more.

Tucows
http://www.tucows.com
Tucows (The Ultimate Collection of Winsock Software) is one of the biggest collections of shareware on the internet. Here you can find most of the latest Windows, Macintosh and OS/2 shareware. Tucows claims to check all the software for viruses and quality.

ZD Net
http://www.zdnet.com
If the software you are looking for is not here, the site will probably tell you where to find it. The site lists software for many different systems including as Dos, Windows and Macintosh.

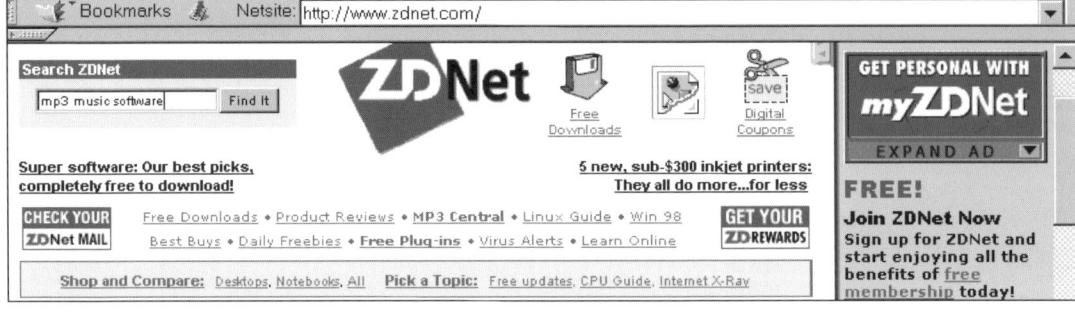

Appendix: Your safe use of the internet

In this appendix we will explore:

- *viruses and the web*
- *The reliability of information on the web*
- *electronic copyright*
- *privacy on the internet*
- *children and the web*
- *FAQ – frequently asked questions*

Viruses and the web

1. When browsing the world wide web, you should always take some basic precautions. These should include:
2. Never set your browser to automatically open or run downloaded files.
3. Never run a program without checking it for viruses.
4. Prevent word processing and other software from automatically executing macros when document opens.
5. Make regular backups of important data.

A computer crash never seems a danger until it actually happens – then it can be too late. The Melissa virus, for example, is a macro, which infects Word documents, and there are a number of other macro viruses that also affect Word files; all of them, and many others, can be received as email attachments. If you receive an attachment, do not open it. If you need to view it, save it to a floppy disk first then virus check the disk with an **up-to-date** virus checker. Last year's software is no use unless it has been updated in the last month or so.

Other Word processors can also be affected; in fact any program such as Excel which allows advanced macros may be susceptible to viruses. The only way you can realistically keep up with new strains of virus is by regularly updating your antivirus software.

An excellent and free antiviral program for PCs is f-prot. This can be downloaded from

> http://www.simtel.net/pub/simtelnet/msdos/virus

Full instructions for using f-prot come with the downloaded package – download it and **use** it!

The reliability of information on the web

There is a large and increasing number of authoritative and genuine

Safe use of the internet

sites on the internet but there are many more that are pure rubbish. Even some of the major companies see the internet as only needing a token presence and don't bother to update information. Often they leave the same old news there for years. Other sites are little more than a patchwork of oddball opinions, rumours or plain lies.

Here are some tips for evaluating the usefulness of a site:

- ▶ If a deal seems to be too good to be true, it probably is.

- ▶ Good sites will have a date of modification on each page – make sure this is recent.

- ▶ If the content of the site is badly designed, has bad spelling, atrocious grammar, or poorly laid out text, avoid it. If someone has something of value, it is almost always well presented.

- ▶ The longer the URL, the less professional the site. Serious sites will pay for a special internet address, which is usually something like http://www.mycompany.com. If you find something like http://dspace.dial.pipex.com/town/plaza/yix56/members/page1.html (My old home page which had a picture of my house and my cat and little else of value), the site is probably of little use. You can find excellent sites constructed by dedicated enthusiasts but they are few and far between.

- ▶ If in doubt about the information on a site, check it with that on other sites or from other sources such as newspapers and journals.

Electronic copyright

Copyright is defined as: the exclusive legal right to reproduce, publish, and sell a piece of literary, musical, or artistic work. Copyright usually belongs to the creator of the work such as a writer, artist or musician. Sometimes the copyright belongs to a company such as a newspaper or a record company. If you try to use a piece of work that is copyrighted, you run the risk of being prosecuted.

There have been many cases where fans of pop-stars have been warned to remove music clips off their site or risk legal action. There have been other similar cases where pictures or text have been taken from another site without permission and prosecutions have followed. It is true that there is a lot of content on the internet that is not copyrighted but never assume that you can use it – ask the owner of the site or work for permission.

If you are a writer or artist putting your work on the internet, it is very simple for other people to copy and distribute your work. Prosecuting people who copy your material without permission is very difficult, especially if they live in another country.

Fig. 61. The Copyright Website deserves a round of applause for tackling one of the most controversial topics to do with the internet.

When your work is in a fixed format such as CD-rom or a multimedia product, the law is relatively easy to enforce. The internet, however, is more of a challenge. At present, trying to protect work on the internet is like trying to stop a neighbour playing loud music late at night – a polite request may work, but it may need a lengthy period of protesting and the arbitration of some legal body.

Tips

1. If your work is valuable, don't put it on the internet.
2. Have a copyright statement on every page that contains work you want to protect.
3. Do not copy pages or images off the internet without permission of the copyright owner.

For more information go to:

The Copyright Website
http://www.benedict.com

Edward Barrow's unofficial internet copyright pages
http://www.plato32.demon.co.uk/Edward

Privacy on the internet

The invisible eavesdroppers
With normal telephone conversations, you can find a private place to talk and the conversation is over once you hang up the telephone.

The internet is different. You leave a trail behind you that can last many months or even years. Others can read your email messages, they can

Safe use of the internet

trace your surfing habits, and the posts you make to newsgroups will be stored, and some may even be published in books or on web sites. The question some ask is, 'If you have nothing to hide why should you need privacy?' Let me ask a question in reply – are you willing to let anyone read your private letters or listen to your telephone conversations? Not many people would answer yes to that question but, unless legislation has been introduced after this book has been printed, the British police can intercept and read your email without prior notification and without a court order.

It is not only the police that have this power. When you look at a web site, the chance is that information is being compiled in a log about who you are and what parts of the site you visit. The records in the log are made accessible to anybody who knows how to view them. Web-browsing programs are designed to give this information away. Companies like Netscape and Microsoft can afford to give away web browsers, because the real customers are the people who use this collected information, such as corporations and other large organisations.

If we just limit speculation to the marketing uses of the information, companies can put together a detailed dossier on your personal online habits, and your interests and preferences. Advertising can then be specifically targeted for the best results – to part you with your money. The scenario becomes more sinister when you realise that not all companies are going to use this information for purely commercial purposes. There are cases where companies target children and use private information about them to gain their trust and thereby get credit card and address details of the parents. No child would give away credit

Fig. 62. Anonymizer allows you to become 'invisible' online by using technology to keep your identity hidden while you are using the internet. Is this a good thing? Go over to the site and see for yourself.

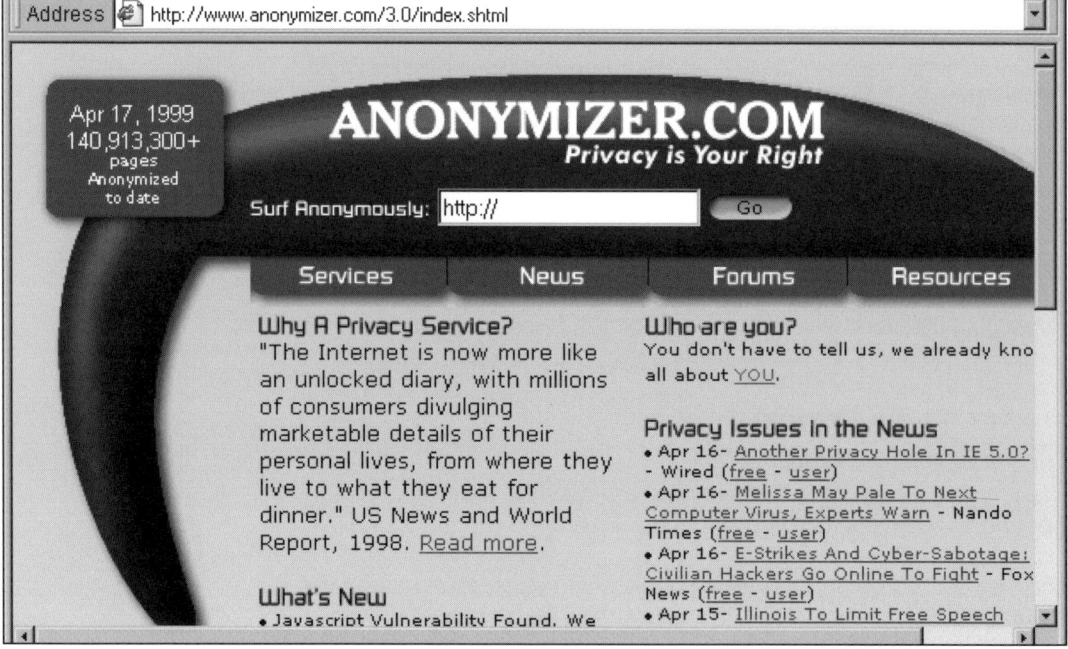

Anonymous surfing

card details, but what if there was an animated cartoon frog on the site that knew the child's name and interests? Privacy is a complex problem and will probably not be resolved for many years.

What can we do?

Anonymous mailing services preserve your privacy by acting as a go-between when you browse or send email messages. Such services slow your internet experience but if your information is sensitive, the sacrifice is worthwhile.

Anonymizer
http://www.anonymizer.com
Anonymizer lets you know just how much information you are giving away when you browse. Once you have recovered from the shock, it allows you to surf anonymously. Sending email also puts information in the hands of anybody who cares to look. The company claims to be the most secure way, apart from the military, to use email in the world. Just visit the site, type your message and let Anonymizer send it securely.

Net Freedom
http://www.netfreedom.org
Internet Freedom is opposed to all attempts to censor and regulate the internet from newsgroup bans to the use of PICS (see page 165). Did you know that armed with a copy of Internet Explorer and a computer you could bring down the US government? That seemed to be the view of the White House early in 1999. At around the same time in the UK the police were in 'secret' talks with ISPs trying to persuade them to allow them to intercept private email messages.

Zero Knowledge
http://www.zeroknowledge.com
ZKS is a Canadian company that sells a software package called Freedom, which allows users to use the internet while remaining anonymous. The system works by a combination of encryption and pseudonyms that are wrapped around the user's email messages so that the content and the sender remain private. Freedom also takes control of the 'cookies' that many web sites leave on your hard disk.

▶ *Cookies* – small files left on your hard disk by a web site. Information in cookies often includes your name and interests. The next time you connect to the website, it can use this information in many ways – for instance it can welcome you by name and then show you information that suits your interests.

Children and the web

If you are accessing the internet from home, you are likely to have uncensored and unfiltered access. If you have, you are bound to come across many sites on the net that you would not want your children to see. Indeed, some of those sites would shock even the most liberal-minded adult.

Safe use of the internet

One of the areas you may want to keep your children away from is that of gambling. The combination of a child, a credit card and an online casino is enough to make any parent shiver. On the internet, there is no way to know a person's real age, nor can you tell if a credit card number has been submitted by the rightful owner or not. The control must, therefore, be exerted in the home on your own computer. A different kind of horror is that of pornography, especially child or sadistic pornography. No matter how illegal pornography is, there will still be places on the internet where there is a risk of coming across it by accident.

There are three main ways you can protect your children:

1. Use blocking software, which gives access to the web but monitors the connection and filters out any sites containing keywords you have marked as undesirable.
2. Enable the ratings system, which uses information about the content of a site to decide whether it is acceptable or not. The unacceptable sites are filtered out.
3. Parental guidance. For example, by only allowing the use of the computer in a communal area such as the kitchen where people are likely to be near or pass by regularly.

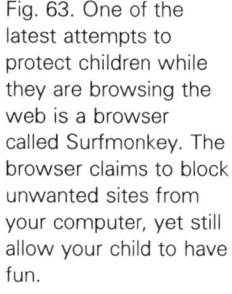

Fig. 63. One of the latest attempts to protect children while they are browsing the web is a browser called Surfmonkey. The browser claims to block unwanted sites from your computer, yet still allow your child to have fun.

Blocking software

The disadvantage of blocking software is that you have to try to be aware of all the various rude words and banned sites yourself – a difficult task. And how do you know if an image is undesirable unless you look at it first? Could you really justify banning all of the sites that

Children & the web

contained the word 'pussy' for example?

SurfMonkey
http://www.surfmonkey.com
Perhaps the best kind of blocking software is that which is both unobtrusive and fun. SurfMonkey is a browser that is based on Internet Explorer but is designed to be user friendly to younger children. There is a helper, a monkey that pops up to offer advice and tips. The main screen has the appearance of the inside of a space ship with simple navigation buttons on the console. As with all good cartoon space ships, there are also some simple 'weapons'. This has a bomb button, which 'explodes' the web page being viewed, and a splat button, which throws coloured globs onto it. There are, of course, various filtering options. Before a site is visited, it is checked against a blacklist of sites which the SurfMonkey company updates daily. This, combined with a large number of pre-stored sites, combines to make SurfMonkey a worthwhile browser. You can download it for free.

CyberSitter
http://www.solidoak.com/cysitter.htm
CyberSitter is Windows 95 program that lets you block access to common types of graphic files and specific files and programs. You can set the software to block or sound an alarm when your child tries to access the blocked items. From their site: 'Working secretly in the background, CyberSitter analyses all internet activity. Whenever it detects activity the parent has elected to restrict, it takes over and blocks the activity before it takes place. If desired, CyberSitter will maintain a complete history of all internet activity, including attempts to access blocked material.'

Netnanny
http://www.netnanny.com
Net Nanny lets you limit access to inappropriate material, prevent the threat of Cyber Strangers, and deny the misuse of personal information. It can also monitor the internet, email, IRC chat programs, newsgroups and offline applications. They claim, 'Net Nanny gives the parent or administrator complete control over what is being accessed on your PC.'

Ratings

A rating system is based on an internationally agreed set of tools that can control who sees what kind of content. Web sites rate themselves and include the rating information hidden on their web pages so that browsers can access this information and decide whether the site is acceptable to the user or not. Sites with unacceptable content are not shown. For the rating system to work, you must be using a browser capable of being configured for ratings and you must set these rating to the levels of tolerance you want it to exert.

PICS (Platform for Internet Content Selection) is now widely accepted as the main way to implement these ratings. The most used set of

Safe use of the internet

standards for screening material was developed by the RSACi (Recreational Software Advisory Council on the Internet). This rates material according to the degree of sex, violence, nudity, and bad

Level	Violence	Nudity	Sex	Language
0	Harmless conflict, some damage to objects	No nudity or revealing attire	Romance, no sex	Inoffensive slang; no profanity
1	Creatures injured or killed; damage to objects; fighting	Revealing attire	Passionate kissing	Mild expletives
2	Humans injured, or small amounts of blood	Partial nudity	Clothed sexual touching	Expletives; non-sexual anatomical references
3	Humans injured or killed	Non-sexual frontal nudity	Non-explicit sexual activity	Strong, vulgar language; obscene gestures; racial epithets
4	Wanton and gratuitous violence; torture; rape	Provocative frontal nudity	Explicit sexual activity; sex crimes	Crude or explicit sexual references; extreme hate speech

language depicted. The levels and categories of the PICS/RSACi rating are shown in the following table:

The vast majority of sites on the web do not, and may never, use any ratings. Unless you allow your browser software to view unrated sites, your child will be blocked from many of the best sites on the web.

The rating system is politically sensitive because internet cafés and schools are increasingly forcing users to have PICS enabled if they wish to use their machines and browsers. This is little more than covert censorship of publicly available information. For more information, go to Internet Freedom at http://www.netfreedom.org. Internet Freedom is

Fig. 64. Did you know that if you use a computer in a library or a college to view the internet, what you see is probably being censored? No? Visit this site and you will see some shocking revelations.

FAQ

'opposed to all attempts to censor and regulate the internet – from newsgroup bans to the use of PICS'.

Parental control

A third alternative relies on parental guidance. As with a television, if a computer is in the child's bedroom, there is no foolproof way of ensuring that your child is not accessing something dubious or harmful. And you should always assume that your child knows more about the internet than you do. If you suspect your child of wandering towards pornographic or other negative sites, you could move the computer into the open and keep an eye on what is happening. If all else fails, you can lock it away when you leave the child alone in the house for any length or time – even that may not work.

FAQ – Frequently Asked Questions

Q. *When I try a keyword search, even though I follow the rules and use AND, OR and quotes, I still can't narrow the search down.*

A. Not all search engines or directories use the same syntax rules – some use single quotes, others double, some will not accept either. Some engines use AND, others use a plus sign. Refer to the instructions on the site or try another search engine. Your keywords may be

- ▶ spelt wrongly
- ▶ too specific
- ▶ terms that are not in common use

Could the keywords have an American variation? Try 'center' instead of 'centre', 'sidewalk' instead of 'pavement', and so on.

Q. *Why do I need a search engine?*

A. For the same reason that you need an index in a book or a card catalogue in a library. It would be impossible to examine all the books in a library yourself so a card index or computer index is necessary. There are millions of pages on the web – try keeping track of all those yourself! The search engines and directories help you find the specific information you need.

Q. *What's a wild card and how do I use it?*

A. A wild card is a special character that can be added to a word to make the search engine look for all possible endings to that word. For instance, you might want to find information about brewing beer. Pages that contain the words brew, brewing, brewery may all be relevant. If the search engine you want to use allows wild cards, you would enter 'brew*'. The asterisk is the wild card and pages that contained words that started with 'brew' would be listed.

Q. *How do I narrow a search?*

Safe use of the internet

A. The special keyword 'and' is probably the best way to narrow a search. For example, with 'bread and butter', a search engine will list pages that have both of these words present in a document. It will ignore those that just have the word 'bread' in it (e.g. baking bread) and it will also ignore pages with just the word 'butter' in it (e.g. melted butter, Irish butter). It will only list pages if both of the words are present – although they don't have to be beside each other on the page. To narrow the search even further, you can use 'and' more than once. For example, 'bread and butter and pudding' would limit your search even more since all three terms would have to be present before a link would be made to the document. The keyword 'not' narrows the search by excluding certain words. For example, 'bread not brown' would list pages on bread but not if the word 'brown' was present. You can combine the two different keywords. For example the phrase 'bread and butter and pudding not recipes' would give you information on bread and butter pudding but no pages with recipes, since the 'not' term specifically excludes that word.

Q. How do I widen a search?

A. The keyword 'or' will broaden your search. For example, if you were looking for information on a herb but you were not sure of the spelling of its name, you could use 'or' to include different variations of the spelling. By entering 'pennywart or pennywort', the search engine would provide a link to any site that had either of those words present. For even wider searches, you can use 'or' more than once. For example, 'pennywart or pennywort or pennyroyal or pennygrass' would provide a larger list.

Further reading

Web pages

Many sites contain useful and in-depth information about the internet itself. Referring to these sites will ensure that you have the latest information and that it is written by people in the know. The information will not always be in plain language, but most of it is readable.

Finding Information on the Internet
http://www.lib.berkeley.edu/TeachingLib/Guides/Internet/FindInfo.html
A tutorial taking you through how to find information on the internet using basic to advanced techniques; from general to advanced web searching. Includes a glossary of internet jargon and things to know before starting a search.

Glossary of Internet Terms
http://www.matisse.net/files/glossary.html
For a more extensive glossary of internet terms, look at this site. For a short version see the glossary on page 173.

Guide to Effective Searching of the Internet
http://thewebtools.com/searchgoodies/tutorial.htm
A tutorial on finding information on the internet. It covers directories, search engines and search strategies. Also covers the basics of internet searching, keywords, Boolean, and advanced searching.

Internet Detective
http://sosig.ac.uk/desire/internet-detective.html
This interactive tutorial will help you evaluate the quality of an internet resource.

Internet Handbooks
http://www.internet-handbooks.co.uk
The web site of the publishers of this book. The site contains practical and easy-to-follow information on various aspects of using the internet.

Searching, Sleuthing and Sifting
http://www.angelfire.com/in/virtuallibrarian/ismain.html
Here you will find a set of tutorials on searching methods and techniques, covering subjects such as the types of information available (graphics, audio clips, software etc), indexes and directories, how to use search engines, and an introduction to metasearch engines.

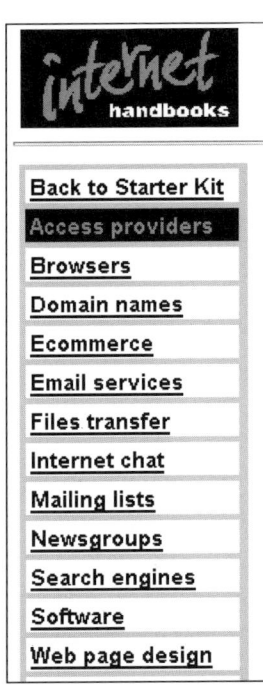

Further reading – traditional books

Casting Your Net: A Student's Guide to Research on the Internet
H. Eric Branscomb
UK list price £23.95 paperback. February 1997. Allyn & Bacon. ISBN 0205266924.
Biased towards academic research, 'this book has been designed as a

Further reading

supplement to standard first-year handbooks or research paper tests. It assumes some familiarity with standard research procedures, but assumes little experience with the internet.'

Finding Information on the Internet
Howard Lake
£6.95 paperback, 140 pages. June 1998. Aurelian Information Ltd. ISBN 1899247114.

Finding It on the Internet: The Internet Navigator's Guide to Search Tools and Techniques
Paul Gilster
£22.50 paperback. January 1996. Wiley. ISBN 0471126950.
This is a guide to business-related information on the internet. It shows how to find information about individuals, companies and public sector activities.

How to Search the Web: A Quick-Reference Guide to Finding Things on the World Wide Web
£7.78 US paperback. May 1998. Want Pub. ISBN 094200888X.

How to Search the World Wide Web Efficiently
J. Shelley
£6.99 paperback, 112 pages. September 1998. Bernard Babani Publishing Ltd. ISBN 0859344533.

The Internet at a Glance: Finding Information on the Internet
Susan E. Feldman & Larry Krumenaker
£5.98 US edition, paperback. March 1996. Learned Information. ISBN: 1573870242.

An Internet Education: A Guide to Doing Research on the Internet
Cheryl Harris
£26.99 paperback, 320 pages. December 1995. Integrated Media Group. ISBN: 0534258514.

Internet Research Companion
Geoffrey W. McKim
£22.95 paperback, 266 pages. March 1996 Que E&t. ISBN: 1575760509.

The Internet Research Guide
Timothy K. Maloy
UK price £14.95. Allworth Press New York. Paperback 1996. ISBN 188059455. A concise, friendly and practical handbook for anyone researching in the wide world of cyberspace.

The Official Netscape Guide to Internet Research: For Windows & Macintosh
Tara Calishain & Jill Nystrom
£27.50 paperback, 391 pages. 2nd edition. April 1998. International

.... **Further reading**

Thomson Publishing. ISBN 1566048451. As the official Netscape Guide, this book only covers searching on the internet using Netscape software.

The On-Line Research Handbook (Concise Guides Series)
Hayden Mead & Andy Clark
£3.60 paperback, 208 pages. April 1997. Berkley Publishing; ISBN: 0425156672 US edition.

Researching on the Internet: The Complete Guide to Finding, Evaluating, and Organizing Information Effectively (Prima Online)
Robin Rowland & Dave Kinnaman
£27.49 paperback. May 1995. Prima Publications. ISBN 0761500634.

The Student's Guide to Doing Research on the Internet
David R. Campbell, Mary Campbell, Dave Campbell
£12.99 paperback, 349 pages. July 1995. Addison Wesley Pub Co. ISBN 0201489163.

Technical or more academic books

Internet Research: Theory and Practice
Ned L. Fielden & Maria Garrido
£22.50 paperback. September 1998. McFarland & Co. ISBN 0786405384.

Internet Users' Guide to Network Resource Tools
M. Isaacs (Trans-European Research and Education Networking Association)
£11.95 paperback, 224 pages. April 1998. Addison Wesley Longman Higher Education. ISBN 0201360551.

Research on the Net
Kevin McGuinness & Tom Short
£19.95 paperback, 385 pages. 1998. Old Bailey Press. ISBN 1858362695.
Biased toward the law practitioner.

Searching & Researching on the Internet and World Wide Web: The Information Specialist's Guide
Ernest Ackermann & Karen Hartman
£17.99 paperback, 488 pages. October 1998. ABF Content. ISBN 1887902317 US edition.

Glossary of internet terms

Access provider – The company that provides you with access to the internet. This may be an independent provider or a large international organisation such as AOL or CompuServe. See also **internet service provider**.

Adobe Acrobat – A piece of software required for reading PDF files. You may need Adobe Acrobat when downloading large text files from the internet, such as lengthy reports or chapters from books.

Address book – A directory in a web browser where you can store people's email addresses. This saves having to type them out each time you want to email someone.

AltaVista – One of the half dozen most popular internet search engines. Just type in a few key words to find what you want on the internet.

AOL – America OnLine, still the world's biggest internet service provider, with more than fifteen million subscribers. Because it has masses of content of its own – quite aside from the wider internet – it is sometimes referred to as an 'online' service provider rather than internet service provider. It has given away vast numbers of free CDs with the popular computer magazines to build its customer base.

Agent – This is a searching tool that acts on your behalf to find out information across the internet. An agent is usually a separate programme, such as WebFerret.

Ask Jeeves – A popular internet search engine. Rather than just typing in a few key words for your search, you can type in a whole question or instruction, such as 'Find me everything about online investment.' It draws on a database of millions of questions and answers, and works best with fairly general questions.

ASP – Active Server Pages, a filename extension for a certain type of web page.

Attachment – A file sent with an email message. The attached file can be anything from a word processed document to a database, spreadsheet, graphic, or even a sound or video file. For example you could email someone birthday greetings, and attach a sound track or video clip.

Bandwidth – The width of the electronic highway that gives you access to the internet. The higher the bandwidth, the wider this highway, and the faster the traffic can flow.

Banner ad – This is a band of text and graphics, usually situated at the top of a web page. It acts like a title, telling the user what the content of the page is about. It invites the visitor to click on it to visit that site. Banner advertising has become big business.

Baud rate – The data transmission speed in a modem, measured in bps (bits per second).

BBS – Bulletin board service. A facility to read and post messages on a particular web site.

Glossary

Blue Ribbon Campaign – A widely supported campaign supporting free speech and opposing moves to censorship of the internet by national governments and other agencies of control.

Bookmark – A file of URLs of your favourite internet sites. – Bookmarks are very easily created by bookmarking (mouse-clicking) any internet page you like the look of. If you are an avid user, you could soon end up with hundreds of them!

Boolean search – A search in which you type in words such as AND and OR to refine your search. Such words are called 'Boolean operators'. The concept is named after George Boole, a nineteenth-century English mathematician.

Browser – This is the program that you use to access the world wide web. Your browser is your window to the internet, and will normally supplied by your internet service provider when you first sign up. The most popular browsers are Netscape Communicator and Microsoft Internet Explorer. Both can be downloaded free from their web sites and are found on the CD-Roms stuck to the computer magazines. It won't make much difference which one you use – they do much the same thing.

Bulletin board – A type of computer-based news service that provides an email service and a file archive.

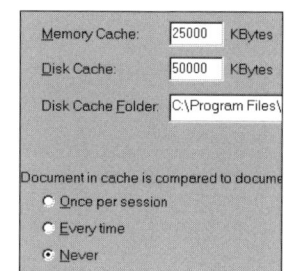

Cache – A file storage area on a computer. Your web browser will normally cache (copy to your hard drive) each web page you visit. When you revisit that page on the web, you may in fact be looking at the page originally cached on your computer. To be sure you are viewing the current page, press **reload** or **refresh** on your browser toolbar. You can empty your cache from time to time, and the computer will do so automatically whenever the cache is full.

Certificate – A computer file that securely identifies a person or organisation on the internet.

Client – This is the term given to the program that you use to access the internet. For example your web browser is a web client, and your email program is an email client.

Closed areas – Those areas of a web site that only registered users can enter.

Community – The internet is often described as a net community. This refers to the fact that many people like the feeling of belonging to a group of like-minded individuals. Many big web sites have been developed along these lines, such as GeoCities which is divided into special-interest 'neighbourhoods', or America OnLine which is strong on member services.

Compression – Computer files can be electronically compressed, so that they can be uploaded or downloaded more quickly across the internet, saving time and money. If an image file is compressed too much, there may be a loss of quality.

Crash – What happens when a computer program malfunctions. The operating system of your PC may perform incorrectly or come to a complete stop ('freeze'), forcing you to shut down and restart. A crash is more likely to happen when you have several windows and several

Glossary

software programs running simultaneously.

Credit scoring – When you apply for a loan or a credit card information about you and your financial status is given a score. This helps financial institutions quickly assess the level of risk they are taking on.

Currency converter Thinking about buying a villa on the Algarve, but not sure about the Portuguese currency? Thinking about buying some Swiss francs, but not sure about the rate of exchange? Then use a currency converter. This is a web page where you can easily convert any currency into another. You type in the amount, the currency it is in, and the currency you want to convert to, and the calculator instantly displays the result. To find one, just type 'currency converter' into your favourite search engine.

Cybercash – This is a trademark, but is also often used as a broad term to describe the use of small payments made over the internet using a new form of electronic account that is loaded up with cash. You can send this money to the companies offering such cash facilities by cheque, or by credit card. Some internet companies offering travel-related items can accept electronic cash of this kind.

Cyberspace – Popular term for the intangible 'place' where you go to surf – the ethereal and borderless world of computers and telecommunications on the internet.

Dial in account – This allows you to connect your computer to your internet provider's computer remotely.

Digital – Based on the two binary digits, 1 and 0. The operation of all computers is based on this amazingly simple concept. All forms of information are capable of being digitalised – numbers, words, sounds and images – and then transmitted over the internet.

Domain – A domain is a specific area on the internet and identifies to the computers on the rest of the internet where to access particular information. Each domain has a name. The domain for Internet Handbooks for instance is: www.internet-handbooks.co.uk

Download – 'Downloading' means copying a file from one computer on the internet to your own computer. You do this by clicking on a button that links you to the appropriate file. Downloading is an automatic process, except you have to click 'yes' to accept the download and give it a file name. You can download any type of file – text, graphics, sound, spreadsheet, computer programs, etc.

E-cash – Short for electronic cash. See cybercash.

Email – Electronic mail: anything you send from your computer to another computer using your 'email client' program (such as Eudora or Microsoft Outlook).

Encryption – Encoding for security purposes. Email and any other data can now be easily encrypted using PGP and other freely available programs. Modern encryption has become so amazingly powerful as to be to all intents and purposes uncrackable. Law enforcers world wide are pressing their governments for access to people's and organisations' passwords and security keys. Would you be willing to hand over yours?

Glossary

Excite – A popular internet directory and search engine used to find pages relating to specific keywords which you enter. See also Yahoo!.

E-zines – The term for magazines and newsletters published on the internet.

FAQ – Frequently Asked Questions. You will see 'FAQ' everywhere you go on the internet. If you are ever doubtful about anything check the FAQ page, if the site has one, and you should find the answers to your queries.

Favorites – The rather coy term for **bookmarks** used by Internet Explorer, and by America OnLine.

File – A file is any body of data such as a word processed document, a spreadsheet, a database file, a graphics or video file, sound file, or computer program.

Firewall – A firewall is special security software designed to stop the flow of certain files into and out of a computer network.

Form – A means of collecting data on web pages, using text boxes and buttons. For example quite a few commercial sites will ask you to register by completing an online form.

Forums – Places for discussion on the internet. They are rather like usenet newsgroups and allow you to read, post and reply to messages. See also **bulletin board services.**

Frames – A web design feature in which web pages can be divided into several areas or panels, each containing separate information. A typical set of frames in a page includes an index frame (with navigation links), a banner frame (for a heading), and a body frame (for text matter).

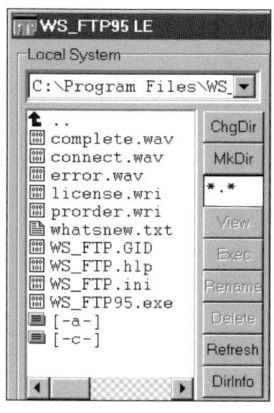

FTP – File transfer protocol, the method the internet uses to speed files back and forth between computers. Your browser will automatically select this method, for instance, when you want to download your bank statements to reconcile your accounts. In practice you don't need to worry about FTP unless you are thinking about creating and publishing your own web pages: then you would need some of the freely available FTP software.

Hacker – Someone who makes or seeks to make an unauthorised entry into someone else's computer system or network.

History list – A record of visited web pages. Your browser probably includes a history list. It is handy way of revisiting sites whose addresses you have forgotten to bookmark – just click on the item you want in the history list. You can normally delete all or part of the history list in your browser.

Hits – The number of times a web site has been visited.

Host – A host is the computer where a particular file or domain is present.

HotBot – This is a popular internet search engine used to find pages relating to any keywords you decide to enter. 'Bot' is short for robot. In internet terms it means a piece of software that performs a task on the internet, such as searching.

HTML – Hypertext markup language, the universal computer language

Glossary

used to create pages on the world wide web. It is much like word processing, but uses special 'tags' for formatting the text and other content, and for creating hyperlinks to other web pages.

Hyperlink – See **link**.

Infoseek – One of the most popular internet search engines.

Internet – The broad term for the fast-expanding network of global computers that can access each other in seconds by phone and satellite links. If you are using a modem on your computer, you too are part of the internet. The general term 'internet' encompasses email, web pages, internet chat, newsgroups, gopher and telnet. It is rather like the way we speak of 'the printed word' when we mean books, magazines, newspapers, newsletters, catalogues, leaflets, tickets and posters. The 'internet' does not exist in one place any more than 'the printed word' does.

Internet Explorer – The world's most popular browser software, a product of MicroSoft and keen rival to Netscape (recently taken over by America OnLine).

Internet service providers – ISPs are commercial, educational or official organisations which offer people ('users') access to the internet. The best known ones include AOL, CompuServe, BT Internet, Freeserve, GlobalNet, Demon and Virgin Net. Commercial ISPs may levy a fixed monthly charge, though the world-wide trend is now towards free services. Services typically include access to the world wide web, email and newsgroups, as well as news, chat, and entertainment. You should be aware that your internet service provider will know everything you do on the internet – emails sent and received, web sites visited, information downloaded, key words typed into search engines, newsgroups visited and messages posted. This is why many of them are willing to offer their services free. What do they do with all this data? Do they store it? Do they share or sell it? Do they make it clandestinely available to enforcement agencies? These are major issues of personal privacy and data protection, at both a national and European level. At the very least, check out your service provider's privacy statement.

ISDN Integrated Services Digital Network. This is a high speed telephone network that can send computer data from the internet to your PC faster than a normal telephone line.

JavaScript – A simple programming language that can be put onto a web page to create interactive effects such as buttons that change appearance when you position the mouse over them.

Key shortcut – Two keys pressed at the same time. Usually the 'control' key (Ctrl), 'Alt' key, or 'Shift' key combined with a letter or number. E.g. To use 'Control-D', press – 'Control', tap the 'D' key once firmly then take your finger off the 'Control' key.

Link – A hypertext phrase or image that calls up another web page when you click on it. Most web sites have lots of hyperlinks, or 'links' for short. These appear on the screen as buttons, images or bits of text (often underlined) that you can click on with your mouse to jump to another site on the world wide web.

Glossary

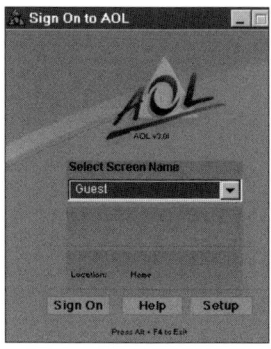

Linux – A new widely available operating system for personal computers, and challenger to Microsoft.

Log on You may be asked to 'log on' to certain sites and particular pages. This normally means entering your user ID in the form of a name and a password.

Log on/log off – To access/leave a network. In the early days of computing this literally involved writing a record in a log book.

Lurk – The slang term used to describe reading a newsgroup's messages without actually taking part in that newsgroup. Despite the connotations of the word, it is a perfectly respectable activity on the internet.

Mail server – A remote computer that enables you to send and receive emails. Your internet access provider will usually act as your mail server.

Mailing list – A forum where messages are distributed by email to the members of the forum. The two types of lists are discussion and announcement. Discussion lists allow exchange between list members. Announcement lists are one-way only and used to distribute information such as news or humour. A good place to find mailing lists is Liszt (http://www.liszt.com). You can normally quit a mailing list by sending an email message to request removal.

Marquee – A moving ('scrolling') line of text on a web site, often used for eye-catching advertising purposes.

Media Player – Software on a personal computer that will play sounds and images including video clips and animations.

Metasearch engine – A site that sends a keyword search to many different search engines and directories so you can use many search engines from one place.

Modem – An internal or external piece of hardware, one end of which is plugged into your PC. The other end is plugged into a standard phone socket, thereby linking you to the internet. The word is short for Modem MOdulator/DEmodulator.

Mortgage calculator – A web page where you easily find out the cost of a repayment mortgage. You type in the amount you want to borrow, the interest rate, and term of years, and the calculator instantly tells you how much you will have to pay in interest, and repayments, each month and each year. No more waiting around for written quotes. To find one, type 'mortgage calculator' into your favourite search engine.

MP3 – MPEG Audio Layer 3 – an audio format that compresses music to create files that are small yet whose quality is almost as good as CD music. See http://mpeg.org for further technical information. At time of writing, MP4 – even faster to download – was being developed.

Navigate – To click on the hyperlinks on a web site in order to move to other web pages or internet sites.

Net – A slang term for the internet. In the same way, the world wide web is often just called the web.

Netiquette – Popular term for the unofficial rules and language people follow to keep electronic communication in an acceptably polite form.

Glossary

Netscape – After Internet Explorer, Netscape is the most popular browser software available for surfing the internet. An excellent browser, Netscape has suffered in the wake of the rise of Microsoft's Internet Explorer, mainly because of the success of Microsoft in getting it pre-loaded on most new PCs. Netscape Communicator comes complete with email, newsgroups, address book and bookmarks, plus a web page composer, and you can adjust its settings in all sorts of useful ways. Netscape has recently been taken over by American OnLine for $4 billion.

Netscape Communicator

Newsgroup – A Usenet discussion group. Each newsgroup is a collection of messages, usually unedited and not checked by anyone. Messages can be placed within the newsgroup by anyone including you. The ever-growing newsgroups have been around for longer than the world wide web, and are an endless source of information, gossip, news, entertainment, resources and ideas. The 30,000-plus newsgroups are collectively referred to as usenet.

News reader – A type of software that enables you to search, read, post and manage messages in a newsgroup. It will normally be supplied by your internet service provider when you first sign up.

News server – A remote computer (eg your internet service provider's) that enables you to access newsgroups. If you cannot get some or any newsgroups from your existing news server, use your favourite search engine to search for 'open news servers' – there are lots of them freely available. When you have found one you like, adjust the news server settings in your browser or news reader software.

Online – Being connected to the internet.

PGP – Pretty Good Privacy. A method of encoding a message before transmitting it over the internet. With PGP, a message is first compressed then encoded with the help of keys. Just like the valuables in a locked safe, your message is safe unless a person has access to the right keys. Many governments would like to ban or control its use.

PoP – Point of presence. This refers to the dial up phone numbers available from your ISP. If your ISP does not have a local point of presence (ie local access phone number), then don't sign up – your telephone bill will rocket because you will be charged national phone rates. All the major ISPs have local numbers covering the whole of the UK.

Portal site – Portal means gateway. A portal site is one that loads into your browser as soon as you connect to the internet. It could for example be the front page of your internet service provider such as AOL, CompuServe, BT Internet, Freeserve, Demon or Virgin Net. Or you can set your browser to make it some other front page, for example a search engine such as Yahoo, or even your own home page if you have one.

Post, to – The common term used for sending ('posting') messages to a newsgroup. Posting messages is very like sending emails, except of course that they are public and everyone can read them. Also, newsgroup postings are archived, and can be read by anyone in the world years later.

Protocol – Technical term for the method by which computers commu-

Glossary

nicate, for example http (hyper text transfer protocol) or ftp (file transfer protocol). It's not something to worry about in ordinary life.

Quicktime A software program from Apple Computers that will play sounds and images including video clips and animations on both Apple Macs and personal computers.

Register You may have to give your name, personal details and financial information to some sites before you can continue to use the pages. This is done so that site owners can produce a mailing list to offer you products and services. It is also done to reduce use of the site by people who are not really interested. An additional benefit of registering is that it can help increase security, since the owners of the site know details of everyone using it.

Registered user – Someone who has filled out an online form and then been granted permission to access a restricted area of a web site. Access is usually obtained by logging on: entering a password and user name.

Search engine – A search engine is a means of finding something on the internet, though it is not an 'agent' (qv). Popular search engines are big web sites in their own right and include Alta Vista, Excite, Infoseek, Lycos and Yahoo!.

Secure servers – The hardware and software provided so that people can use their credit cards and leave other details without the risk of others seeing them online.

Shareware – Software that you can try before you buy. Usually there is some kind of limitation to the program such as a time limit or limited features. To get the registered (uncrippled) version, you must pay for the software. A vast amount of shareware is now available on the internet.

Shockwave – A popular piece of software produced by Macromedia, which enables you to view animations and other special effects on web sites. You can download it free and in a few minutes from Macromedia's web site. The effects can be fun, but they slow down the speed at which the pages load into your browser window.

Signature file This is a computer file in which you can place your address details, and which you can add to email and newsgroup messages. You only need to create a signature file once and you can then append it to your emails as often as you like.

Spam – The popular term for electronic junk mail – unsolicited and unwelcome email messages sent across the internet. – There are various forms of spam-busting software which you can now obtain to filter out unwanted messages.

Subscribe – Term for accessing a newsgroup in order to read and post messages in the newsgroup. There is no charge, and you can subscribe, unsubscribe and resubscribe at any time at the click of your mouse. Unless you post a message, no-one in the newsgroup will know that you have subscribed or unsubscribed.

Surfing – Slang term for browsing the internet, especially following trails of links on pages on the world wide web.

Glossary

TCP/IP – Transmission Control Protocol/Internet Protocol, the essential technology of the internet. It's not normally something you need worry about.

Thread – An ongoing topic in a usenet newsgroup or mailing list discussion. The term refers to the original message on a particular topic, and all the replies and other messages which spin off – from it. With news reading software, you can easily 'view thread' and read the related messages in a convenient batch.

UNIX This is an operating system that has been in use for many years, and still is used in many larger systems. Most ISPs use this operating system.

URL – Uniform resource locator the address of each internet page. For instance the URL of Internet Handbooks is http://www.internet-handbooks.co.uk

Usenet – The collection of well over 40,000 active newsgroups that make up a substantial part of the internet.

Virus – A computer program maliciously designed to cause havoc to people's computer files. Viruses can typically be received when downloading program files from the internet, or from copying material from infected disks. Even Word files can now be infected. You can protect yourself from the vast majority of them by installing some inexpensive anti-virus software.

Wallet – An electronic purse that you can fill up with e-cash for spending online.

Webcrawler – A popular internet search engine used to find pages relating to specific keywords entered.

Webmaster The person who runs a particular web site.

Windows – The ubiquitous operating system for personal computers developed by Bill Gates and the Microsoft Corporation. The Windows 3.1 version was followed by Windows 95, and most recently Windows 98.

WWW – The world wide web. Since it began in 1994 this has become the most popular part of the internet. The web is made up of hundreds of millions of often highly designed web pages with numerous hyperlinks to other pages. Developed by a British computer scientist, Tim Berners-Lee, its growth has been exponential and is set to continue.

Yahoo! – Probably the world's most popular internet directory and search engine.

Zip/unzip – Many files that you download from the internet will be in compressed format, especially if they are large files. This is to make them quicker to download. These files are said to be zipped or compressed. Unzipping these compressed files generally refers to the process of returning them to their original size on receipt. Zip files have the extension '.zip' and are created (and unzipped) using WinZip or a similar popular software package.

Index of Web Sites

1st Ski, 139

4colds, 76

5W, 144

A List Apart, 47
A2B Travel, 116
AA, 121
Abbey National, 59
ACATS, 91
Achoo, 76
Aidsmap, 82
Air Sickness Bag Virtual Museum, 123
All-Movie Guide, 149
Alta Vista, 21, 25
Alzheimer's Association, 80
Amazon Books, 104
Amnesty International, 73
Anagram Fun, 85
Ancient Sites, 43
Anonymiser, 163
Anonymizer, 50
Applied Space Resources, 51
Architectural Association, 39
Architectural Web Sites, 39
ArgoSphere, 87
Art Review Magazine, 40
Art-Connection, 39
Artres, 40
Artwell's Oracula, 99
ASH, 80
Ask an Astronaut, 29
Ask Dr. Internet, 47
Ask Grammar Queen, 29
Ask the Doctor, 30
AskA Locator, 28
ASR, 51
Assorted Encyclopaedias, 34
Astrology – Astrodienst Atlas Database, 99
Astrology.net, 99
Atlapedia, 128
Autobytel, 106
Autotrader, 106

Babyworld, 81
Balesworld, 117
Ballet.co, 37
Bank of England, 59
Bank of Scotland, 59

Barclays, 59
Bargain Holidays, 123
Barnes and Noble, 105
Battersea Dog's Home, 147
BBC News, 149
BBC Radio, 152
Beeb, 149
Beer Info, 92
Beer.com, 91
Beers Direct, 115
Berry Bros, 115
Better Business, 60
Bibliofind, 105
Bigfoot, 145
Bignote, 94
Billboard Online, 97
Bizarre Stuff You Can Make in Your Kitchen, 85
Blackwell's, 105
Blind Date, 144
Bonnington.com, 139
BookBrowse.com, 34
Bookwire, 34
Botany.com, 55
Boxing Monthly, 142
BritArt, 40
British Army, 66
British Athletics, 139
British Council, 130
British Diabetic Association, 80
British Journal of Photography, 40
British Library, 34
British Monarchy, 131
British Politics Page, 71
British School of Motoring, 121
British Tourist Authority, 126
British Watersports, 140
Britnet, 63
Brits Abroad, 113
Buy.co.uk, 110

Cancerhelp, 80
Capital Radio, 152
Car Lounge, 107
Carsource, 107
Cartoon Network, 134
Castle Search, 108
Cat Fancy, 147
Catholic Encyclopaedia, 97
CCTA, 131
CDnow, 94

Index of web sites

Certes, 66
Channel 4, 150
Channel 5, 150
Chapter And Verse Online, 97
Charles Schwab Europe, 60
Cheap Flights, 123
Cheltenham Racecourse, 143
Chemistry, 52
Children's Candlelight Stories, 87
Children's Software Review, 158
Chopstix, 92
Christianity Online Games, 86
Christianity Today magazine, 98
Church of England, 97
CIA World Fact Book, 132
Classic Car Source, 122
Classic Cars World, 107
Club 18-30, 144
CNET, 47
CNN, 156
CNN: Sci-Tech, 45
Cola, 140
Colouring, 89
Communications Business, 63
Company Sleuth, 63
Computerworld, 48
Condomania, 83
Confetti.co.uk, 82
Co-operative Bank, 59
Coppernob, 113
Coral Cay Conservation, 117
Cornucopia, 41
Coronation Street, 151
CricInfo, 138
Crime Scene, 86
Crufts, 147
Customs and Excise, 71
CyberSitter, 165

Dateline, 144
Deckchair, 123
Deja.com, 32
Dell, 112
Demolition Derby, 142
Department for Education and Employment, 70
Department of Health, 119
Dinosaur Interplanetary Gazette, 55
Disaster Relief, 132
Dixons, 112
Dog Breed Information Centre, 147
Dotmusic, 94
Drudge Report, 155
Drug InfoNet, 30

Durex World, 83
DVLA, 120

eBay, 104
eBid, 104
Eclectic, 81
E-Conflict World Encyclopaedia, 133
Ecovolunteer, 117
Edward Barrow's unofficial Internet copyright pages, 161
eFUSE.com, 48
Electronic Emissary, 28
Electronic Telegraph, 153
Electronic Yellow Pages, 64
Electronic Zoo, 148
Elonex, 112
English National Ballet, 38
Enterprise City, 102
Epicurious food, 92
Epicurious Travel, 12, 124
Euro calculator, 130
Eurodocs, 43
European Space Agency, 52
Exchange and Mart, 110
Excite, 26, 124, 128
Experiment in International Living, 145

Fantasy League, 136
FashionMall, 113
FashionUK, 113
Federal Express, 64
FIFA Online, 136
FilePile.Com, 26
Film Finder, 91
Financial Times, 153
FIND, 61
FinestWine, 115
First Call, 91
First Direct, 59
Fishing World, 140
Fitness Online, 77
FitnessLinks, 136
Flight Bookers, 124
Flightline, 125
Flowers Direct, 110
Fodor's Travel Online, 117
Football 365, 137
Football News, 137
Foreign Office, 12
Foreign Office Warnings, 119
Formula 1, 142
FOTA, 142
FreeSpeech, 73

Index of web sites

Freeway, 106
French Wines, 116
Fresh Food, 114
Friends of the Earth, 73
FriskyPet, 148
Fromages, 114
FT.com, 61
FunTrivia.com, 86

Gamblers Anonymous, 80
Garden Web, 90
Gay.com, 83
Gift Store, 110
Gingerbread, 83
Global Earthquake Response Centre, 133
Global Tickets, 111
Go Ask Alice, 30
Go Edinburgh, 130
Going for Green, 74
Golden Square, 66
GolfWeb, 139
Google, 25
Gradfinder, 68
Greenfingers, 90
GreenNet, 74
Greenpeace, 74

Harley-Davidson, 122
Headlice.org, 81
Healself Network, 84
HEBS, 77
Hindu Universe, 98
Hitch Hiker's Guide to the Internet, 134
Hitched, 83
Home Directory, 108
Homework help, 29
Horse Planet, 148
Horse Racing, 140
Hotel Guide, 126
Hotel Reservation Service, 126
Hotels and Travel on the Net, 12
House Directory, 108
How Stuff Works, 135
Hubble Space Telescope Public Pictures, 53
Human Anatomy Online, 55
HumourNet, 135
Hyperhistory, 44

ICA, 41
IDrink, 92
Imperial War Museum, 57
Infant Explorer, 89
InfoNation, 133

Inland Revenue, 61
Insomnia, 77
Interactive Investor, 61
Interactive Music and Video Shop, 95
Interflora, 110
International Amateur Athletic Federation, 140
International Federation of Aromatherapists, 84
International Olympic Committee, 140
International Vegetarian Union, 92, 93
Internet Banking, 59
Internet Chef, 92
Internet for Schools, 70
Internet Freedom, 166
Internet Garden, 90
Internet Mental Health, 80
Internet Movie Database, 151
Introduction, 145
Is Today Monday, 44
Islamic Digest, 98
ITN, 150

Janes Defence, 56
JobServe, 67

Kids @ National Geographic, 89
KidsConnect, 29
KidsFun, 88

La Cuisine de Veronique, 93
La Redoutte, 113
Lastminute, 102, 125
Law Talk, 63
Liszt, 31, 32, 33
Live Online, 95
Lloyds, 59
Lodging.com, 126
London Student, 68
London transport, 119
Loot, 106
Lords, 138
Lycos Jobs, 67
Lycos Music Search, 95

MacDonalds, 114
MacWarehouse, 112
Magixl, 157
MapQuest, 129
Matchfacts, 137
Medic-alert foundation, 81
MedicineNet, 78
Medscape, 78
Meningitis Research Foundation, 81
Mental Health, 80

185

Index of web sites

MG, The Classic Marque, 122
Michael Page, 67
Microsoft Expedia, 125
Midland, 59
Millions2000, 86
Mini Site, 122
Ministry of Agriculture, Fisheries and Food, 71
Ministry of Defence, 131
Moneyworld, 62
MoneyXtra, 62
Monster Board, 67
Morgans, 104
MP3.com, 96
Multi Media Mapping, 129
Multiple Sclerosis Foundation, 81
Muscular Dystrophy Association, 81
Museum of London, 42
Museum of Science and Industry, 42
MuseumNet, 41
Museums and Galleries Commission, 42
Music Rough Guide, 95
MusicMatch, 96
Muslim News, 99
My Yahoo, 19
MyTaxi, 102

NASA Spaceflight, 53
NASA Spacelink, 53
NASA's Quest Projects, 53
National Association of Youth Theatres, 88
National Express, 119
National Gallery, 42
National Geographic, 53
National Health Service, 79
National Kidney Foundation, 81
National Library for the Blind UK, 35
National Portrait Gallery, 43
National Trust, 127
National Westminster, 59
National Zoo Web Cams, 148
Nationwide, 59
NATO, 71
Natural History Museum, 42
Nature, 46
Need a Nanny, 81
Net Freedom, 163
Netnanny, 165
New British Artists, 41
New Car Net, 106
New Century Nutrition Online, 77
New Scientist, 47
New York Times, 154
NewsNow, 156

NJ NIE Project, 28
NME, 97
NoWonder, 48
Number Ten, 71

O & A Converter, 130
Obesity.com, 77
Office of Fair Trading, 102
Off-Road.com, 120
On This Day in History, 45
One World, 156
OneLook, 36
Online Interactive Alcoholics Anonymous, 80
Online Surgery, 56
OnNow, 49
OperaData, 38
Operation Desert Storm Debriefing Book, 57
Ordnance Survey, 127
Oxford University, 69

Package Holidays, 117
Paper Currency, 133
ParaScope, 100
Parliament, 72
Patient Information, 77
PCgame, 158
PeakHealth.net, 78
PGP home page, 51
Physics Time-Line, 54
PhysicsWeb, 54
Pickable Brains list, 28
Planet Rugby, 139
Plus Lotto, 86
Press Association, 156
Priceline, 103
Private Eye, 154
Project Gutenberg, 36
Property Live, 108
PropertySight, 108
Psychology, 56
Pure Fiction, 17
Puzzability, 86

QXL, 104

RAC, 121
Racenews, 141
Radio Tower, 152
RailTrack Travel Information, 119
Rain or Shine, 157
Ramblers' Association, 127
RealPlayer, 151
Reference.com, 33

Glossary

Religious Freedom, 100
Renaissance, 45
Resort Sports Network, 141
Reuters, 156
RFU, 138
Richard Kimber, 72
Rolling Stone, 97
Royal & ancient Golf Club of St Andrews, 139
Royal Air Force, 68
Royal Bank of Scotland, 59
Royal Insight, 132
Royal Mail, 65
Royal National Institute for the Blind, 81
Royal Navy, 68
Royal Opera, 38
Royal Shakespeare Company, 39
Royal Society for the Prevention of Accidents, 121
Royalty Magazine, 132
RSPCA, 148
Rugby Club, 139
Runnersworld, 142

SafeKids, 88
Sail Online, 142
Sainsburys, 114
Salem Tarot, 100
Samaritans, 78
Science Frontiers, 47
ScreenTalk, 151
Scrum.com, 138
Secret Kingdom, 57
Self Assess, 63
Shakespeare Birthplace Trust, 36
Shakespeare Online, 37
Shockwave, 42
Shopguide, 103
Shopping City, 102
Silicon News, 49
Simpsons, 157
Sky, 151
Snowboarding, 142
SoccerNet, 137
Software Warehouse, 113
Soil Association, 85
Somerfield, 114
Spacestation.com, 54
Speedtrap Registry, 121
Spider's apprentice, 23
SportsWeb, 136
Staples, 110
Statewatch, 74
Strolling.com, 128

Student UK, 69
Subway Navigator, 119
Sunday Times, 155
SurfMonkey, 165

Tariff On Line, 111
Tasty Bits, 49
TeaTime, 93
Techtronics, 96
Teen Talk, 82
Telephone Directories on the Web, 146
Teletubbies, 89
Tennis, 143
TerraServer, 133
Tesco, 114
The Arthur C Clarke Foundation, 51
The British Stammering Association, 76
The Copyright Website, 161
The Economist, 152
The Edinburgh Engineering Virtual Library, 52
The Electric Gallery, 40
The Euro, 60
The European, 153
The Exploratorium, 45
The Guardian Network, 153
The History Channel, 44
The History of Plumbing, 90
The Human Body: An Online Tour, 55
The Independent, 153
The Insulin-Free World Foundation, 80
The Internet Classics Archive, 35
The Internet Public Library, 28
The Internet Sleuth, 27
The Junction, 88
The London Science Museum, 46
The London Stock Exchange, 62
The Louvre, 41
The Met Office, 157
The Mirror, 154
The Motley Fool, 63
The Natural Handyman, 91
The Natural Health Guide, 84
The Online Books Page, 36
The Privacy Site, 51
The Response Centre, 68
The Runic Journey, 100
The Scotsman, 155
The Sidewalk, 12
The Stage, 38
The Star, 155
The Times, 155
The Treasury, 72
The Ultimates, 26, 146

Index of web sites

The Virtual Garden, 91
The Whisky Shop, 116
TheBiz, 58
TheSite, 88
Thomas Cook, 125
Thomas the Tank Engine, 88
Tibetan Buddhism, 99
Ticket Links, 111
Time Machine, 151
Time Out, 130
Timewarp Records, 95
TNT, 65
Top Gear, 121
Top Magazine, 97
Topmarks, 88
Trainline, 120
Travel Guides, 130
Travel Health Online, 12, 119
Travel Resources, 117
Travelocity, 12, 125
Travlang, 126
TripSpot, 117
Trivia Treasure Trove, 87
Trouble, 82
TSB, 59
Tucows, 158
Tudor England, 45

U.K. Directory, 19
UK Directory, 58
UK Map of Universities, 69
UK Property Gold, 109
UK Property Register, 108
UK street Map Page, 128
UK Theatre Web, 39
UK Travel, 128
UKwriters, 17
United Nations, 75
UpMyStreet, 109
UselessKnowledge.com, 87

Vatican, 98
Vegweb, 93
Viagra, 84
Victoria and Albert Museum, 43
Virgin Radio, 152
Virtual Bar, 116
Virtual Library, 37
Virtual London, 118

Waterstones, 105
WEA, 69
WebData, 58
WebFerret, 27
Western European Union, 72
Westminster Abbey, 128
What's New, 118
WhatIs, 135
Where To Eat, 93
Whitehouse, 73
Whole Earth, 85
WhoWhere, 147
Wine Cellar, 116
Wine Pages, 93
WineNet, 116
WirePlay, 87
World Flag Database, 133
World in Action, 156
World Snooker, 143
World Wide Arts Resources, 39
World Wildlife Fund, 148
Worldwide Tourism Directory, 118
Yahoo, 20
Yahoo People Search, 146
Yahoo UK, 26
Yearling's TV guides, 151
Youth 2 Youth, 82
Youth Hostel Association, 126

ZD Net, 158
Zero Knowledge, 51, 163

Index

accommodation, 69, 116, 117, 121, 123, 125, 126, 130, 144
addictions, 80, 85, 89
agriculture, 75
aircraft, 56, 125
airports, 109, 116, 117, 124, 125, 128
Alzheimer's disease, 80
animals, 42, 43, 85, 147, 148
anonymous mailing services, 163
archaeology, 47
architecture, 39, 40
aromatherapy, 84
art, 39, 40, 41, 42, 43, 45, 56, 121
astrology, 99
astronomy, 45, 47
astrophysics, 35
athletics, 139
auctions, 21, 22, 23, 104, 107, 110, 125, 137
babies, 81
ballet, 37, 38, 91
banking, 58, 59, 61, 98
beer, 91, 92
biology, 34, 46, 47
anatomy, 55
human, 43
blocking software, 164, 165
books, 10, 12, 13, 19, 20, 26, 32, 34, 35, 36, 51, 53, 74, 91, 93, 104, 105, 106, 114, 146, 154, 162, 167
botany, 55
boxing, 142, 143
braille, 35
British Army, 66
Buddhism, 99
building societies, 58
business, 20, 27, 29, 31, 34, 38, 39, 58, 60, 61, 63, 64, 74, 76, 91, 95, 101, 104, 109, 110, 112, 122, 130, 146, 149, 153, 156
buying a house, 22
buying products, 101
cache, 17
calculators, 62, 110, 121, 130
calendars, 44, 45, 49, 54, 91, 118, 136, 140
careers, 66
cars, 89, 103, 105, 106, 107, 110, 121, 122, 142, 149
cartoons, 134, 157
chemistry, 52
childbirth, 81
children, 19, 29, 42, 55, 76, 81, 85, 87, 88, 89, 91, 134, 158, 162, 163, 164, 165
Christianity, 28, 86, 98
churches, 82, 97
cinemas, 91
classics, 35, 36, 39, 107, 113
clubs, 107, 122, 137
colleges, 69, 109
companies, 11, 60, 63, 64, 66, 68, 71, 80, 95, 101, 109, 110, 160, 162
competitions, 82, 129, 141, 142, 147, 149, 155
computers, 11, 12, 15, 16, 17, 20, 26, 45, 47, 49, 58, 66, 74, 77, 85, 86, 89, 95, 96, 104, 110, 112, 114, 121, 128, 130, 148, 151, 153, 156, 159, 163, 164, 167
technical support, 48
computing, 34
cookery, 92
copyright, 36, 160, 161
cosmology, 34, 54
couriers, 64, 65
courses, 69, 70, 139
crafts, 34
cricket, 138
crime, 86, 109
cultures, 34
dance, 37, 38, 39, 111
databases, 25, 27, 30, 55, 58, 125
diabetes, 80, 85
dictionaries, 36, 55, 90, 92
dinosaurs, 43, 55
directories, 3, 4, 19, 20, 21, 24, 25, 26, 58, 61, 80, 102, 108, 117, 118, 146, 147, 167, 169
disability, 80
DIY, 90, 91
drink, 20, 91, 93, 113, 116, 128, 153
driving, 120, 121, 126, 142
drugs, 30, 77, 78, 79, 82, 88
ecology, 43, 117
economics, 34, 43

Index

education, 3, 19, 21, 28, 30, 34, 39, 54, 55, 66, 67, 70, 77, 88, 89, 99, 127, 128
email, 12, 13, 64, 82, 146, 147
email addresses, 145
encryption, 51, 163
encyclopaedias, 55, 89, 97, 114, 133
engineering, 52, 53
entertainment, 15, 20, 38, 42, 83, 86, 111, 118, 130, 149, 156
environment, 34, 71, 73, 74, 85, 89, 109, 117, 158
estate agents, 108
Europe, 42, 43, 45, 52, 61, 71, 72, 74, 75, 90, 94, 111, 115, 153, 157
events, 27, 38, 39, 41, 43, 44, 45, 46, 48, 49, 54, 71, 84, 91, 98, 107, 111, 118, 122, 130, 131, 136, 138, 139, 140, 142, 147, 151
exhibitions, 39, 40, 41, 43, 46, 107, 111
experts, 13, 24, 27, 28, 30, 32, 49, 78, 107, 113, 116, 140, 142
farming, 71, 85, 114
fashion, 81, 113, 153
festivals, 92, 114, 130, 143
film, 46, 91, 153
films, 15, 41, 45, 53, 56, 91, 149, 151
finance, 11, 28, 34, 59, 60, 61, 62, 63, 70, 72, 75, 106, 153, 156
firearms, 56
fitness, 66, 76, 77, 78, 83
flights, 12, 19, 102, 103, 116, 117, 122, 123, 124, 125, 130
flowers, 55, 102, 103, 110
food, 71, 73, 85, 91, 92, 93, 113, 114, 119, 128, 153
football, 33, 136, 137, 152
forums, 13, 30, 31, 32, 38, 77, 90, 91, 117, 122, 133, 137, 147
free Internet access, 19, 59, 112, 114
friendship, 144
galleries, 40, 41, 42, 43
gambling, 80, 164
games, 20, 26, 42, 43, 47, 66, 85, 86, 87, 88, 89, 92, 95, 103, 110, 122, 134, 136, 139, 140, 149, 158
gardening, 55, 90, 91, 153
geography, 34, 53, 54, 128, 133
geology, 47
golf, 139

government, 11, 19, 27, 59, 70, 71, 72, 73, 81, 100, 128, 130, 131, 163
hacking, 50
health, 12, 30, 69, 71, 75, 76, 77, 78, 79, 80, 82, 83, 84, 88, 119, 121, 147, 153
hinduism, 98
history, 3, 28, 34, 37, 38, 42, 43, 44, 45, 46, 51, 55, 71, 79, 80, 83, 90, 92, 93, 99, 100, 116, 117, 122, 128, 132, 136, 138, 140, 142, 143, 147, 148, 151, 158, 165
hobbies, 34
holidays, 11, 12, 116, 117, 118, 122, 123, 125, 126, 127, 128, 130, 139, 149
homework, 12, 29
hotels, 11, 12, 103, 116, 117, 121, 123, 124, 125, 126, 128
houses, 16, 21, 22, 23, 40, 92, 108, 109, 125, 160, 167
HTML, 47
human rights, 50, 73, 74, 156
humour, 91, 134
industry, 34, 42, 46, 59, 61, 66, 93, 96, 97, 106, 107
intelligence, 57, 75
internet security, 49
investment, 60, 61
islam, 99
ISP, 16, 74, 105, 113
java, 55, 66, 86, 87
javascript, 52, 55, 71
jobs, 11, 28, 34, 39, 46, 47, 54, 66, 67, 68, 71, 72, 91, 97, 114, 127, 147, 153
jokes, 63, 83, 135
keywords, 20, 21, 22, 23, 24, 25, 26, 27, 28, 32, 62, 92, 103, 149, 156, 164, 167, 168, 169
law, 63
libraries, 3, 12, 17, 20, 27, 28, 29, 34, 35, 37, 43, 52, 53, 69, 76, 89, 107, 127, 129, 133
mailing lists, 30, 31
maps, 45, 53, 69, 90, 109, 117, 119, 124, 126, 127, 128, 129, 133, 147, 156, 157
marriage, 82, 83, 135
maths, 34, 47
medals, 56
medicine, 34, 46, 76, 79, 84
meningitis, 81
mental health, 80

Index

metasearch tools, 24, 26
monarchy, 4, 131, 132
money, 19, 59, 60, 63, 69, 88, 125, 126, 133, 153, 162
mortgages, 61, 103
motoring, 120, 121
MP3, 3, 95, 96, 97
multiple sclerosis, 81
muscular dystrophy, 81
museums, 41, 42, 43, 46, 56, 57, 119, 123
music, 20, 32, 35, 41, 81, 82, 91, 94, 95, 96, 97, 103, 110, 151, 152, 158, 160, 161
mysticism, 34
mythology, 34
NASA, 30, 53, 55
NATO, 71, 72
natural history, 42
news, 12, 15, 17, 18, 19, 26, 31, 32, 34, 38, 40, 42, 43, 45, 46, 47, 48, 49, 51, 54, 55, 57, 58, 60, 61, 62, 63, 64, 66, 68, 72, 73, 74, 75, 77, 80, 83, 87, 88, 92, 97, 99, 107, 113, 114, 117, 118, 119, 122, 131, 132, 133, 137, 138, 139, 140, 141, 142, 143, 148, 149, 150, 151, 152, 153, 154, 155, 156, 160
newsgroups, 13, 30, 31, 32, 33, 52, 162, 163, 165, 166
newspapers, 108, 152, 155, 156, 160
nutrition, 77, 78, 142, 147, 148
offline viewing, 17
online business, 19
opera, 38, 39, 91, 95, 111, 112
organisations, 80
Outlook Express, 32
paintings, 40, 42
parents, 81, 82, 83, 88, 158, 162
peace, 74, 145
pensions, 62
PGP, 51
philosophy, 34
photography, 40, 46
physics, 34, 47, 54
PICS, 163, 165, 166
pictures, 15, 26, 43, 45, 53, 82, 89, 92, 122, 128, 135, 139, 143, 144, 148, 155, 160
plants, 43, 55, 85
plays, 37, 39, 143, 151
plumbing, 90
poetry, 37, 81
politics, 71, 72, 145, 153
pornography, 19, 164
portals, 58, 63, 151, 152
privacy, 50, 51, 161, 163
psychology, 56
publishing, 34
quizzes, 87, 139, 149
racing, 89, 107, 136, 140, 141, 142
radio, 4, 73, 97, 151, 152
ratings, 165
recipes, 77, 92, 93, 114, 116, 168
religion, 34, 97-98, 100, 133
research, 12, 19, 43, 48, 53, 60, 69, 76, 77, 79, 81, 85, 125, 127, 132
restaurants, 12, 20, 93, 117, 121, 128, 152
road safety, 120
romance, 144
Royal Air Force, 68
Royal Navy, 68
rugby, 138, 139
samaritans, 78
schools, 68, 70, 84, 109, 166
science, 29, 45, 46, 47, 51, 54, 56, 85
sculpture, 40
security, 50, 51, 72, 75
self-assessment, 11, 63
self-employment, 60
sex, 88, 145, 166
Shakespeare, 3, 36, 37, 39
shares, 60
shareware, 26, 85, 158
shopping, 19, 49, 90, 94, 102, 103, 109, 113, 136
skiing, 11, 136, 139, 140, 141
small businesses, 48, 60, 63
smoking, 77, 80
spirituality, 83
sports, 19, 34, 45, 68, 91, 103, 136, 139, 140, 141, 142, 143, 149, 151
stock, 11, 19, 58, 59, 63, 153
stock market, 11, 153
stories, 23, 62, 87, 89, 94, 135, 138, 141, 147, 150, 153, 155, 156
students, 29, 39, 46, 53, 55, 68, 69, 70, 73, 135
surgery, 56
tax, 61, 62, 63, 71, 98, 109
teachers, 28, 29, 39, 46, 53, 56, 70, 88
teaching, 46

Index

technology, 20, 31, 41, 45, 46, 48, 49, 56, 57, 60, 66, 90, 97, 112, 135, 149, 156
military, 56
teenagers, 81
telecommunications, 75
television, 15, 32, 46, 53, 73, 89, 140, 144, 149, 150, 151, 156, 157, 167
tennis, 143
terrorism, 19
theatre, 28, 38, 39, 88, 91, 111, 118
tickets, 12, 33, 38, 111, 118, 120, 122, 124, 130, 157
timelines, 44
tourism, 128, 131
trains, 119, 120
transport, 12, 119

travel, 4, 12, 19, 27, 31, 55, 71, 78, 103, 116, 117, 118, 119, 122, 123, 124, 125, 126, 128, 130, 139, 144, 145
universities, 11, 30, 39, 69, 88
URL, 16, 17, 21, 63, 64, 101, 147, 160
usenet, 13, 30, 31
virtual tours, 41, 43
viruses, 85, 158, 159
war, 44, 56, 57, 58, 71, 86, 131
weather, 11, 12, 19, 26, 58, 87, 90, 122, 124, 133, 141, 142, 156, 157
wild card, 167
wine, 93, 115, 116
women, 81, 144
world wide web, 11, 15, 20, 58, 90, 159
young people, 81, 82, 88